Frommer's®

Las Vegas
day BY day™

1st Edition

by Mary Herczog

WILEY
Wiley Publishing, Inc.

Contents

Published by:

Wiley Publishing, Inc.

111 River St.
Hoboken, NJ 07030-5774

ISBN: 978-0-470-13469-6

Editor: Naomi P. Kraus
Production Editor: Lindsay Conner
Photo Editor: Richard Fox
Cartographer: Elizabeth Puhl
Production by Wiley Indianapolis Composition Services

For information on our other products and services or to obtain technical support, please contact our Customer Care Department within the U.S. at 800/762-2974, outside the U.S. at 317/572-3993 or fax 317/572-4002.

Wiley also publishes its books in a variety of electronic formats. Some content that appears in print may not be available in electronic formats.

Manufactured in China

5   4   3   2   1

A Note from the Publisher

Organizing your time. That's what this guide is all about.

Other guides give you long lists of things to see and do and then expect you to fit the pieces together. The Day by Day guides are different. These guides tell you the best of everything, and then they show you how to see it *in the smartest, most time-efficient way*. Our authors have designed detailed itineraries organized by time, neighborhood, or special interest. And each tour comes with a bulleted map that takes you from stop to stop.

Hoping to hit it big at the blackjack tables, visit the dolphins at The Mirage, take in a major production show, or just stroll the Strip? Planning a walk through Downtown, or dinner and drinks where you can rub shoulders with the rich and infamous? Whatever your interest or schedule, the Day by Days give you the smartest routes to follow. Not only do we take you to the top attractions, hotels, and restaurants, but we also help you access those special moments that locals get to experience—those "finds" that turn tourists into travelers.

The Day by Days are also your top choice if you're looking for one complete guide for all your travel needs. The best hotels and restaurants for every budget, the greatest shopping values, the wildest nightlife—it's all here.

Why should you trust our judgment? Because our authors personally visit each place they write about. They're an independent lot who say what they think and would never include places they wouldn't recommend to their best friends. They're also open to suggestions from readers. If you'd like to contact them, please send your comments my way at mspring@wiley.com, and I'll pass them on.

Enjoy your Day by Day guide—the most helpful travel companion you can buy. And have the trip of a lifetime.

Warm regards,

Michael Spring
Publisher
Frommer's Travel Guides

About the Author

Mary Herczog lives in Los Angeles and works in the film industry while also attending graduate school. She is the author of *Frommer's New Orleans, California For Dummies, Frommer's Portable Las Vegas for Non-Gamblers,* and *Las Vegas For Dummies,* and she has contributed to *Frommer's Los Angeles.* Craps make her nervous so she sticks to blackjack even if she still is never sure when to hit on 13.

Acknowledgments

The correct billing on this book should read "by Mary Herczog and Naomi Kraus," because as the editor, Naomi shaped an ungainly manuscript (and an even more feckless author) into a book. I can't thank her enough. Thanks also go to Frommer's, whose continued support during difficult times is a gift. Thank you to Bianca Arvin for all her massive efforts and Arlene Wszalek and Lisa Derrick for further help. Rick Garman keeps it all in perspective with the latest giggle-inducing Vegas news. No award-winning Vegas meal tastes good unless I eat it with Steve Hochman.

An Additional Note

Please be advised that travel information is subject to change at any time—and this is especially true of prices. We therefore suggest that you write or call ahead for confirmation when making your travel plans. The authors, editors, and publisher cannot be held responsible for the experiences of readers while traveling. Your safety is important to us, however, so we encourage you to stay alert and be aware of your surroundings.

Star Ratings, Icons & Abbreviations

Every hotel, restaurant, and attraction listing in this guide has been ranked for quality, value, service, amenities, and special features using a **star-rating system.** Hotels, restaurants, attractions, shopping, and nightlife are rated on a scale of zero stars (recommended) to three stars (exceptional). In addition to the star-rating system, we also use a **kids icon** to point out the best bets for families. Within each tour, we recommend cafes, bars, or restaurants where you can take a break. Each of these stops appears in a shaded box marked with a coffee-cup-shaped bullet ☕ .

The following **abbreviations** are used for credit cards:

AE	American Express	DISC	Discover	V	Visa
DC	Diners Club	MC	MasterCard		

Frommers.com

Now that you have this guidebook to help you plan a great trip, visit our website at **www.frommers.com** for additional travel information on more than 3,600 destinations. We update features regularly to give you instant access to the most current trip-planning information available. At Frommers. com, you'll find scoops on the best airfares, lodging rates, and car-rental bargains. You can even book your travel online through our reliable travel booking partners. Other popular features include:

- Online updates to our most popular guidebooks
- Vacation sweepstakes and contest giveaways
- Newsletter highlighting the hottest travel trends
- Online travel message boards with featured travel discussions

A Note on Prices

In the "Take a Break" and "Best Bets" sections of this book, we have used a system of dollar signs to show a range of costs for 1 night in a hotel (the price of a double-occupancy room) or the cost of an entree at a restaurant. Use the following table to decipher the dollar signs:

Cost	Hotels	Restaurants
$	under $100	under $20
$$	$100–$150	$20–$40
$$$	$150–$200	$40–$75
$$$$	over $200	over $75

An Invitation to the Reader

In researching this book, we discovered many wonderful places—hotels, restaurants, shops, and more. We're sure you'll find others. Please tell us about them, so we can share the information with your fellow travelers in upcoming editions. If you were disappointed with a recommendation, we'd love to know that, too. Please write to:

Frommer's Las Vegas Day by Day, 1st Edition
Wiley Publishing, Inc. • 111 River St. • Hoboken, NJ 07030-5774

Bonus Online Update

Everything in this book was correct at press time, but Las Vegas is a city in flux. For current updates to the text, head online to www.frommers.com/go/lasvegasdaybyday.

15 Favorite **Moments**

15 Favorite **Moments**

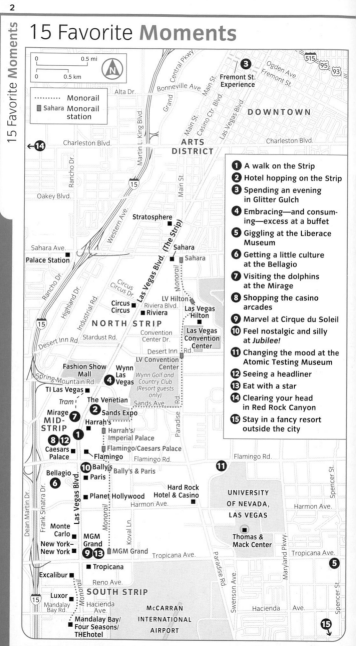

0   0.5 mi
0   0.5 km

········· Monorail
▓ Sahara Monorail
   station

DOWNTOWN

ARTS DISTRICT

Fremont St. Experience

Charleston Blvd.

Stratosphere

Sahara

LV Hilton
Las Vegas Hilton

Circus Circus Dr.

Circus Circus
Riviera

NORTH STRIP

Las Vegas Convention Center

LV Convention Center

Wynn Las Vegas
Wynn Golf and Country Club (Resort guests only)

Fashion Show Mall

TI Las Vegas

The Venetian
Sands Expo

Mirage
MID-STRIP
Harrah's
Harrah's/Imperial Palace

Caesars Palace
Flamingo/Caesars Palace
Flamingo

Bellagio

Bally's
Paris
Bally's & Paris

Planet Hollywood

Hard Rock Hotel & Casino

UNIVERSITY OF NEVADA, LAS VEGAS

Monte Carlo

New York–New York

MGM Grand

Thomas & Mack Center

Excalibur

SOUTH STRIP

Luxor

Mandalay Bay/Four Seasons/THEhotel

Tropicana

McCARRAN INTERNATIONAL AIRPORT

Palace Station

1 A walk on the Strip
2 Hotel hopping on the Strip
3 Spending an evening in Glitter Gulch
4 Embracing—and consuming—excess at a buffet
5 Giggling at the Liberace Museum
6 Getting a little culture at the Bellagio
7 Visiting the dolphins at the Mirage
8 Shopping the casino arcades
9 Marvel at Cirque du Soleil
10 Feel nostalgic and silly at *Jubilee!*
11 Changing the mood at the Atomic Testing Museum
12 Seeing a headliner
13 Eat with a star
14 Clearing your head in Red Rock Canyon
15 Stay in a fancy resort outside the city

Previous Page: The Las Vegas Strip at night.

Elvis sang "Viva, Las Vegas," wishing there were more than 24 hours in the day to spend in the city that sets his soul on fire. But some respond by saying, "Yeah, it's not my kind of thing." For me, that's like saying the Grand Canyon isn't your kind of thing. Sure, the latter is one of the great natural wonders of the world, but Las Vegas is *the* great unnatural wonder of the world. It's a life experience like no other. It has to be seen to be believed, and to see it is to experience it. And once you have, you may be singing along with the King, because even in a 24/7 kind of town there aren't enough hours to handle it all. My favorite picks should help you manage this sprawling mass of fun.

The Venetian is one of the Strip's best re-created locales.

1 Walking on the Strip. The heart of the city, a 13-block stretch of Las Vegas Boulevard South, is lined left and right with behemoth hotel casino resorts, all wonders of excess and each with its own particular absurd delight, from gaudy outside decor to attention-grabbing free attractions to a theme run amok. It's less spectacular during the day, but the lights at night are so head-spinning you might be too distracted to take it all in. Truth be told, it's too far to walk in one go, so plan to do it in stretches. See p 42.

2 Hotel hopping on the Strip. It's Vegas, after all, and even if you don't want to drop a dime (though isn't that partly what you came here for?), you'll want to see what's inside those flashy facades. The trend has been toward resort spas on steroids—what would be quiet good taste were it on a smaller scale—but there is still plenty, from ancient Egypt and Rome to medieval Venice to a scaled-down New York City to keep you agog. Remember, in other cities, hotels are built *near* the attractions. In Vegas, they *are* the attractions. See p 42.

3 Spending an evening in Glitter Gulch. The original heart of the city, the pedestrian-only section of Fremont Street comes as a relief after the overwhelming Strip. Sure, there's still sensory overload, but the scale is such that by comparison, it's practically small-town Main Street. Each casino is an easy distance from the next, the crowds seem less

Mustang Sally is among Glitter Gulch's most famous icons.

daunting, and you don't have to jostle for position to view the overhead Fremont Street Experience light show. *See p 60, bullet* **14**.

4 Embracing—and consuming—excess at a buffet. All-you-can-eat, low-cost buffets have long been a symbol of the city's bargain vacation status. Vegas is no longer a bargain, but the buffets remain, though similarly increased in price. Still, the sight of rows of prep stations, offering varieties of international and American cuisine, not to mention mounds of shrimp and prime rib, remains a sybaritic treat. And though prices have gone up, so has quality—and it's still cheaper than multicourses at a costly restaurant. The Buffet at Wynn Las Vegas is tops in appeal, though also in price. *See p 98.*

5 Giggling at the Liberace Museum. For a city that reinvents itself every 5 minutes, it's nice to see some level of appreciation for the past. And nothing says Vegas quite like a performer who appreciated the town's glitter and applied it to himself—literally. Marvel at the wonder and glory of the human performance project that was Liberace, not to mention his sequined clothing, rhinestone-coated piano, and

jewels—faux and fabulous alike. *See p 15, bullet* **1**.

6 Getting a little culture at the Bellagio. Vegas still remains too busy with the bang and the bustle to really dedicate itself to the quieter arts, but the Bellagio Gallery of Fine Art continues to defy the odds and offers excellent retrospective shows on everything from photography (Ansel Adams) to fine art (Monet). Ducking into a gallery from a casino is nearly an exercise in cognitive dissonance, but a little intellectual nutrition helps keep your balance in a city designed to throw you off same. *See p 16, bullet* **3**.

7 Visiting the dolphins at the Mirage. An unexpected oasis in the midst of the Strip's pleasurable madness. Visitors can watch these playful mammals swim and frolic in a meticulously designed environment; they'll even interact a bit thanks to cute and lively trainers, glorying in the best job in Vegas. Take as long as you like to enjoy the dolphins' company; if you are really lucky, they might even play ball with you. *See p 16, bullet* **5**.

Stuff yourself silly at one of the city's many buffets; it's a quintessential Vegas experience.

8 Shopping the casino arcades. Vegas is a shopper's paradise only if you don't demand cute, quirky, and original stores. In other words, chains and other recognizable names rule the day, but rule they do, in shopping centers largely attached to the casino hotels and every bit as extravagantly designed. From Versace to Old Navy, there is something for every budget, and in the case of the Forum Shops, it's all set in an overblown Roman streetscape that adds fanciful (if not tasteful) glamour. Buy some shoes in between rounds of blackjack—maybe your winnings will pay for it! *See p 72.*

9 Marveling at Cirque du Soleil. The tacky postvaudevillian variety shows that were once the standard for Strip entertainment have almost entirely vanished in favor of a great many offerings from the idiosyncratic human circus Cirque du Soleil. Truth be told, there can be too much of a good thing, and at five and counting (at least two more productions are ramping up at press time), not every one is worth the high ticket price. But the good ones certainly are, so much so that it's hard to choose. Right now, my favorite is *KÀ* at the MGM-Grand, a near-perfect blend of Cirque artistry, athleticism, visuals, and storytelling. *See p 115.*

10 Feeling nostalgic and silly at *Jubilee!* Classic, over-the-top (not to mention topless) Vegas revues are a dying breed, hedged out by special-effects-laden modern productions and just a modicum of good taste. But if you are nostalgic for some old-fashioned glamour and barely naughty fun, come see the pinnacle of what was once the dominant theatrical art form in town, the shameless and delightful *Jubilee! See p 116.*

You haven't really done Las Vegas properly if you haven't seen one of the city's famous showgirls; Jubilee! *Is the best place in town to check them out.*

11 Changing the mood at the Atomic Testing Museum. With the Atomic Testing Museum, the city delivers something unexpected and otherwise unique. For 4 decades, Sin City's neighbor was the country's primary nuclear weapons testing ground. This admirable facility offers perspectives, technical and personal, on the science and implications of the work done there. *See p 15, bullet* **2**.

An exhibit inside the Smithsonian-affiliated Atomic Testing Museum, one of the best museums in the city.

⑫ **Seeing a headliner.** Time was, all the names in show business did stands of varying lengths in Vegas. And though the decline of the Rat Pack left a longtime hole in the name-brand entertainment market, big deals such as Barry Manilow, Elton John, and even Prince (with Bette Midler to join them any minute) have lately taken up residency at various showrooms. Ticket availability varies, as do the performance schedules. If you can splurge on only one, make it Elton. *See p 116.*

⑬ **Eating with a star.** A Michelin-starred chef, that is. Any number of celebrity chefs have set up outposts in town, but only at Joël Robuchon at the Mansion (in the MGM Grand) can you dine on the work of the youngest chef in history to win three consecutive Michelin stars. It'll cost you, make no mistake about it, but it's also been hailed by the country's most prominent food critics as some of the finest French food on the continent. You won't regret spending the big bucks. *See p 94.*

⑭ **Clearing your head In Red Rock Canyon.** Less than 20 miles from the overstimulated artifice of Vegas is one of the great wonders of the natural world, an impossible set of sandstone monoliths stretching across an unspoiled vista. Take a car through the 13-mile (21km) scenic drive, or hike around on your own and marvel at what is possible given a mere 300 million years or so. *See p 19, bullet ①.*

⑮ **Staying in a fancy resort outside the city.** There are so many Vegas hotel experiences, but my favorite one isn't actually in the city. The remarkable Ritz-Carlton Lake Las Vegas is set right on the titular lake, with a backdrop of desert mountains and an interior of gracious pampering luxury. There are plenty of perks (free yoga lessons) and activities (fly-fishing!) to make this a true resort experience, but it's also a short drive away from all the Vegas action you could want. *See p 133.* ●

The Ritz-Carlton Lake Las Vegas offers a luxury resort atmosphere that's far more sedate than the hubbub of the Strip.

1 The Best Full-Day Tours

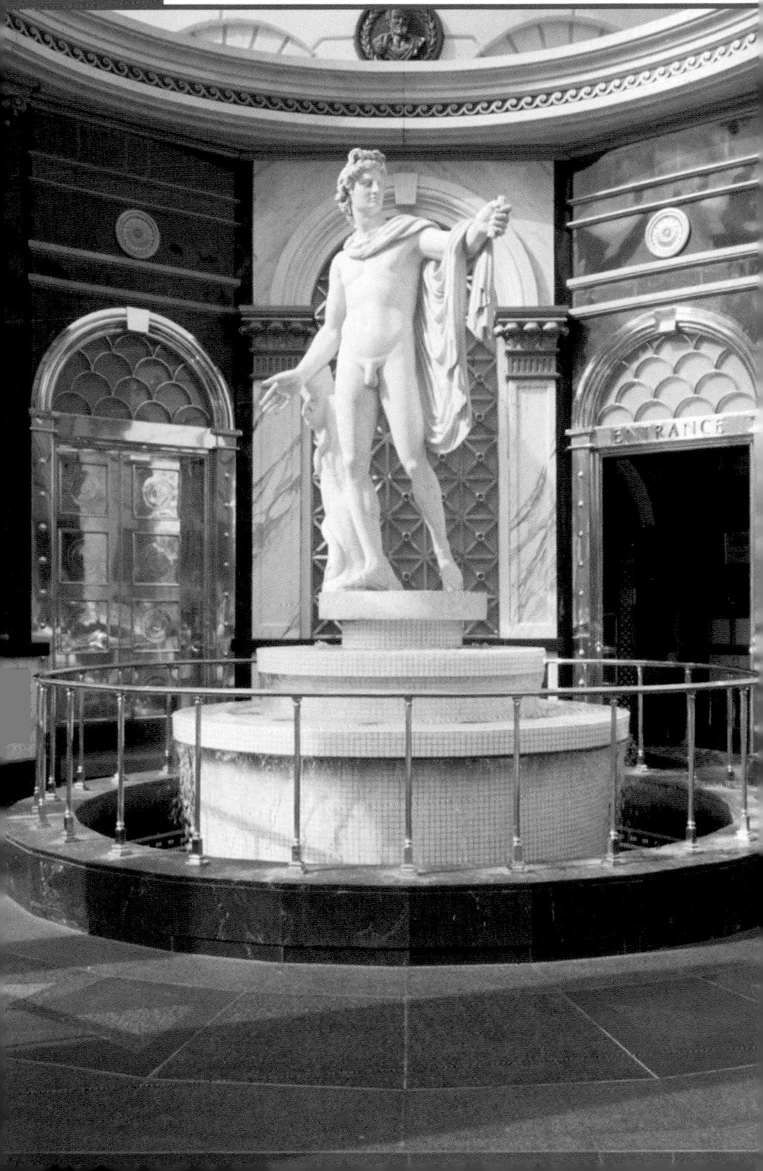

The Best **in One Day**

The Best Full-Day Tours

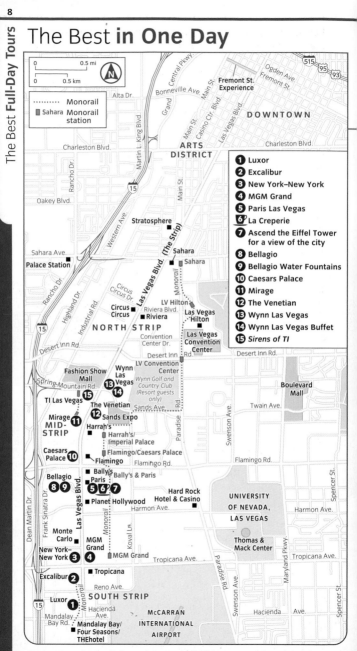

1 Luxor
2 Excalibur
3 New York–New York
4 MGM Grand
5 Paris Las Vegas
6 La Creperie
7 Ascend the Eiffel Tower for a view of the city
8 Bellagio
9 Bellagio Water Fountains
10 Caesars Palace
11 Mirage
12 The Venetian
13 Wynn Las Vegas
14 Wynn Las Vegas Buffet
15 Sirens of TI

Previous Page: Caesars Palace, a prime example of the Las Vegas theme hotel.

If all you know of Las Vegas is the Strip, that's okay—that's really all you need to know. This stretch of Las Vegas Boulevard South is the heart of the city—sometimes it's mistaken for the city itself. That's an understandable error, because here is what Vegas is all about: mammoth hotel casinos, glittering with electricity both real and metaphorical. See nothing else and you will see Las Vegas. START: **The main entrance to the Luxor.**

❶ ★ Luxor. With its glass pyramid-shaped main building (designed by noted architect Veldon Simpson), complete with a 315,000-watt light beam emanating from its peak, this hotel is an appropriate introduction to all things Vegas. There's a touch of historical accuracy (say howdy to those replicas of the Sphinx and Cleopatra's Needle), there's more than a bit of braggadocio (that light beam is allegedly visible from space), and it's all a bit weirdly wrong. (Did I mention the 30-story pyramid is made of glass?) ⏱ *20 min. 3900 Las Vegas Blvd. S.* ☎ *888/777-0188 or 702/262-4000. www.luxor.com.*

❷ Excalibur. Though its interior's King Arthur mythology has been toned down over the years, this castle-shaped resort is still one of the largest in Vegas, and continues to give a sense of what the city was like at its kitsch-and-cash height. Note the battlements, the drawbridge, and even a moat, though the spoilsports have ditched the larger-than-life Merlin that used to overlook the realm. ⏱ *5 min. 3850 Las Vegas Blvd. S.* ☎ *800/937-7777 or 702/597-7700. www.excalibur.com.*

❸ ★★ New York–New York. Take the Big Apple's skyline, squash it down and turn it into a hotel exterior, and presto—you have this pinnacle of over-the-top fantasy Vegas. The Empire State and Chrysler buildings, a half-scale Statue of Liberty, and more are represented in brightly colored, semicartoon detail—and a roller coaster (whose cars appropriately resemble NYC taxis) swooshes through it all. Ridiculous and fantastic all at once. ⏱ *20 min. 3970 Las Vegas Blvd. S.* ☎ *800/693-6763 or 702/740-6969. www.nynyhotelcasino.com.*

Excalibur is the city's tacky but entertaining take on the Arthurian legend.

An immense bronze lion, the largest statue in the United States, guards the entrance to the equally mammoth MGM Grand hotel.

4 MGM Grand. The biggest of the big, the MGM Grand's emerald interior (left over from its original incarnation as an homage to MGM's most beloved *Wizard of Oz*) is garish in the daytime, glowing at night, and enormous at all times. Possibly the biggest hotel in the U.S. (figures vary), it certainly is the greenest. A stately 100,000-pound bronze lion guards the entrance beneath high-tech video screens. Once upon a time, this was the pinnacle of the ill-conceived—and hastily discarded—"Vegas is for families" campaign, but today it caters to more adult-oriented tastes. ⏱ *15 min. 3799 Las Vegas Blvd. S.* ☎ *800/929-1111 or 702/891-7777. www.mgmgrand.com.*

5 Paris Las Vegas. More reproductions of famous landmarks (including a two-thirds replica of the Arc de Triomphe), though without

much regard to actual geographical location, as the Hôtel de Ville is crammed on top of the Louvre. The $785-million resort at least has something of a proper French pedigree; Catherine Deneuve lit it up for the first time when the hotel opened in 1999. ⏱ *15 min. 3655 Las Vegas Blvd. S.* ☎ *888/BONJOUR (266-5687) or 702/946-7000. www.parislv.com.*

Sidewalk creperies are everywhere in Paris, so continue your ooo-la-la mood and grab a traditional snack, with either sweet or savory filling, at **6 La Creperie.** *Inside Paris Las Vegas; see bullet 5.* ☎ *702/946-7000. $.*

7 Ascend the Eiffel Tower for a view of the city. It's half the size of the original (540 ft. tall/165m, to be specific), and probably has about that same percentage of the romance. But the view from the top of the Bellagio

The view from the top of Paris Las Vegas's re-creation of the Eiffel Tower is superb.

The dancing fountains that front the Bellagio are the best free attraction in Las Vegas.

fountains and the Strip in general is pretty swell. Plus the guides here give you all kinds of details about the structure, the kind of re-creation that Vegas used to boast more of, both in the bragging sense and in the possessing sense. Be warned that on windy days, the tower may be shut down for safety reasons. ⏲ *30 min., unless you hang out longer. In Paris Las Vegas; see bullet ❺. Admission Mon–Thurs $9 adults, $7 seniors over 65 & children 6–12; Fri–Sun $12 adults, $10 seniors & children 6–12. Daily 9:30am–12:30am, weather permitting.*

❽ **Bellagio.** The turning point for modern-day Vegas, this elegant cross between hotel as attraction and hotel on steroids set back original owner/visionary Steve Wynn about $1 billion. As you stroll by, admire the ever-so-slightly classy strip mall version of a charming Italian village strung along an 8-acre (3.2-hectare) invo-cation of Lake Como. ⏲ *15 min. 3600 Las Vegas Blvd. S.* ☎ *888/ 987-6667 or 702/693-7111. www. bellagio.com.*

❾ ★★★ **Bellagio Water Fountains.** The best free show in Vegas. Giant spouts send water, shooting (as high as 250 ft./76m in the air), dancing, swaying, and even twirling to music ranging from Sinatra to symphonic. A sophisticated lighting array adds a dash of color to the pro-ceedings. You may think it sounds a bit silly, but catch a show and see if you can stop with just one; for a cine-matic preview, check out the foun-tains' action in the 2001 remake of *Ocean's Eleven.* ⏲ *30 min., to allow for two different shows. In front of the Bellagio; see bullet ❽. Shows every half-hour starting early after-noon; every 15 min. 7pm–midnight, weather permitting.*

❿ ★ **Caesars Palace.** Vegas's original, simultaneously goofy and romantic hotel—and one of the old-est venues (it opened in 1966) still extant on the Strip. It's expanded so much that the Rat Pack wouldn't recognize it, but you should still enjoy the tacky and over-sized replicas of Greco-Roman statuary that decorate the front. Watch for the four-sided Bhrama shrine, an

8,000-pound (3,629kg) replica of the venerated Thai Buddhist good-luck landmark, on the north lawn. ⏲ *15 min. 3570 Las Vegas Blvd. S.* ☎ *877/427-7243 or 702/731-7110. www.caesars.com.*

⓫ ★ **Mirage.** The hotel that, in 1989, kicked off the "more is more" modern Vegas era. This gleaming gold structure cost $630 million (a record when it was built) and set the pattern for pretty much every hotel that followed, down to its mirrored facade and Y shape, to say nothing of the attention-getting outdoor free attractions. The volcano out front doesn't spew lava, but it does set off fire, lights, and smoke every 15 minutes after dark. ⏲ *10 min. 3400 Las Vegas Blvd. S.* ☎ *800/627-6667 or 702/791-7111. www.mirage.com.*

The jaw-dropping lobby of the Venetian is loaded with marble and exquisitely detailed frescoes.

The Mirage kicked off the modern hotel era in Las Vegas and still holds its own today.

⓬ ★ **The Venetian.** Another excellent continuation of the be-in-Vegas-but-pretend-you-are-else-where architecture craze; in this case, a rather admirable (and $1.5-billion) simulation of Venice. There's part of the Doge's palace, there's the Campanile, there's St. Mark's Square, there are even guys in gondolier outfits. All that is missing is the smell from the canals and those pesky attack pigeons. And unlike similar storybook lands at New York–New York and Paris, you can actually wander this Italian cityscape. ⏲ *20 min. 3355 Las Vegas Blvd. S.* ☎ *888/2-VENICE (283-6423) or 702/414-1000. www. venetian.com.*

⓭ ★ **Wynn Las Vegas.** A nearly $3-billion, 60-story effort from Steve Wynn, the man who transformed Las Vegas forever. Disappointingly, you can't see that much from the out-side; unlike Wynn's previous efforts, the eye-catching accouterments—in this case, a 150 foot-tall (46m) man-made mountain—can be properly viewed only from inside. Spoilsport! ⏱ *15 min. 3400 Las Vegas Blvd. S.* ☎ *800/627-6667 or 702/791-7111. www.wynnlasvegas.com.*

⓮ **Wynn Las Vegas Buffet.** For the most part, buffets are no longer the bastion of budget Vegas (itself a thing of the past), but they're still cheaper than dining at one of the city's fabled high-end, celebrity-chef restaurants (and a Vegas tradition, to boot). The buffet at Wynn is a fancy affair, with options running from tandoori chicken to Southern specialties, complete with an active pastry chef on duty—how else to explain a dessert option of floating islands (a sublime meringue-and-cream confection)? *See p 98 for full details on the restaurant.*

⓯ *Sirens of TI.* A free live-action show on the Strip is pretty irre-sistible, and if the kid-friendly stunts that used to be the focus of the entertainment departed this attrac-tion when Treasure Island changed from G-rated to R, adults won't mind switching from rooting for

The Sirens of TI walk the planks outside TI Las Vegas every night.

the buccaneers to leering at the lingerie-clad lovelies who are now the "villains" of this show. ⏱ *20 min. In front of TI Las Vegas, 3300 Las Vegas Blvd. S.* ☎ *702/894-7111. www.treasureisland.com. Shows nightly at 5:30, 7, 8:30 & 10pm.*

Getting Something for Nothing

Vegas used to be the land of freebies—or at least, stuff so cheap it seemed free. Those days are an increasingly dim memory, but many hotels still offer free attractions designed to lure you into their casinos, where they can separate you from even more of your cash. The best of the loss-leaders on the Strip include the **Bellagio Conservatory** (p 53, bullet ❸), the **Bellagio Water Fountains** (p 11, bullet ❾), the **volcano** at the Mirage (bullet ⓫), the **Atrium** (p 55, bullet ❶) at Wynn Las Vegas, and the **fountain shows** at the Forum Shops (p 49, bullet ❹ & p 5, bullet ❺).

One off-Strip number that's worth your while is the **Masquerade in the Sky** show in the Rio (p 133), where carnival-themed floats fly over-head as Mardi Gras-by-way-of-Rio costumed extras toss beads to the cheering crowds. It runs daily at 3, 4, 5, 6:30, 7:30, 8:30, and 9:30pm.

The Best **in Two Days**

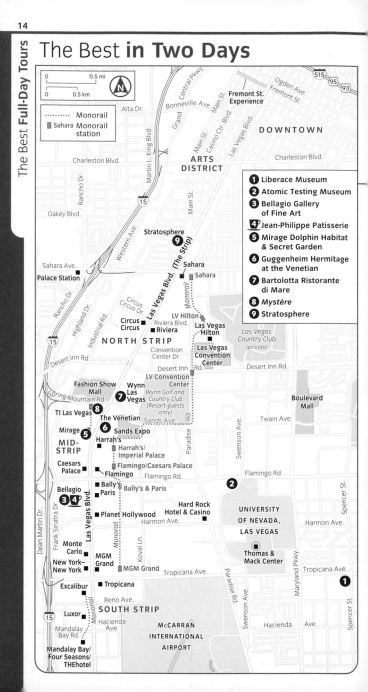

1 Liberace Museum
2 Atomic Testing Museum
3 Bellagio Gallery of Fine Art
4 Jean-Philippe Patisserie
5 Mirage Dolphin Habitat & Secret Garden
6 Guggenheim Hermitage at the Venetian
7 Bartolotta Ristorante di Mare
8 *Mystère*
9 Stratosphere

.... Monorail
▯ Sahara Monorail station

Vegas doesn't have a lot of "cuhl-cha," but it does have four compelling and wildly different museums, each with its own charms—two are located on casino property! Today, I'll also give you a glimpse of life off the Strip, which might reinforce why most visitors rarely leave Las Vegas Boulevard South; except for a few architectural bright spots, design imagination seems to have been exhausted and what remain are mostly strip malls. The treasures found inside, however, should more than make up for the bland exteriors. **START: Liberace Museum (1775 E. Tropicana Ave.). It's best to drive here from your hotel; you can park in the free lot outside the museum.**

The Liberace Museum houses its namesake's flamboyant costumes, cars, and other memorabilia.

❶ ★★ Liberace Museum. Only outsized personalities can leave their imprint on Vegas, and Wladziu Valentino Liberace (1919–87) certainly did that, bless his jewel-encrusted heart. This campy gem helps define "fabulous," and it does it with sequin-twinkle. Pass through the entrance, dominated by a giant pink piano, and get ready to thrill to the Maestro's dazzling collection of outfits, cars (check your hair in that mirrored Rolls-Royce), pianos (former owners include George Gershwin and Chopin), and jewelry—all lovingly preserved and displayed. Don't miss the 50-pound (23kg) rhinestone—as if you could. ⏲ 1 hr. 1775 E. Tropicana Ave. (at Spencer St.). ☎ 702/798-5595. www.liberace.org. Admission

$13 adults, $8.50 seniors over 65 & students with valid school ID, free for children 10 & under. All children must be accompanied by adult. Tues–Sat 10am–5pm; Sun noon–4pm. Closed Mon., Thanksgiving, Dec 25 & Jan 1.

❷ ★★ Atomic Testing Museum. Nevada, in addition to its other dubious contributions to the cultural history of the world, was the primary location for the testing of atomic weapons from 1951 to 1992. Indeed, above-ground blasts at the nearby Atomic Testing Site were once a tourist attraction in the way hotel implosions are today. This Smithsonian-affiliated museum soberly and carefully explores the development and implications of 40 years of nuclear weapons development. Particularly affecting is a rather intense simulation of an explosion. The docents (some of them former site

Las Vegas once promoted nuclear test explosions as a tourist attraction; check out this part of the city's history at the Atomic Testing Museum.

Few things in the city are more fun than visiting the residents of the Mirage's Dolphin Habitat.

employees) are chock-full of information, so quiz them at will. 🕐 *1 hr. 755 E. Flamingo Rd.* ☎ *702/794-5161. www.atomictestingmuseum.org. $12 adults; $9 seniors, military & students with ID; free for children 6 & under. Mon–Sat 9am–5pm; Sun 1–5pm.*

❸ Bellagio Gallery of Fine Art. Originally opened as a showcase for former owner Steve Wynn's personal art collection, this small gallery now hosts often critically lauded temporary exhibits, ranging from fine art to Ansel Adams retrospectives. It's pricey, but it's good to rest your eyes on something of true value and quiet impact in a town that's renowned for its loud and busy landscape. 🕐 *45 min. In Bellagio, 3600 Las Vegas Blvd. S.* ☎ *702/ 693-7871. www.bgfa.biz. Reservations suggested, but walk-ins taken every 15 min. Strollers & packages are forbidden in the gallery, but there are no storage facilities. Admission $15 adults; $12 seniors & students with ID. Audio tour included with admission. Daily 9am–10pm.*

Have a sandwich or, best of all, a delectable dessert at the award-winning **❹ Jean-Philippe Patisserie,** whose signature attraction is a 27-foot-tall (8.2m) chocolate fountain that Willie Wonka would love. *In Bellagio, 3600 Las Vegas Blvd. S.* ☎ *702/693-8788. $.*

Drive to The Mirage, park your car, and walk until further notice.

❺ ★★★ Mirage Dolphin Habitat & Secret Garden. My favorite attraction in Vegas, partly because it's so unexpected. You can get fairly close to some good-looking white tigers and lions at **The Secret Garden,** the daytime quarters for some of Siegfried & Roy's animals (they really live on the duo's ranch). But the best thing here is the **dolphin exhibit,** where a number of the delightful mammals (all born in captivity) live in a state-of-the-art habitat, designed to their specifications. There are no shows per se, but you can watch the dolphins happily cavort with their doting trainers to your heart's content. 🕐 *1 hr. In The Mirage, 3400 Las Vegas Blvd. S.* ☎ *702/791-7111. www.mirage habitat.com. Admission $15 adults; $10 children 4–10; free for children under 10 if accompanied by adult. Mon–Fri 11am–5:30pm; Sat–Sun 10am–5:30pm. Hours vary seasonally.*

❻ ★★ Guggenheim Hermitage at The Venetian. This historic co-venture between New York's Guggenheim and the State Hermitage Museum in St. Petersburg is a complete folly for Vegas and, thus, all the more culturally treasured. The venue hosts regular retrospectives, not infrequently of masterworks rarely (if ever) seen outside of Russia. The free audio guide is excellent, but if a docent-led tour is scheduled, give it a whirl—they are always worthwhile. One thing to look for: The museum's ultracool metal walls allow it to hang pictures with magnets instead of using the usual techniques. ⏱ *45 min. In The Venetian, 3355 Las Vegas Blvd. S. ☎ 702/414-2440. www. guggenheimlasvegas.org. Admission $20 adults, $15 seniors, $13 students with ID, $9.50 children 6–12, free for children under 6. Audio guide included with admission. Daily 9:30am–8:30pm.*

❼ Have dinner at the super Bartolotta Ristorante di Mare.

To get the full Vegas experience, you need to dine with at least one celebrity chef, and it's better to dine with James Beard–nominated Paul Bartolotta, who is actually likely to be in his kitchen. Plus, this beauty of a multilevel restaurant, featuring simple yet not simplistic classic Italian seafood cuisine, is a jewel box in its own right. Worth every dime. ⏱ *At least 2 hr. In Wynn Las Vegas, 3131 Las Vegas Blvd. S. ☎ 888/352-3463 or 702/248-3463. www.wynnlasvegas. com. See p 89 for details on the restaurant.*

❽ ★★★ Mystère. The artistically superb productions of the world-famous Cirque du Soleil have largely

Even in a restaurant mecca such as Vegas, Bartolotta Ristorante di Mare stands out thanks to its superb Italian cuisine.

Mystère launched the onslaught of Cirque du Soleil productions in Las Vegas.

replaced the old Vegas jiggle top revues. This is the first and most representative of classic Cirque, before it went nuts (happily) with the possibilities afforded by a big budget and elaborate staging. The result is a weird and wonderful mix of choreography, acrobatics, and music. ⏱ *1½ hr. In TI Las Vegas, 3300 Las Vegas Blvd. S. ☎ 800/963-9634 or 702/796-9999. www.cirquedusoleil.com. Tickets $60–$95 (plus tax). Shows Mon–Wed & Sat 7 & 9:30pm, Sun 4:30 & 7pm. No shows Thurs–Fri.*

Take the TI shuttle back to The Mirage (or walk to the parking lot) and drive to the Stratosphere.

❾ Stratosphere. The tallest building west of the Mississippi (1,149 ft./350m) offers eagle's-eye views of the desert, the mountains, and the Strip from its observation deck. Access stays open until 1am, and though lines to get up here can be lengthy, you can stay as long as you like. The panorama up here can't be beat, as the lights of this ridiculous and marvelous city twinkle below and around you. If you want, you can have a drink at the deck's Top of the World bar. Check out the adjacent restaurant (the desserts aren't bad); it revolves, which is a retro hoot. ⏱ *30 min. if you stay for a drink. 2000 Las Vegas Blvd. S. ☎ 702/380-7777. Admission to observation deck: $10 adults; $6 seniors, hotel guests & children 4–12; free for children 3 & under. Sun–Thurs 10am–1am; Fri, Sat & holidays 10am–2am. Hours vary seasonally.*

The Best **in Three Days**

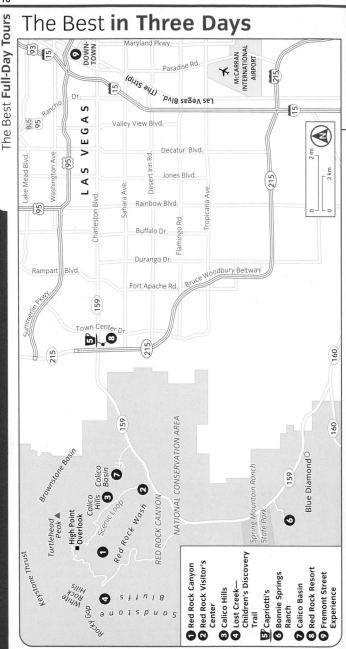

1. Red Rock Canyon
2. Red Rock Visitor's Center
3. Calico Hills
4. Lost Creek—Children's Discovery Trail
5. Capriotti's
6. Bonnie Springs Ranch
7. Calico Basin
8. Red Rock Resort
9. Fremont Street Experience

Even the most dedicated gambler needs to get outside for some real oxygen, so today I start you off with some of the natural wonders surrounding Vegas before whisking you back to Old Vegas for a look at the city the way it used to be. This tour has a lot of wholesome, child-appropriate activities, but adults need not fear—there's also a stop at a casino hotel, in case you need a fix. **START: Drive west from the Strip on Charleston Boulevard, which becomes NV 159, until you get to the Red Rock Canyon Visitor Center.**

① ★★★ **kids Red Rock Canyon.** In startling contrast to the sparkling madness of a city that sheds its skin about once every 10 years is this geological wonder, a mere 600 million years in the making. Sandstone monoliths—yes, some of them are quite red, though others are, frankly, sand-colored—rugged canyons, cliffs, and other topographical thrills thrust up from the desert thanks to serious fault action. The **Red Rock Canyon National Conservation Area** consists of 197,000 acres (79,720 hectares), accessible to the public via a 13-mile (21km) scenic driving loop and 19 hiking trails. In addition to even better photo ops and encounters with local flora and fauna, the hikes provide opportunities to view petroglyphs and pictographs. Red Rock is also one of the most popular rock-climbing destinations in the world. ⏱ *30 min., unless*

The magnificent natural scenery of Red Rock Canyon is only 30 minutes from the Strip.

you stop to take photos or hike. On NV 159. ☎ *702/515-5350. www.nv. blm.gov/redrockcanyon. Admission: $5 for 1-day vehicle pass. Daily 6am–7pm Oct 1–Mar 31, 6am–8pm Apr 1–Sept 30.*

② **kids Red Rock Visitor's Center.** Stop here for brochures, suggestions for hikes, and other practical advice. The center has a small exhibition hall that helpfully illustrates the natural history of Red Rock. If you time it right—spring and summer—you can also visit with Mojave Max, a 65-plus-year-old desert tortoise, who is the charismatic star of the center. ⏱ *30 min. Just past the park entrance on the scenic loop. Daily 8am–4:30pm.*

③ **Calico Hills.** The parking lot at the start of the second trail along the scenic loop provides one of the two best views at the red rocks that give this area its name. ⏱ *20 min. for photographs or 3 hr. to hike, depending on level of fitness. Look for route marker just under a mile (1.6km) from the Visitor's Center.*

④ **kids Lost Creek—Children's Discovery Trail.** The easiest of the park's trails, with no more than a 200-foot (61m) gentle elevation, lasts only about an hour round-trip (depending on how fast you go). It's perfect for kids and anyone who doesn't want to commit to a more demanding hike. Vegetation here is a bit more lush, due in part to the year round stream, and there are some pictographs and an agave (a plant that was once a major source of food for local tribes) roasting pit. 🕐 *1 hr. to hike. Look for route marker, approximately 7 miles (11km) from Visitor's Center.*

Take advantage of the picnic tables at the start of the Lost Creek—Children's Discovery Trail by splitting a sandwich you picked up before entering the park, at **5** **Capriotti's**, the justly lauded local submarine sandwich place. Its outlet in the Red Rock Resort is on the drive in from the Strip to the park. *11011 W. Charleston Blvd., Las Vegas, NV 89135.* ☎ *866/ 767-7773 or 702/797-7625. $.*

6 🔳 **Bonnie Springs Ranch.** A deliberately hokey re-creation of an old Western town, where it's hard to tell if the weather-beaten look is authentic or the sign of a somewhat aging attraction. The regular satirical dramatic skits provide old-fashioned fun; not slick, but sweet and silly. Play cowboys with your kids as you wander past the saloon, the mill, and the old general store. Next door is a petting zoo, a maze of (scrupulously clean) wire pens with goats, rabbits, snooty llamas, elderly deer living in fat retirement, and a couple of wolves. The aviary provides glimpses of peacocks, while a riding stable offers trail rides into the mountains. 🕐 *1–2 hr. NV 159, 5 miles (8km) past Red Rock Canyon.* ☎ *702/875-4191. www. bonniesprings.com. Admission $20 per car. Daily Nov–April 10:30am–5pm, until 6pm the rest of the year.*

7 **Calico Basin.** About 2 miles west of the turnoff into the Red Rock scenic loop is a half-mile-long boardwalk trail, an alternative way for travelers with disabilities or for those with other mobility issues to get out of the car and into the scenery. Look for wild flowers and the foundations of an old cabin. 🕐 *1 hr. Look for signs*

2 miles (3.2km) west of park entrance, on north side of Charleston Blvd.

8 **Red Rock Resort.** This fancy new resort is the getaway of choice for the famous of face to hide in Vegas. It's a good spot to ease yourself back into a Vegas frame of mind with a drink, and maybe even a little gambling. 🕐 *30 min. & up, depending on whether you gamble. 11011 W. Charleston Blvd.* ☎ *866/767-7773 or 702/797-7625. See p 132 for more information on the resort.*

9 🔳 **Fremont Street Experience.** In the heart of Downtown Vegas is a pedestrian-only zone that's covered with a video screen about five football fields in length. The screen's 12.5 million LED modules, and a 500,000-watt sound system, deliver a rotating light-and-sound show. It's the best free show in Vegas after the Bellagio fountains (p 11, bullet **9**). 🕐 *20 min., unless you see more than one show. Fremont Street, between Main St. & Las Vegas Blvd. S.* ☎ *702/678-5777. First show at 8:30pm, then at the top of the hour through midnight.* ●

Its glory days might be in the past, but Bonnie Springs Ranch still offers lots of old-style fun, especially for families.

2 The Best Special-Interest Tours

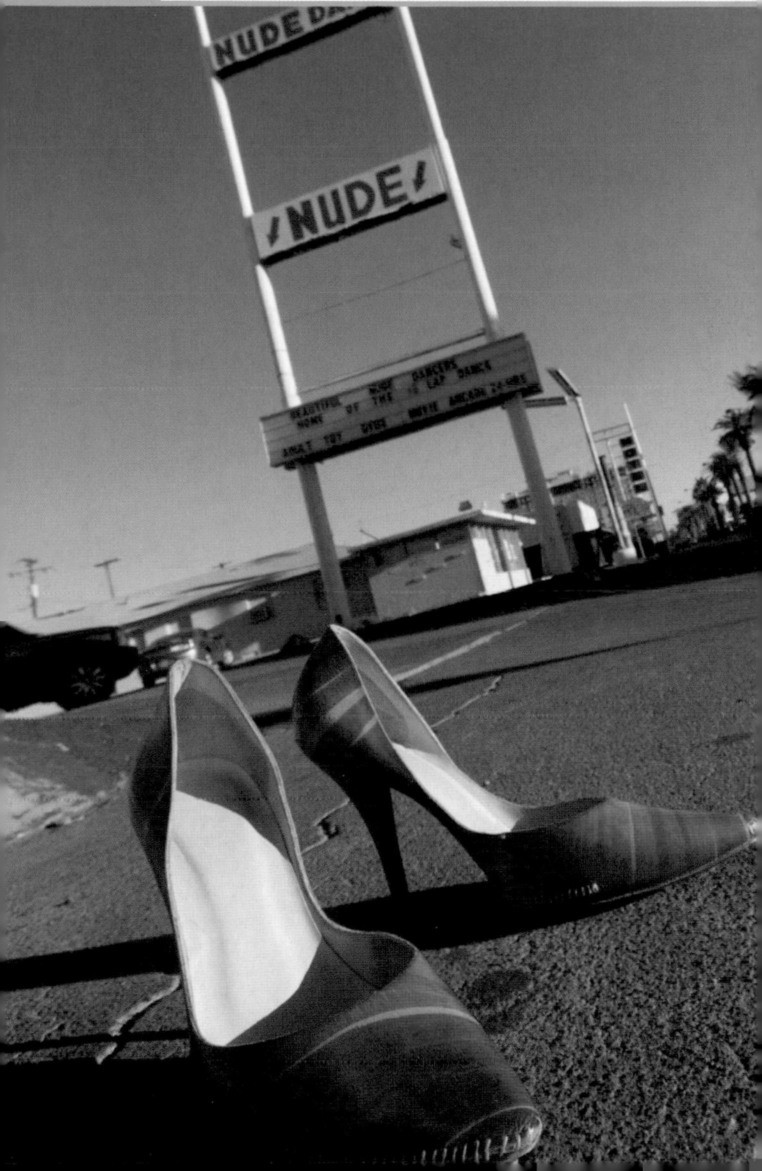

Las Vegas for **Sinners**

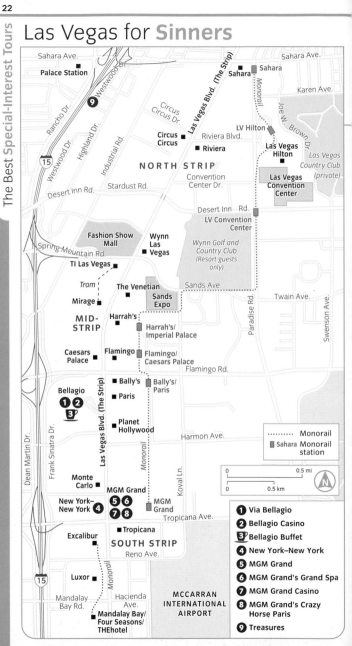

Sahara Ave.

Palace Station

Sahara Ave.

Sahara

Sahara

Karen Ave.

Westwood Dr.

9

Rancho Dr.

Highland Dr.

Westwood Dr.

15

Circus Circus Dr.

Las Vegas Blvd. (The Strip)

Joe W. Brown Dr.

Circus Circus

Riviera

Riviera Blvd.

LV Hilton

Las Vegas Hilton

Monorail

Las Vegas Country Club (private)

NORTH STRIP

Convention Center Dr.

Las Vegas Convention Center

Industrial Rd.

Desert Inn Rd.

Stardust Rd.

Desert Inn Rd.

LV Convention Center

Spring Mountain Rd.

Fashion Show Mall

Wynn Las Vegas

Wynn Golf and Country Club (Resort guests only)

Paradise Rd.

Twain Ave.

Swenson Ave.

TI Las Vegas

Tram

Sands Ave.

The Venetian

Mirage

Sands Expo

MID-STRIP

Harrah's

Harrah's/ Imperial Palace

Caesars Palace

Flamingo

Flamingo/ Caesars Palace

Flamingo Rd.

Bellagio

❶❷
❸

Bally's

Bally's/ Paris

Paris

Las Vegas Blvd. (The Strip)

Frank Sinatra Dr.

Dean Martin Dr.

Planet Hollywood

Harmon Ave.

Monorail

Koval Ln.

Monte Carlo

MGM Grand

New York–New York ❹

❺❻
❼❽

MGM Grand

Tropicana Ave.

Tropicana

Excalibur

SOUTH STRIP

Reno Ave.

15

Luxor

Monorail

Mandalay Bay Rd.

Hacienda Ave.

Mandalay Bay/ Four Seasons/ THEhotel

MCCARRAN INTERNATIONAL AIRPORT

.... Monorail

🚉 Sahara Monorail station

| 0 | | 0.5 mi |
| 0 | | 0.5 km |

N

❶ Via Bellagio
❷ Bellagio Casino
❸ Bellagio Buffet
❹ New York–New York
❺ MGM Grand
❻ MGM Grand's Grand Spa
❼ MGM Grand Casino
❽ MGM Grand's Crazy Horse Paris
❾ Treasures

Previous Page: Las Vegas's nickname as Sin City is well deserved; don't wear your shoes out as you hop from indulgence to indulgence.

A dmit it . . . you didn't come here to have a good time. You came here to have a naughty time. More power to you. Vegas is ready to accommodate, having shifted over to a much more, let's say, adult perspective toward rest and relaxation. In fact, let's see if we can fit in all seven deadly sins, shall we? **START. Drive to Bellagio; there is a convenient parking lot by the far entrance to Via Bellagio, so you need not navigate the distance from Bellagio's main parking structure.**

❶ ★★ Via Bellagio. Start your day off with a little envy, as you window-shop such high-priced outlets as Tiffany, Chanel, Hermes, Dior, Prada, and more. There are plenty of shopping malls all over Vegas, and in just about every hotel, but there is something so classy, so high-end about this one that it gives off the impression that you can't even afford the oxygen. And yet, you are surrounded by people who can. ⏱ *45 min. In Bellagio, 3600 Las Vegas Blvd. S.* ☎ *702/693-7871. www.bellagio.com. Daily 10am–midnight.*

❷ Bellagio Casino. Not jealous enough? Drop by the high rollers section of the Bellagio casino, where well-heeled types drop $500 on one pull of a slot. Notice how even the machines look fancier here, appearing to be encased in marble and wood. Now slink off and go find some nickel slots. Bummer. ⏱ *20 min. See p 79.*

New York–New York is loaded with re-created Big Apple landmarks, including the Brooklyn Bridge; see p 24, bullet ❹.

If you have to ask how much it costs, you probably can't afford it at the mucho upscale Via Bellagio.

Nothing says gluttony like a meal at a Vegas buffet. The **3** ★★ **Bellagio Buffet** is particularly large and especially indulgent, with elaborate pastas, duck and game hen, mounds of cold seafood, and more. *In Bellagio, see bullet* **8**. ☎ *877/234-6358. $$–$$$.*

4 New York–New York. Summon up the wrath felt by locals stuck in a NYC gridlock as you wander around this remarkable re-creation of Manhattan. Outside, the famous skyline is squashed down into a multicolored pastiche. Inside, all the famous neighborhoods are similarly crammed together, from Central Park to Times Square to the Village. It's a remarkable simulation, but it's also a bit of a nightmare to navigate, as there is no way to avoid rambling through the intricately designed twists and turns. Toss in a few thousand (at minimum) other visitors, not to mention the inevitability of getting turned around and heading in the wrong direction, and you'll feel pretty steamed. It won't help if you just lost at blackjack, either. ⏲ *45 min. 3790 Las Vegas Blvd. S.* ☎ *702/740-6969. www.nynyhotelcasino.com.*

5 MGM Grand. This gleaming mass of green houses the largest casino in town, and even if the hotel itself is no longer quite the biggest in the world, it's still pretty darn big. Realize there is truth to the phrase "size does matter" and why those who created and own this might feel more than a bit of pride. Oddly enough, the powers that be sometimes demur about the vastness of the place, having found that people began to be daunted by the sheer acreage. Consequently, one is now told that this isn't the largest casino in town, because its 171,500 square feet have been divided into "four"

Take a breather from the buzz of the Strip at the ultra-relaxing Grand Spa.

smaller casinos. Misplaced use of humility, if you ask me. ⏲ *30 min. 3799 Las Vegas Blvd. S.* ☎ *702/891-7777. www.mgmgrand.com.*

6 ★★ MGM Grand's Grand Spa. Get your sloth on with a pampering treatment at this Asian Zen–themed tranquil spa. It's a minimalist wonder. The Red Lotus Love Ritual, for couples, includes Tibetan ingredients and massage techniques, while the signature Nirvana massage tries to indulge all the senses. ⏲ *1½ hr. In MGM Grand, 3799 Las Vegas Blvd. S.* ☎ *702/891-3077. No children under 12. Ages 12–18 must be accompanied by an adult. Non-hotel guests may use spa Mon–Thurs. Massages $150–$290. Open daily 6am–8pm.*

7 MGM Grand Casino. Go ahead, play those slots or try a hand or two at the tables. And when you win, play some more . . . you greedy thing. ⏲ *30 min.—or many hours. See p 81.*

8 MGM Grand's *Crazy Horse Paris.* A classy way to finish up the list with some lust, this production showcases the "art of the nude."

Stripping 101

Want to learn to work a pole like a pro, get in touch with your inner vixen, or strut sexily in those stilettos you love? Stripping, when done right (think more tease than strip), is actually hard work, and **Stripper 101,** in the Miracle Mile Mall, 3663 Las Vegas Blvd. S. (☎ 702/260-7200; www.stripper101.com), teaches this very Vegas art form to women (sorry guys, you're strictly *verboten!*) ranging from 50-year-old housewives to 20-something celebrities. The hour-long classes are actually pretty nifty and confidence boosting, showing you the proper way to strut, slide down that pole, and give a lap dance. The shy shouldn't worry; you keep your clothes on for the entire experience. And you'll also burn a couple of hundred calories, so you can go sin without guilt at a buffet afterward. Classes cost $30 (they throw in a drink) and you must be at least 18 years of age.

Flawlessly figured girls perform cleverly designed burlesque numbers that tease as they strip down to a wee, letter-if-not-the-spirit strategically placed modesty patch. It really is as artistic as it is sexy. ⏱ 1½ hr. See p 117, for full details on the show.

❾ ★★★ Treasures. You can never have too much of a good thing, so continue your lustfest at this fancy strip joint, whose interior looks like it's straight out of a Victorian sporting house. The stage is strictly modern, as gals twirl in some actual routines on light-up poles, action often complete with fog machines and other effects. Be careful about prices and hidden fees, lest you fall victim to someone else's greed! ⏱ 1 hr., or all night. 2801 Westwood Dr. (parking is hard to spot after dark; use Highland Dr. & keep your eyes peeled). ☎ 702/257-3030. No unescorted women. Topless. Cover $45 & up (includes drinks). Lap dances $10 & up. Open Sun–Thurs 4pm–6am, Fri–Sat 4pm–9am.

Treasures is among the classiest of Sin City's famous strip clubs.

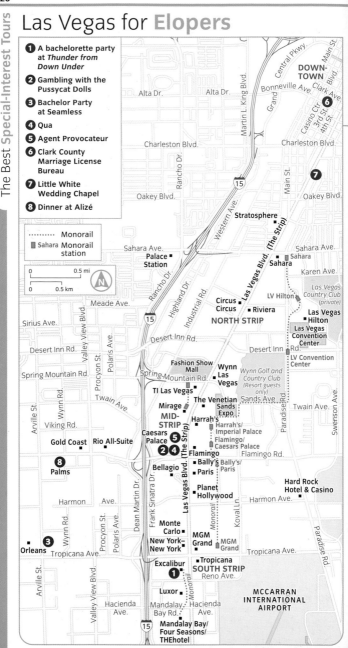

Las Vegas for **Elopers**

1 A bachelorette party at *Thunder from Down Under*

2 Gambling with the Pussycat Dolls

3 Bachelor Party at Seamless

4 Qua

5 Agent Provocateur

6 Clark County Marriage License Bureau

7 Little White Wedding Chapel

8 Dinner at Alizé

·········· Monorail

■ Sahara Monorail station

0   0.5 mi
0   0.5 km

It's quite easy to get married in Vegas. Too easy. There is little, apart from good sense, to prevent you from getting married to a total stranger, and given those free drinks handed out to anyone playing the slots, after a short time you might not even have much of that. If you want to join the more than 100,000 couples who have walked down the aisle before you, here's a traditional 24-hour tour of Vegas-style wedding action. START: **Brides-to-be should drive or take a taxi to Excalibur; grooms should head for Caesars Palace.**

❶ A bachelorette party at *Thunder from Down Under.*
Gals, check out the hunky action at this Aussie male strip revue, featuring some of the cheekiest—and I mean that in all ways—performers you can imagine. Hilarious as well as handsome, they know how to work a room. ⏲ *80 min. In Excalibur, 3850 Las Vegas Blvd. S. ☎ 702/597-7600. www.thunderfromdownunder.com. Must be at least 18 years old. Ages 18–20 must be accompanied by adult. Gentlemen welcome. General Admission $40, plus tax. VIP admission $50, plus tax. Shows Sun–Thurs 9pm; Fri–Sat 9 & 11pm.*

The Aussie hunks in Excalibur's Thunder from Down Under are a very popular diversion for women.

❷ Gambling with the Pussycat Dolls.
An understanding bride-to-be might feel comfortable sending her intended off to gamble at the **Pussycat Dolls Pit** at Caesars

Gambling is undoubtedly entertaining when the Pussycat Dolls perform in their namesake pit at Caesars Palace.

Palace, where the dealers are dressed like America's current favorite burlesque act–turned–band, and go-go dancers suspended in cages above try to make you forget if you should hit or hold at 17. ⏲ *45 min., or until your money runs out. In Caesars Palace, 3570 Las Vegas Blvd. ☎ 702/731-7110. www.caesars.com. Open 24 hr.*

❸ Bachelor Party at Seamless.
Really understanding brides-to-be won't mind if their men head for this rocking high-tech strip club, not least because at 4am the clothes go back on the dancers and the place turns into an after-hours club. Women, feel free to join your men—nothing says "Vegas wedding" more than a hangover and a really late night. ⏲ *1 hr., or more. 4740 S. Arville St. ☎ 702/227-5200. www. seamlessclub.com. Cover: $30 if you arrive by taxi, $20 if you drive yourself. Open 24 hr.*

The luxe Qua spa is the perfect place to relax after a night out on the town.

4 Qua. As soon as you can drag yourself out of bed in the morning, head to this lush new spa at Caesars Palace. Get a special treatment or just sit in the blissful Roman bath area, moving from ice room (where you can exfoliate with shaved ice), to sauna, to plunge pools of varying temperatures, before finally collapsing in a heated lounge chair. Qua's salon also does hair and makeup to make you picture-perfect. *In Caesars Palace, 3570 Las Vegas Blvd. S. (on the 2nd level of the Augustus Tower).* ☎ *866/QUA-0655. www.quabath andspa.com. Full-body massage $140*

Couples from all over the world come to the very convenient Clark County Marriage License bureau to secure permission to get hitched.

& up. All treatments must be reserved in advance. Daily 6am–8pm.

5 Agent Provocateur. If you really did come to Vegas in a hurry, and you want to wear something, ahem, special for your wedding night, check out this British import's line of classy but naughty lingerie. 🕐 *30 min. In The Forum Shops at Caesars Palace.* ☎ *702/696-7174. www.agent provocateur.com. See p 67.*

6 Clark County Marriage License Bureau. Ready to go? You can't until you've made sure what you are about to do is legal. Get your license here. It's no longer open round-the-clock, which is probably just as well, but the entire process should take no more than an hour—and possibly as little as 10 minutes. Once you have that important piece of paper, you're good to go—there's no set waiting period. 🕐 *10 min.– 1 hr. Busiest days are Fri–Sat; slowest period is first thing in the morning on weekdays. 201 Clark Ave.* ☎ *702/671-0600. www.co.clark.nv.us/clerk/ marriage_information.htm. Must be at least 18 years old & have valid proof of age & a Social Security number. Couples must be male–female. License is $55, cash only. Open daily 8am–midnight, including holidays.*

For Your Honeymoon . . .

It should come as no surprise that a city that holds as many weddings as this one does has plenty of hotel options for that must-have romantic honeymoon. Many hotels offer special packages for newlyweds, so ask when you book. For my favorite properties in Vegas, including some ultraromantic possibilities, see p 122.

Wedding Tip

If you want something a little more traditional . . . or outrageous for your big day, see p 119 for a rundown of my favorite wedding chapels in Las Vegas.

❼ Little White Wedding Chapel. Hotel chapels tend to be prettier and more traditional, but if you came to Vegas for the kitsch, your search will be best fulfilled by this famous wedding factory. It was good enough for Michael Jordan, Demi Moore and Bruce Willis, and Brittany Spears (though "good" in these cases may be a debatable term). Plus, for those particularly in a hurry, it has a drive-up window. ⏲ 10 min.–1 hr., depending on how busy

If you like your weddings kitschy and fast, the Little White Wedding Chapel is the best place to get married in Vegas.

For a romantic dinner in Las Vegas, you can't beat Alizé.

they are & if you made a reservation in advance. 1301 Las Vegas Blvd. S. (between E. Oakley & Charleston blvds.). ☎ 800/545-8111 or 702/382-5943. www.alittlewhitechapel.com. Base chapel rate $55; add-ons (everything from garters to Elvis) & complete packages are available at extra cost. Open 24 hr.

❽ ★★★ Dinner at Alizé. Hold your wedding feast at the city's most romantic restaurant, with nearly floor-to-ceiling windows on three sides, and a virtually unobstructed view of the city and desert. Though surely you won't take your eyes off each other. ⏲ 2 hr. See p 87 for more details on the restaurant.

Las Vegas **with Kids**

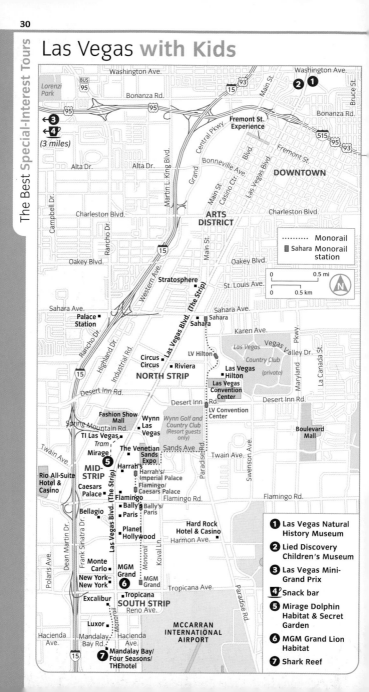

Legend:

- ·········· Monorail
- ■ Sahara Monorail station

0 ——— 0.5 mi
0 ——— 0.5 km

1. Las Vegas Natural History Museum
2. Lied Discovery Children's Museum
3. Las Vegas Mini-Grand Prix
4. Snack bar
5. Mirage Dolphin Habitat & Secret Garden
6. MGM Grand Lion Habitat
7. Shark Reef

Don't kid yourself; Vegas isn't for children. Nowadays, the city markets itself strongly as a haven for distinctly adult pursuits and entertainment. This is obvious when you look at the sides of several of the casino hotels, often featuring multistory adverts for girlie shows in the form of shapely, nearly bare bottoms. But there are some activities appropriate for the younger set, so if you have kids in tow, your vacation won't come up a loser in the short run. START: **Drive to Las Vegas Natural History Museum and park in the museum lot.**

❶ ★ Las Vegas Natural History Museum. Hardly high-tech, this throwback to the era of dioramas of taxidermy animals comes off as small-town when compared to more venerable—and well-funded—institutions found in New York or Los Angeles. But your dinosaur-crazy kid will enjoy it, and you'll enjoy the relaxed pace. Among the hands-on, interactive exhibits is an installation that allows participants to experience life as a nocturnal critter—and not in the Vegas way! ⏱ *90 min. 900 Las Vegas Blvd. N. (at Washington Ave.; adjacent to Cashman Center).* ☎ *702/384-3466. www.lvnhm.org. Admission $7 adults; $6 seniors, military & students; $3 kids 3–11; free for kids 2 & under. Daily 9am–4pm*

The relaxed Las Vegas Natural History museum is loaded with life-size fossils and animal exhibits.

❷ ★★ Lied Discovery Children's Museum. An excellent facility that provides tons of sugar (all kinds of playful, clever, interactive

exhibits) to help the medicine—that is, education about physics, nature, the human body, history, and more—go down. Kids are probably savvy enough to realize it's good for

Both kids and parents love the interactive exhibits at the Lied Discovery Children's Museum.

Future Formula One stars can get their speed on at the delightful Las Vegas Mini-Grand Prix.

them, but by the time they are launching tennis balls into the air, they probably won't care they are also learning about air pressure. There is even a special section for the 5-and-under set. ⏱ *2hr. 833 Las Vegas Blvd. N. (½ block south of Washington Ave., across the street from Cashman Field).* ☎ *702/382-3445. www.ldcm.org. Admission $8 adults; $7 seniors, military & kids 1–17. Open Tues–Fri 9am–4pm, Sat 10am–5pm, Sun noon–5pm. Closed Mon, except school holidays.*

③ ★★★ Las Vegas Mini-Grand Prix. Now that the kids have gotten a little education, let 'em have some fun! This attraction is part arcade, part go-kart racetrack; though the former is well stocked, it's the latter that holds the most appeal. Not only is it a rare outdoor non-water-related activity, but your offspring can work off nervous energy on four different tracks. One is the longest road track in Vegas, full of twists and turns, while another is a high-banked oval where the goal is to make other drivers take a spill on the grass. Well, maybe that's just me . . . and only to the mean kids who deserve it. ⏱ *2 hr. 1401 N. Rainbow Rd., just off U.S. 95 N.* ☎ *702/259-7000. www.lvmgp. com. Ride tickets $6.25 each, $29 for 5. Minimum height requirement for rides is 36 in. Sun–Thurs 10am–10pm; Fri–Sat 10am–11pm.*

The pizzas at the **④ snack bar** are triple the size and half the price of those you'll find in your hotel or on the Strip. And pretty tasty, too! *In Mini-Grand Prix, 1401 N. Rainbow Rd.* ☎ *702/259-7000. $.*

⑤ ★★★ Mirage Dolphin Habitat & Secret Garden. There is an actual zoo in Vegas, but I am sending you here because it's more of a highlight, short-attention-span choice. Plus, the inhabitants are just so cool. Siegfried & Roy's show may have come to an abrupt and rather ignominious end, but the furry stars of their show are still on display in this lush setting. It's aesthetically pleasing—more so than a regular zoo—because of its size, which also allows for some fairly up-close encounters with white tigers and the like. (None of the cats lives here, instead putting in regular "shifts" before returning to their expansive digs at their owners' ranch.) The best part is the dolphin habitat, an expensive, carefully constructed and maintained 2.5-million-gallon tank where these most delightful of mammals frolic. Trainers dote on them, stimulating their charges. If you are really lucky, you might be around for a session of ball. Very little pleases a kid more than trying to catch a wet ball flipped to them by a dolphin snout. ⏱ *1 hr. See p 16, bullet ⑤.*

No Children Allowed!

When I said Vegas no longer throws out the welcome mat to families, I wasn't kidding. Be advised that many hotels will not allow children who aren't staying on their property through the front door (they'll demand a room key as proof of occupancy). And don't even think about allowing your children to linger anywhere near a casino floor . . . they'll be shooed away pretty quickly. This tour will keep your youngsters happy for a day in the city, but as a long-term family vacation destination, Vegas falls short of ideal. If you have little ones, I strongly advise you to look elsewhere for a long break.

6 ★★ **MGM Grand Lion Habitat.** More cooing at kitties for the kiddies, as visitors to this free exhibit gather around a glassed-in enclosure to watch big cats lounge. Gather under the glass tunnel, the top of which is a favorite napping spot, and check out the underside of a lion. Hold up your kid's paw to the feline above you and marvel at the size and power. Prepare to go "aww" when the trainers, who spent a lot of time becoming accepted as one of the pack, wrestle, play with, and lavish love on their furry companions. The time you spend will depend on how much action the trainers are stirring up. ⏱ *20 min. In MGM Grand, 3799 Las Vegas Blvd. S.* ☎ *702/891-7777. www.mgmgrand. com. Free admission. Daily 11am–10pm.*

7 ★ **Shark Reef.** Guests travel through a tunnel that runs through the middle of this giant aquarium, designed to look like a sunken ancient temple. The sharks (plus other finny friends) glide smoothly and somewhat sinisterly up and around you. It's more active than the MGM lions (see **6**, above), but has less personality. It also doesn't take much time to navigate, which is probably just as well, because you—if not the kids—will probably be fairly tuckered out by this point. ⏱ *45 min. The aquarium is in a remote area of Mandalay Bay, a difficult trek for those with mobility problems. In Mandalay Bay, 3950 Las Vegas Blvd. S.* ☎ *702/632-4555. www.mandalaybay.com. Admission $16 adults, $11 children 5–12, free for children 4 & under. Daily 10am–11pm. Last admission at 10pm.*

Children love watching the MGM Grand's signature lions carouse in their glass-enclosed habitat.

Las Vegas for **Adrenaline Junkies**

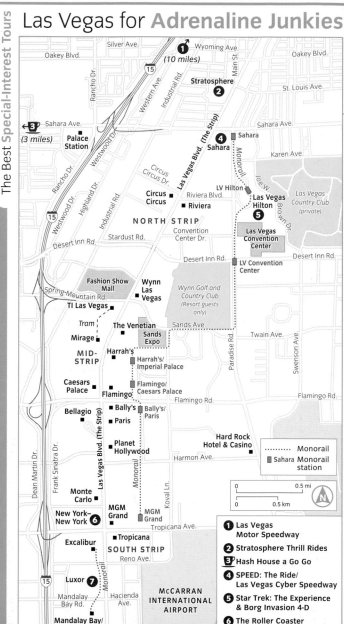

Silver Ave.

Oakey Blvd.

1 (10 miles)

Wyoming Ave.

Oakey Blvd.

Stratosphere 2

St. Louis Ave.

3 Sahara Ave. (3 miles)

Palace Station

4 Sahara

Sahara

Karen Ave.

LV Hilton

Las Vegas Hilton

Las Vegas Country Club (private)

Circus Circus Dr.

Circus Circus

Riviera Blvd.

Riviera

NORTH STRIP

Convention Center Dr.

5

Stardust Rd.

Las Vegas Convention Center

Desert Inn Rd.

LV Convention Center

Desert Inn Rd.

Fashion Show Mall

Wynn Las Vegas

Wynn Golf and Country Club (Resort guests only)

Spring Mountain Rd.

TI Las Vegas

Tram

The Venetian

Sands Expo

Sands Ave.

Twain Ave.

Swenson Ave.

Mirage

MID-STRIP

Harrah's

Harrah's/ Imperial Palace

Caesars Palace

Flamingo

Flamingo/ Caesars Palace

Flamingo Rd.

Flamingo Rd.

Bellagio

Bally's

Bally's/ Paris

Paris

Hard Rock Hotel & Casino

Planet Hollywood

Harmon Ave.

Monte Carlo

MGM Grand

MGM Grand

Tropicana Ave.

New York–New York **6**

Excalibur

Tropicana

SOUTH STRIP

Reno Ave.

Luxor **7**

McCARRAN INTERNATIONAL AIRPORT

Mandalay Bay Rd.

Hacienda Ave.

Mandalay Bay/ Four Seasons/ THEhotel

	Monorail
▣ Sahara	Monorail station

0   0.5 mi

0   0.5 km

1 Las Vegas Motor Speedway

2 Stratosphere Thrill Rides

3 Hash House a Go Go

4 SPEED: The Ride/ Las Vegas Cyber Speedway

5 Star Trek: The Experience & Borg Invasion 4-D

6 The Roller Coaster

7 IMAX Theater and Ridefilm

The thrills in Vegas don't come solely from games of chance. While efforts to sustain full-blown amusement parks have failed, there are still plenty of rides and other what-a-rush-type activities scattered about the city. Many of the hotels, in an effort to lure business, have some kind of attraction designed to make some of us nauseous and others exhilarated. If you have balance or nerve issues, this ain't the tour for you. START: **Drive to Las Vegas Motor Speedway.**

For speedy thrills, racing fans flock to the Las Vegas Motor Speedway to watch the pros rev their engines.

① ★★ **Las Vegas Motor Speedway.** Just about anything with wheels that goes really, really fast can be found here in one form or another. A $200-million state-of-the-art motorsports entertainment complex, this 176,000-seat facility serves up drag racing and super-speed courses in the viewing department. If participation is more your thing, get your speed fix at the go-kart tracks, driving schools, and other attractions. ⏱ *At least 2 hr. 7000 Las Vegas Blvd. N., directly across from Nellis Air Force base (take I-15 N to Speedway exit 54).* ☎ *702/644-4443 or 800/644-4444 for ticket information. www.lvms.com. Tickets $10–$75. Race days vary.*

② ★★ **Stratosphere Thrill Rides.** The Stratosphere tower is the tallest building west of the Mississippi. That's 1,149 feet up, for those keeping track. So naturally, one puts thrill rides on the top of it. The **Big Shot** takes you up the final 160 feet or so of the spire before letting you free-fall back down again. Once your

heart is back where it belongs, you can then try the **X-Scream,** a giant teeter-totter that teeters and totters over the edge of the 100-story tower. Try not to throw up on the smart people who stayed safely below on the Strip, okay? Finally, there is **Insanity**—an appropriate moniker, given that the very thought of this ride elicits an "are you nuts?" from me—which whirls you around 1,000 feet in the air. ⏱ *45 min., depending on how long the lines are. In Stratosphere Las Vegas, 2000 Las Vegas Blvd. S.* ☎ *702/380-7777. www.stratospherehotel.com. Admission $8 per individual ride, plus fee to ascend Tower ($10 adults; $6 seniors, hotel guests & kids 4–12; free for those dining in the buffet room or Top of the World. Discount multiride & all-day packages available.*

Zip around the Sahara hotel on SPEED: The Ride, one the city's best coasters; see p 36, bullet **④***.*

Sun–Thurs 10am–1am; Fri, Sat & holidays 10am–2am. Hours vary seasonally. Minimum height requirement for all rides is 48 in.

At **3** **Hash House a Go Go,** the pancakes are just about the size of a large pizza, and the waffles can have bacon baked right into them. Burgers are stuffed, salads come in all varieties, and the menu is extensive. Portions are meant for sharing, which makes the prices reasonable. *6800 W. Sahara Ave. ☎ 702/804-4646. $–$$.*

4 ★★ SPEED: The Ride/Las Vegas Cyber Speedway. This two-parter capitalizes on the increasing popularity of auto racing in America. Part one is a virtual reality ride allowing you to effectively take the wheel of a NASCAR race car and drive it around the Las Vegas Motor Speedway, or through the streets of Vegas. Watch out for that pyramid! Racing fans ought to be in virtual heaven. Part two is a roller coaster that whips around the NASCAR Café and the Sahara hotel, zooms straight

Soar high above the Strip on the Stratosphere's very appropriately named Insanity; see p 35, bullet **2**.

Assimilate some sci-fi culture as you peruse Star Trek memorabilia on your way into the city's best motion simulator at Star Trek: The Experience.

up a 250-foot-tall tower, and then propels you through the whole thing all over again—this time, backward. 🕐 *At least 45 min. In the Sahara, 2535 Las Vegas Blvd. S. ☎ 702/734-RACE (7223). www.nascarcafelas vegas.com. Cyber Speedway simulator $10 (you must be at least 54 in. tall to ride); SPEED: The Ride roller coaster $10 for single ride. $20 for all-day pass on both rides. Sun–Thurs 11am–midnight; Fri–Sat 11am–1am; hours may vary (call 702/737-2875 for up-to-date information).*

5 ★★ Star Trek: The Experience & Borg Invasion 4-D in the Las Vegas Hilton. Obviously, no Trekker worth their Vulcan ears should miss this exhibit, but only the dedicated motion-simulator-ride enthusiast will consider the price and wait thoroughly worthwhile. Then again, the addition of costumed actors, who add to the story line (kept deliberately vague so as not to ruin any surprises), adds an extra fillip of fun to the whole venture, though the quality of the experience depends somewhat on the skill of said actors. The accompanying museum is loaded with *Star Trek* memorabilia and is a must for the sci-fi set. 🕐 *1 hr. In Las Vegas Hilton, 3000 Paradise Rd.* ☎ *888/GO-BOLDLY. www.startrekexp.com. All-day pass including both attractions & museum $39 adults, $36 seniors & kids 12 & under. Purchase tickets online for discounts. Must be 42 in. tall. Daily 11am–8:30pm or 10pm, depending on season (call before you go).*

⑥ The Roller Coaster. I consider this "classic" Las Vegas, not because it harkens back to the Rat Pack days, but because it's a remnant of a "quickly becoming similarly remote" era—that of the Family Friendly promotions. Back, oh, about 10 years ago, the attitude was "why *not* put the Coney Island–themed roller coaster (originally known as the Manhattan Express) right through the lobby and around the outside of the hotel?" Why not, indeed? In any case, it's indisputable that the coaster (which pours on the adrenaline with a 144-ft./44m drop, plus various inversions and twists) does replicate a ride in the New York City cabs its

From its cab-themed cars to its adrenaline-inducing drops, The Roller Coaster perfectly captures New York's breakneck speed.

There's almost always something worthwhile playing at the Luxor's IMAX Theater.

cars resemble—with all that entails 🕐 *10 min., depending on the lines. In New York–New York, 3790 Las Vegas Blvd. S.* ☎ *800/689-1797. www.nyny hotelcasino.com. Must be at least 54 in. to ride. Single-ride pass $13, day pass $25. Open Sun–Thurs 11am– 11pm, Fri–Sat 10:30am–midnight.*

⑦ ★ IMAX Theater & Ridefilm. Both parts of this attraction change features regularly. The theater offers standard IMAX films (one almost always deals with Egypt in some form or another), plus 3-D and motion simulator rides. The Ridefilm runs different-themed adventures, but most are decidedly cheesy and not worth the price. *In Luxor Las Vegas, 3900 Las Vegas Blvd. S.* ☎ *702/262-IMAX. www.luxor.com. Admission $12 & up (prices vary depending on movie) for IMAX Theater; $10 for IMAX Ridefilm. Can be purchased as part of an all-attractions package for $35. Sun–Thurs 9am–11pm; Fri–Sat 9am–midnight. IMAX showtimes vary & are subject to change without notice.*

Las Vegas for **Museum Lovers**

NORTH STRIP
Desert Inn Rd.
LV Convention Center
Riviera
0   0.5 mi
0   0.5 km
Fashion Show Mall
Spring Mtn. Rd.
Wynn Las Vegas
Wynn Golf and Country Club (Resort guests only)
······· Monorail
■ Sahara Monorail station
Tram
TI Las Vegas
The Venetian
Sands Ave.
Mirage
MID-STRIP
Harrah's/ Imperial Palace
Flamingo/ Caesars Palace
Twain Ave.
Caesars Palace
Flamingo
Flamingo Rd.
Flamingo Rd.
Bellagio
Bally's/ Paris
Bally's/ Paris
Planet Hollywood
Hard Rock Hotel & Casino
Harmon Ave.
UNIVERSITY OF NEVADA, LAS VEGAS ④
Harmon Ave.
Monte Carlo
MGM Grand
MGM Grand
Thomas & Mack Center
New York-New York
Tropicana Ave.
Tropicana Ave.
Excalibur
Tropicana
SOUTH STRIP
Reno Ave.
Luxor
MCCARRAN INTERNATIONAL AIRPORT
Hacienda Ave.
Mandalay Bay Rd.
Hacienda Ave.
Mandalay Bay/ Four Seasons/ THEhotel
Paradise Rd.
Swenson St.
Maryland Pkwy.
Spencer St.
Eastern Ave.
Koval Ln.
Paradise Rd.
③' →
(15 miles)
②
①→

① Clark County Heritage Museum
② Liberace Museum
③' Freed's Bakery
④ Marjorie Barrack Museum
⑤ Atomic Testing Museum
⑥ King Tut Museum
⑦ Guggenheim Hermitage Museum
⑧ Madame Tussaud's in the Venetian

⑤ ⑥ ⑦ ⑧

L as Vegas isn't much for history, but a few intrepid places hold on to the past, local and otherwise. It's hard to keep up with a place that changes nearly as completely and thoroughly, and just about as often, as a showgirl does when she wipes off her makeup, especially when said place tends to blow up anything that it considers "outdated" (which, for Vegas, could mean something erected in 1987). The following museums (most housed in unpromising strip malls or within hotels) enshrine everything from the sublime to the ridiculous.
START: Drive to Clark County Heritage Museum, and park in lot.

An old-fashioned train depot is just one of the many historic buildings preserved at the Clark County Heritage Museum.

① ★★ **Clark County Heritage Museum.** Charming and cheap, this surprisingly large facility is a collection of restored historic buildings from significant points in Vegas history. There are a train depot, a print shop, a mine, a ghost town, and much more to remind us that up until the days of Bugsy Siegel, Vegas was just another Wild West town, trying to make it in the desert. An exhibit center features changing

The best museum in Las Vegas, the Liberace Museum preserves the memory (and belongings) of one of the city's most beloved (and bejeweled) residents.

displays on different eras in local history. On the downside, it's not particularly close to anything, and because most of it is outside, summer is not an optimum time for a visit unless you go early in the day. 🕐 1 hr. *1830 S. Boulder Hwy., East Las Vegas.* ☎ *702/455-7955. www.co.clark.nv.us/parks/clark_county_museum.htm. Admission $1.50 adults, $1 seniors & kids 3–15, free for kids under 3. Daily 9am–4:30pm.*

❷ ★★★ Liberace Museum.

You can keep your Celine Dions and Manilows. Liberace, now, *there* was a showman, a walking bundle of unashamed, over-the-top glitz and absurdity, all backed up by a classically trained pianist who really knew how to tickle the ivories—and the audience's funny bone. No wonder he was a top Vegas box office attraction during the sequin-drenched 1970s. Here is a shrine to the legend more than the man (you will view plenty of the costumes, jewels, and other excess that made him famous, but you won't learn much about the guy underneath it all). Still, not only is it an only-in-Vegas

kind of place, but it also serves as a reminder that this city needs to stop taking itself so seriously. 🕐 1 hr. See p 15, bullet ❶.

❸ Freed's Bakery,

with its gooey, sugary delights, provides a sort of caloric counterpart to the Liberace way of life. The physical shop itself is nothing special, but the frosting sure is. *4780 S. Eastern Ave. (at Tropicana Blvd.).* ☎ *702/456-7762. $.*

❹ ★ Marjorie Barrack Museum.

Somewhat on the musty side, but worth a stop for those interested in local Native American and Mojave desert natural history. Permanent exhibits include crafts from Hopi, Navajo, and Southern Paiute tribes, plus glass-enclosed displays of local reptiles. Temporary exhibits tend to be a bit spiffier, with the focus on photography and Native American topics. 🕐 45 min. *On the UNLV campus, 4505 S. Maryland Pkwy.* ☎ *702/895-3381. http://hrcweb.nevada.edu/museum. Free admission. Mon–Fri 8am–4:45pm; Sat 10am–2pm.*

A statue of a shaman dancer from the Native American collection at the Marjorie Barrick Museum.

❺ ★★★ Atomic Testing Museum.

Sixty miles from Vegas is a large swath of desolate desert, the perfect place for the testing of nuclear weapons—which is exactly what the government did on that spot for 40 years. Once upon a time, aboveground blasts were a tourist attraction. Such naiveté is part of the

Elvis (okay...his wax replica) hasn't left the building at Madame Tussaud's, and there are lots of other famous people keeping him company.

complicated political, historical, scientific, and moral legacy of the nuclear testing program, and this excellent museum is as much dedicated to trying to sort it all out as it is to preserving this troubled part of Vegas heritage. Look among the excellent displays for the motion-simulator theater that attempts to demonstrate what it feels like to ride out a test blast in a bunker. ⏱ *1½ hr. See p 15, bullet* ❷.

❻ ★★ kids King Tut Museum. This may sound cheesy at first, but it's actually quite a cool little project. A full-scale replica of King Tut's tomb, including many of the wondrous objects discovered therein. Yeah, it's a copy, but it's a really good copy, meticulously hand-crafted by artisans in Egypt. Given the difficulty most would have journeying to see the original, it's a worthwhile substitute. Certainly, it's a

Far from hokey, the King Tut Museum in the Luxor is both cool and educational.

must for any kid who's studying Egypt in Social Studies. ⏱ *30 min. In Luxor, 3900 Las Vegas Blvd. S. ☎ 702/262-4000. www.luxor.com. Admission $10. Daily 11am–11pm.*

❼ ★★ Guggenheim Hermitage Museum. The Hermitage State Museum in St. Petersburg is home to one of the great (and one of the least readily accessible) encyclopedic museum collections in the world, and plenty of rare Russian treasures have been put on display here. Notable past exhibits have included a lauded collection titled "The Pursuit of Pleasure" and a set of Rubens' masterpieces. There have also been superb collaborations with the Guggenheim, such as a comparative display of Mapplethorpe photos and classical figure studies. This is an extraordinary venture, and it's hard to believe it's in Vegas at all, much less inside a casino hotel. ⏱ *45 min. See p 16, bullet* ❻.

❽ ★ kids Madame Tussaud's in The Venetian. A branch of London's legendary wax museum, here you will find lifelike—or creepy, sometimes it's a fine line—replicas of famous folks. Unlike in other museums, you can actually touch the free-standing exhibits. Go ahead, fondle J. Lo's butt or give Brad Pitt a little smooch. ⏱ *45 min. In The Venetian, 3355 Las Vegas Blvd. S. ☎ 702/862-7800. www.madametussauds lv.com. Admission $24 adults, $18 seniors, $15 students, $14 kids 7–12, free for kids 6 & under, $50 family pass for 2 adults & 2 students or children. Daily 10am–10pm, but hours vary seasonally.* ●

The Best
Neighborhood Walks

South Strip

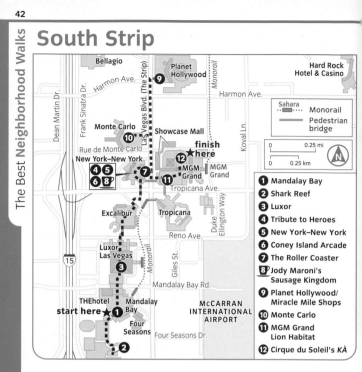

- **1** Mandalay Bay
- **2** Shark Reef
- **3** Luxor
- **4** Tribute to Heroes
- **5** New York–New York
- **6** Coney Island Arcade
- **7** The Roller Coaster
- **8** Jody Maroni's Sausage Kingdom
- **9** Planet Hollywood/Miracle Mile Shops
- **10** Monte Carlo
- **11** MGM Grand Lion Habitat
- **12** Cirque du Soleil's *KÀ*

Of the three major sections of the Strip, this is probably the one with the most variety and the greatest concentration of over-the-top Vegas hotels. Wacky theme hotels are sadly giving way to good-taste resort hotels, which, though grand, are starting to seem a bit cookie-cutter. Not these babies. START: **Mandalay Bay's main lobby.**

1 Mandalay Bay. This is the point, chronologically, when designers began to pull back, if ever so slightly, from full Design Madness. Consequently, the Southeast Asia theme (think Kipling's poem "Mandalay," and the era of British colonialism) is more subdued than I might like. There are still statues, foliage, and a large round aquarium in the lobby, but this hotel's appeal lies more in the whole package. Check out the 11-acre (4.5-hectare)

Mandalay Beach pool area from the casino windows; it's the best in town. And do wander down the hotel's restaurant row, where design has truly run amok. There's a **statue of Lenin** (covered in fake pigeon droppings, and beheaded) outside **Red Square** (p 96), whose interior is covered with the ephemeral trappings of Bolshevik and Stalinist highs and lows. **Aureole** (p 88) has a four-story glass wine tower, accessed by cat-suited wine gals hoisted up on

Previous Page: Dale Chihuly's Fioro di Como *glass sculpture adorns the ceiling of the Bellagio's lobby.*

A headless statue of Lenin marks the entrance to Mandalay Bay's stylish Red Square restaurant.

pulleys. And on it goes, each establishment demonstrating its own level of interior design cleverness. 🕐 *45 min., if you don't stop to eat. 3950 Las Vegas Blvd. S. (at Hacienda Ave.).* ☎ *702/632-7000. www. mandalaybay.com.*

② ★ **Shark Reef.** Don't think this is Animal Planet's "Shark Week" come to life. This is really just a beautifully designed (and expensive) aquarium, though not a particularly large one. But because you travel via a glass tunnel that passes right through the exhibits, it does give you the illusion of joining the fish. It's more peaceful than stimulating, but it's decidedly cool to get that up close and personal with a shark or to see a piranha feed. 🕐 *45 min., unless you are hypnotized by fish-watching. See p 33, bullet* **⑦**.

③ **Luxor.** This Egyptian repro is simultaneously a kitschfest—and I mean that in the best possible Vegas way—and very attractive. Tip your hat to the 30-foot (9.1m) sphinx that guards the entrance before viewing the gloriously over-the-top interior. *See p 47 for a walking tour of this hotel.*

④ **Tribute to Heroes.** At the base of New York–New York's 150-foot-tall (46m) Statue of Liberty, this granite structure holds a permanent collection of notes, pins, and other mementos left outside the hotel post-9/11 to honor the victims and those who so valiantly worked at the tragic site. It's a rare somber note amid the Strip's carefully orchestrated irreverence. *Outside New York–New York, see bullet* **⑤**.

⑤ **New York–New York.** The audacious Manhattan exterior—12 skyscrapers (one-third the size of the originals), including a 47-story Empire State Building, the New York Public Library, Ellis Island, and more—is riveting. It makes me sorry that Vegas hotels now trend toward good taste. Be sure to cross over the one-fifth-size (300-ft.-tall/91m) replica of the Brooklyn Bridge to stroll the hotel's interior, which may have you wondering, "Are they kidding?" From the splendid Art

This lionfish is one of the many denizens of the deep you'll find at Shark Reef.

New York–New York's famous whimsical exterior is dominated by a replica of Lady Liberty.

Deco–inspired reception area and a re-creation of Central Park (complete with trees, streams, and bridges) to detailed mock-ups (check out the graffiti on the walls and cobblestone floors) of Park Avenue, Times Square, and Greenwich Village, this is the most fantastic interior in the city. It's also one of the most confusing and crowded, but surely that's only one more faithful re-creation, this time of midtown during rush hour. *3790 Las Vegas Blvd. S.* ☎ *702/740-6969. www.nynyhotelcasino.com.*

6 Coney Island Arcade. Most Vegas hotels have arcades, partly as a distraction for non-gamblers, especially children, and partly as a way to start indoctrinating said younger set into the ways of gambling. This is the city's most inspired example, because instead of concentrating on video machines, here you have genuine arcade-style money traps—er, games. C'mon, win a stuffed teddy! S'easy! Just above the casino level, in New York–New York. *See bullet* **5**.

7 The Roller Coaster. This 203-foot-tall (62m) roller coaster has classic cars designed to look like old-fashioned checker cabs and swoops not only around the outside of the New York–New York complex (at speeds hovering around 67 mph/108kmph), but right through the interior. Enthusiasts will note that it was the first coaster to feature a 180-degree "heartline" twist and turn. ⏰ *up to 1 hr., depending on lines; ride is only 5 min. Go early in the morning to avoid crowds. See bullet* **5**. *Must be at least 54 in. to ride. Single-ride pass $13, day pass $25. Open Sun–Thurs 11am–11pm, Fri–Sat 10:30am–midnight.*

You won't find as many exotic combinations at the Vegas branch of L.A. fixture **8** ★★★ **Jody Maroni's Sausage Kingdom**, but the quality of the Italian sausage, and even the basic hot dog, makes this gourmet fast food. *In New York–New York, 2nd floor; see bullet* **5**. ☎ *702/740-6969. $.*

9 Planet Hollywood/Miracle Mile Shops. On April 17, 2007, the historic but fiscally troubled Aladdin (the original incarnation of which hosted Elvis and Priscilla's wedding) officially became the Planet Hollywood Resort & Casino, and work began on obliterating its *Arabian Nights* theme in favor of something LA-ish. And its famed Desert Passage mall, one of the better hotel shopping malls, has become the Miracle Mile Shops, which is ridding itself of its charming Middle East kasbah look, and turning it into something a lot more high-tech and generic. Too bad; I like my themes along with my retail therapy. It's unclear at press time exactly what form the latest "wow" factor will take, but if all the promised electronic gizmos really do turn up, it should be quite the glitzy experience. ⏰ *1 hr., depending on how dedicated a shopper you are. 3667 Las Vegas Blvd. S.*

more than a few hours' duty before returning to larger digs) lounge on and around rocks, and often atop a glass tunnel, giving visitors an excellent view of the underside of a lion. It's darn cute when they lounge just like Fluffy at home, or play gently with their trainers. ⏱ *20 min. See p 33, bullet* **6**.

12 ★★★ kids **Cirque du Soleil's KÀ.** This stellar Cirque creation is a superb mix of production values, stage, showmanship, storytelling, and derring-do. And unlike the other Cirque shows in town, this one has a story line (a simple tale about separated royal siblings trying to reunite with one another). The incredible moving stage puts other mechanical theatrical gee-whiz gimmicks to shame, while simultaneously providing just the right literal and figurative platform for Cirque artistry. ⏱ *1½ hr. In MGM Grand, 3799 Las Vegas Blvd. S.* ☎ *866/774-7117 or 702/531-2000. www.cirquedusoleil.com. Shows scheduled Tues–Sat at 7 & 9:30pm. No shows Sun–Mon. See p 115 for more details.*

Modeled on its namesake's famous casino, the Monte Carlo is elegant, but a little bland when compared to its Strip neighbors.

☎ *702/736-0111. www.planet hollywoodresort.com. Hotel is open 24 hr.; mall is open Sun–Thurs 10am–11pm, Fri–Sat 10am–midnight.*

10 **Monte Carlo.** The $344-million project was supposed to be named the Grand Victoria, but MGM Grand objected, so instead, this 44-acre (18-hectare) resort was named after the city in which the Place du Casino (on which this hotel was modeled) resides. It ostensibly captures European elegance (and the grand entranceway on the Strip, loaded with classy statuary and arches, is a great place for a snapshot), but it's not as theme intensive or detailed as its Strip brethren, which sort of makes it the Vegas equivalent of a wallflower. Though a nice wallflower, to be sure. *3770 Las Vegas Blvd. S. (between Flamingo Rd. & Tropicana Ave.).* ☎ *800/529-4828 or 702/730-7777. www.montecarlo.com.*

11 ★★ **MGM Grand Lion Habitat.** A glass enclosure allows for some up-close-and-personal encounters with the MGM's mascot lions. A rotating cast of lions (no cat does

Planet Hollywood's Miracle Mile Shops is one of the best hotel shopping arcades on the Strip.

Luxor Las Vegas

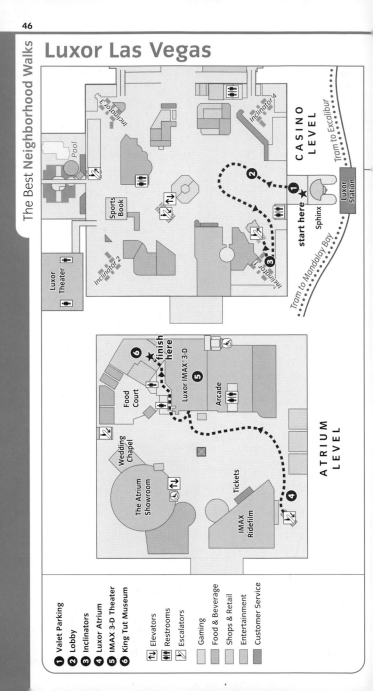

CASINO LEVEL

- Pool
- Inclinator 3
- Inclinator 4
- Sports Book
- Inclinator 2
- Inclinator
- Luxor Theater
- start here
- Sphinx
- Luxor Station
- Tram to Excalibur
- Tram to Mandalay Bay

ATRIUM LEVEL

- finish here
- Food Court
- Luxor IMAX 3-D
- Arcade
- Wedding Chapel
- The Atrium Showroom
- Tickets
- IMAX Ridefilm

Legend:

1. Valet Parking
2. Lobby
3. Inclinators
4. Luxor Atrium
5. IMAX 3-D Theater
6. King Tut Museum

- Elevators
- Restrooms
- Escalators

- Gaming
- Food & Beverage
- Shops & Retail
- Entertainment
- Customer Service

A perfect example of the paradox of Vegas, a city whose highlights are made up of highlights from other cities. In this case, it's a 30-story black glass pyramid—a three-quarter-scale kinda-replica of the famous one at Giza—but then again, Luxor's Sphinx has its nose intact. This South Strip stalwart (it opened in 1993 and was named for the ancient city of Thebes aka Luxor) is one of the best examples of the city's theme-era and late-20th-century postmodern architecture. START: **Valet park your car (it's free) at the hotel, at 3900 Las Vegas Blvd. S. (between Reno and Hacienda aves.).**

Touring Tip

For more information on The Luxor, call ☎ 702/262-4000, surf the Web at www.luxor.com, or check out my hotel review on p 129; for dining opportunities in the hotel, check out chapter 6.

❶ Valet Parking. The fun starts as you step out of your car. If you came in the front entrance, you're standing just behind the massive sphinx that marks the entrance to the hotel.

❷ Lobby. One of the nicest in town, this Art Deco/Egyptian Revival space is dominated by four giant Rameses statues (ostensibly guarding the entrance to that Holy of Holies, the casino). Part of the point of the original Egyptian architecture was to remind mere mortals of their insignificance; it works just as well for the difference between monolithic casino hotels and the average slot player.

❸ Inclinators. See if you can sneak on the best free ride in town, the hotel's "inclinators"—the high-speed elevators that slant up at a 39-degree angle to deliver guests to their rooms. (In theory they're for guests only, but you can often jump on.)

❹ Luxor Atrium. One of the largest atriums in the world, occupying almost 29 million cubic feet. From here you can gaze on the vast inner space of the pyramid and recite

Lose yourself in the Luxor's impossibly immense atrium.

"Ozymandias" to yourself ("look on my works, ye mighty, and despair!").

❺ IMAX 3-D Theater. At least one of the movies playing in this impressive seven-story venue will have something to do with Egypt. When last I was here, there was a first-rate film on the Nile . . . and also an amazing entry on aerial dogfighting. Go figure.

❻ King Tut Museum. A first-rate reproduction of the actual tomb of the famous Egyptian monarch. The 15-minute self-guided audio tour is fascinating and enlightening. *See p 40, bullet ❻.*

Mid-Strip

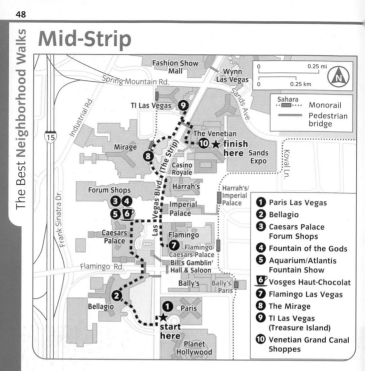

1 Paris Las Vegas
2 Bellagio
3 Caesars Palace Forum Shops
4 Fountain of the Gods
5 Aquarium/Atlantis Fountain Show
6 Vosges Haut-Chocolat
7 Flamingo Las Vegas
8 The Mirage
9 TI Las Vegas (Treasure Island)
10 Venetian Grand Canal Shoppes

Here's the most crowded part of the Strip, though some of the larger casino hotels take up a great deal more space than may first appear. That's because this is, for the most part, the luxury-resort-hotel-on-steroids portion of Vegas. In between are leftovers from Vegas's tacky era. With a few exceptions, most items of interest will be inside, where there are all kinds of distractions designed to keep visitors within the property rather than straying to competitors. **START: Sidewalk in front of the Paris Las Vegas.**

1 **Paris Las Vegas.** After admiring the mashup of the landmarks of Paris outside, take a stroll within, where the feet of the Eiffel Tower replica rest on the casino floor, itself watched over by a ceiling painted to resemble a Parisian spring day. Revolutionary-era facades ring the casino area, and lead to **Le Boulevard,** the hotel's cobblestone shopping area. The original plan was for the smell of fresh bread to waft

through here, complete with the occasional dash of a bike rider ferrying fresh baguettes to the eateries. That attention to detail has been lost, but the Disneyland version of Paris is still in place. It's not romantic so much as it is silly—giggle over the various French-ified signage ("Le Car Rental")—but heavily themed is the way Vegas ought to be; and this $785-million fantasyland certainly fits the bill. *See p 10, bullet* **5**.

2 **Bellagio.** The opening of this lightly themed behemoth in the fall of 1998 marked the beginning of the end of for the Vegas theme trend and the start of the march toward hotel elegance. *See p 11 bullet* **8** *& p 53 for a walking tour of the hotel.*

3 **Caesars Palace Forum Shops.** The first great absurd hotel shopping mall in Vegas, and still The One to See. Walk down corridors designed to look like the streets of ancient Rome—if new and gleaming—with a sky-painted ceiling overhead that tricks you into thinking it's broad daylight when it's really approaching midnight. The 160-store sprawling complex includes a recent, more modern-looking (though just as liberally adorned with Roman statues) expansion featuring a three-story atrium accessed by a spiral shaped escalator. It's a hoot even if you don't care about shopping. *Daily 10am–11pm. See p 72.*

4 **Fountain of the Gods.** This fountain appears to sport the same faux marble statue copies that pop up all over Caesars—until Bacchus, in his drunken glory, comes to creaky animatronic life and delivers a somewhat muffled speech about the wonders of decadence and living it up. The other statues concur. There are some laser effects to try to make it more up-to-date, but it remains cheesy and hokey. It's what passed for a marvel in old Vegas. It's amazing it's still there. ⏱ *8 min. In The Forum Shops, section D on the casino level; see bullet* **3***. Free shows every hour on the hour.*

Stroll beneath a perfectly rendered copy of the Arc de Triumph, then grab a perfectly baked croissant at Paris Las Vegas.

The Fountain of the Gods inside the Forum Shops may not be divine, but it is quite the kitschy diversion; see p 49, bullet **4**.

5 Aquarium/Atlantis Fountain Show. More elaborate and ambitious than the fountain show listed above, this one tells the "story" of the fall of Atlantis. Look for an actual story line, bigger special effects, and correspondingly bigger crowds. For the low-tech and less demanding, behind the fountains is a nifty (and free) 50,000-gallon saltwater aquarium. With luck, you'll arrive during one of the regular (and entertaining) fish feedings. *In The Forum Shops,*

It's not what it was back in Bugsy's day, but the Flamingo is still a Strip mainstay worth seeing.

section F on the casino level; see bullet **3**. *Free 8-min. fountain shows every hour on the hour. Aquarium daily feedings at 1:15 & 5:15pm.*

Get a shot of energy at **6 Vosges Haut-Chocolat**, which, in addition to exotic chocolate-based candy confections, offers a cocoa bar (my favorite: the white chocolate with lavender and lemon myrtle) and fancy ice cream. *In the Forum Shops, section H on the street level.* ☎ 702/836-9866. $.

7 Flamingo Las Vegas. When mobster Bugsy Siegel's $6-million Art Deco–ish baby was born in 1946, all the staff (even the janitors!) wore tuxedos. Siegel met an infamous end in 1947, and little of his original structure remains. The Flamingo no longer rules the Strip roost, but its free wildlife sanctuary (yes, there are flamingos) and gardens are still beautiful and worth a gander. *3555 Las Vegas Blvd. S. (between Sands Ave. & Flamingo Rd.).* ☎ 800/732-2111 or 702/733-3111. www.harrahs.com.

8 The Mirage. Built on the site of the old Castaways hotel, The Mirage made Steve Wynn's rep as the king of Las Vegas hoteliers when it opened in 1989. Say "hi" to the scary-looking statues in front of the resort commemorating magicians Siegfried & Roy, who performed almost 6,000 shows here before Roy Horn was seriously injured onstage in 2003 after a disastrous encounter with one of the famous duo's beloved white tigers. *See p 12, bullet* **11**.

9 TI Las Vegas (Treasure Island). When it opened in 1993, this $450-million property was designed to attract families with a Disneyesque Caribbean pirates theme. That idea walked the plank in 2003 and the property was turned into an adult-oriented resort with nary a trace of theme. And its once kid-friendly free pirate battle now features sexed-up sirens. Yo Ho Hum. *See p 13, bullet* **15**.

10 Venetian Grand Canal Shoppes. Every bit as over-the-top as The Forum Shops, but less cheesy, provided you don't automatically sneer at architectural reproductions (which are wonderfully rendered). Given how well executed the place is—including a rather cunning scaled-down replica of St. Mark's Square and canals with actual gondoliers—and that there are even period costumed performers who actually sing and otherwise interact with customers, it qualifies as a mall-as-theme-park experience, and I mean that in a good way. ⊕ *45 min.; more if you actually shop. 3355 Las Vegas Blvd. S.* ☎ *702/414-1000. www. venetian.com. Daily 10am–11pm.*

Let a gondolier serenade you beneath a fake blue sky as you sail past the stores and restaurants of the Venetian Grand Canal Shoppes.

Bellagio

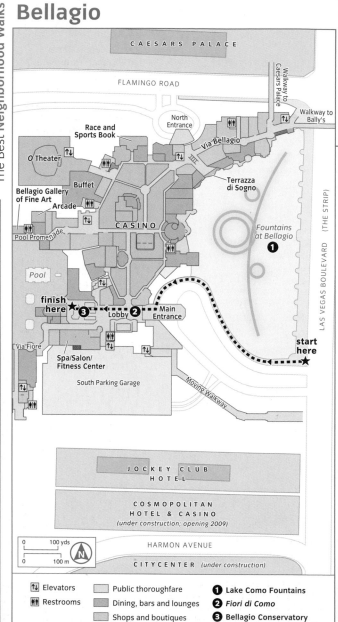

CAESARS PALACE

FLAMINGO ROAD

North Entrance

Walkway to Caesars Palace

Walkway to Bally's

Via Bellagio

Race and Sports Book

O Theater

Buffet

Terrazza di Sogno

Bellagio Gallery of Fine Art

Arcade

CASINO

Pool Promenade

Fountains at Bellagio ❶

Pool

finish here ❸

Lobby ❷

Main Entrance

start here

Via Fiore

Spa/Salon/Fitness Center

South Parking Garage

Moving Walkway

LAS VEGAS BOULEVARD (THE STRIP)

JOCKEY CLUB HOTEL

COSMOPOLITAN HOTEL & CASINO
(under construction; opening 2009)

0	100 yds
0	100 m

N

HARMON AVENUE

CITYCENTER (under construction)

↑↓ Elevators		Public thoroughfare	❶ Lake Como Fountains
🚻 Restrooms		Dining, bars and lounges	❷ *Fiori di Como*
		Shops and boutiques	❸ Bellagio Conservatory

Whalen it opened in 1998 on the site of the old Dunes hotel, this $1.6-billion brainchild of casino magnate Steve Wynn (who's since moved on to properties named for himself) was the most expensive ever built. This is the luxury resort that ushered in the new adults-only elegance epoch in Vegas. It's not quite the relaxing oasis that ads for the hotel make it out to be, but it is probably the closest thing Vegas has to a European casino hotel. And this expensive resort is, ironically, home to some of the best freebies in the city. **START: Valet-park your car (it's free) at the hotel, at 3600 Las Vegas Blvd. S. (at the corner of Flamingo Rd.), then walk to the sidewalk in front of the hotel.**

Touring Tip

For more information on Bellagio, call ☎ 702/693-7111, surf the Web at www.bellagio.com, or check out my hotel review on p 125; for dining opportunities in the hotel, check out chapter 6.

❶ **Lake Como/Fountains.** It's too bad that, after having gone to so much trouble to create this beautiful 8-acre (3.2-hectare) reproduction of Lake Como, the scenic provincial Italian village strung along the lake's banks is not accessible to visitors. Still, it remains a top spot for shutterbugs. If you haven't seen one of the fountain shows that take place on the lake yet and it's past noon, wait for one *See p 11, bullet* ❾ *for more on the fountain shows.*

❷ *Fiori di Como.* This $10-million Dale Chihuly glass sculpture adorns the ceiling of the reception area. When it was commissioned in 1998, this extravagant floral creation, measuring 30 by 70 feet (9.1 by 20m) and containing 2,000 hand-blown flowers, was the largest glass sculpture in the world. Nearly 5 tons of steel affix the sculpture to the ceiling.

❸ ★★★ **Bellagio Conservatory.** The botanical theme is continued in the hotel's 14,000-square-foot (1,300-sq.-m) indoor garden, basking beneath a 55-foot-tall (17m) glass ceiling. As the plants and flowers are freshened daily, and decorations regularly changed in their entirety to correspond to seasons and holidays (Easter and Chinese New Year bring particularly spectacular displays), and given that access to this oasis of life and color is entirely free, this is surely one of the great follies in a town otherwise totally dedicated to commerce. The hotel's yearly bill for all this floral goodness? Close to $8 million. Note that the fountain that stands just outside the conservatory entrance is over 100 years old. ☎ 702/693-7111. www.bellagio. com. Open 24 hrs.

The rotating floral displays inside the Bellagio Conservatory are among the city's best free attractions.

Wynn Las Vegas

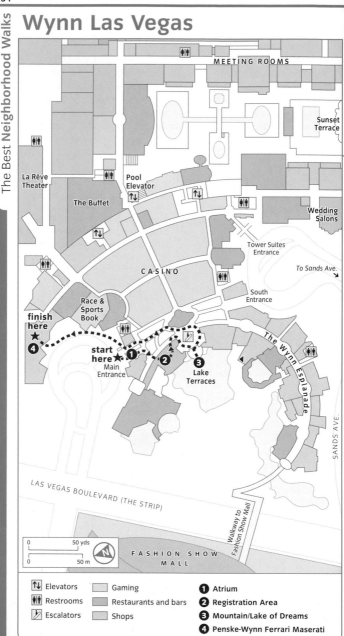

MEETING ROOMS

Sunset Terrace

La Rêve Theater

The Buffet

Pool Elevator

Wedding Salons

Tower Suites Entrance

CASINO

To Sands Ave.

South Entrance

Race & Sports Book

finish here

4

start here
Main Entrance

1

2

3
Lake Terraces

The Wynn Esplanade

SANDS AVE.

LAS VEGAS BOULEVARD (THE STRIP)

Walkway to Fashion Show Mall

0 ____ 50 yds
0 ____ 50 m

N

FASHION SHOW MALL

↑↓ Elevators	Gaming	**1** Atrium
👫 Restrooms	Restaurants and bars	**2** Registration Area
🚶 Escalators	Shops	**3** Mountain/Lake of Dreams
		4 Penske-Wynn Ferrari Maserati

This glitzy $2.7-billion luxury resort is typical in that it's designed to keep visitors just confused enough so that leaving seems like too much effort, but differs from its Strip brethren in that most of its intrigue is on the inside. Named for its creator, legendary casino magnate Steve Wynn, the 215-acre (87-hectare) high-tech resort opened in 2005 on the site of the old Desert Inn and was supposed to revitalize the North Strip, but the area hasn't quite cooperated yet, leaving the Wynn a lone bright spot. START: **Main entrance to the Wynn Las Vegas, 3131 Las Vegas Blvd. S. (at the corner of Sands Ave.).**

Touring Tip

For more information on Wynn Las Vegas, call ☎ 702/770-7100, surf the Web at www.wynnlasvegas.com, or check out my hotel review on p 136; for dining opportunities in the hotel, see chapter 6.

① ★ **Atrium.** It's designed along similar lines as the Bellagio Conservatory (p 53, bullet **③**), though it has a long strolling layout rather than a square one, and its location is more accessible. The botanicals and other ornamentation are less fancy than Bellagio's; but it's still nice to wander through, and the floral mosaic tiles underneath are a pretty touch. *Open 24 hr.*

② **Registration Area.** Though the check-in location is otherwise rather diminutive for such a striking facility, a stop here is called for because examples from Steve Wynn's extraordinary art collection (he owns works by artists ranging from Picasso to Vermeer) are hung on the walls on a rotating basis. *Open 24 hr.*

③ ★ **Mountain/Lake of Dreams.** The 3-acre (1.2-hectare) lake and 70-foot (21m) waterfall at the base of Wynn's 150-foot-tall (46m) man-made mountain are the site of a nightly sound, light, and imagery show that's somewhat psychedelic and really quite weird (and often

rather adult). The only free viewing area is the balcony near the Parasol Bar, which gets quite crowded (and there's no sound). But if you aren't paying to see it by patronizing one of the resort's pricey restaurants or bars, it's worth gawking at, so try to angle your way in there. *Shows run every 20 min., daily 7pm–midnight.*

④ **Penske-Wynn Ferrari Maserati.** Wynn pulled an audacious stunt, putting a car showroom right next to a casino. Nevada's only Ferrari dealership is a must-see for Italian sports car fans, or for anyone who appreciates the artistry of machinery. Or for people who want to see a cool quarter of a million on wheels and are willing to spend $10 for the self-guided tour. Talk about envy. ⏱ *45 min. for the tour.* ☎ *702/770-2000. www.penskewynn.com. Self-guided tour $10. Mon–Sat 10am–9pm, Sun 10am–6pm.*

The free atrium inside the Wynn Las Vegas sports lovely floral arrangements and a gorgeous mosaic floor.

Downtown

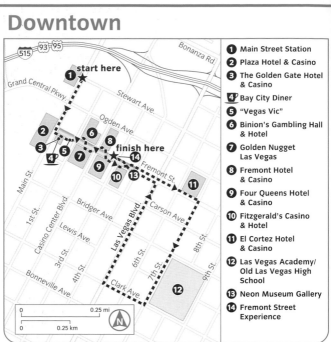

1. Main Street Station
2. Plaza Hotel & Casino
3. The Golden Gate Hotel & Casino
4. Bay City Diner
5. "Vegas Vic"
6. Binion's Gambling Hall & Hotel
7. Golden Nugget Las Vegas
8. Fremont Hotel & Casino
9. Four Queens Hotel & Casino
10. Fitzgerald's Casino & Hotel
11. El Cortez Hotel & Casino
12. Las Vegas Academy/ Old Las Vegas High School
13. Neon Museum Gallery
14. Fremont Street Experience

The former "Glitter Gulch" and glamour spot of Las Vegas, this smaller stretch of correspondingly decreased-in-size hotels and casinos is overlooked in favor of the flashy deal down south. Too bad—you can cover the whole thing so easily, thanks to pedestrian-only Fremont Street; the crowds are friendlier; and the minimum bets are cheaper. START: **Entrance to the Main Street Station; if you're driving, park in one of the many lots off Fremont Street and walk to the hotel.**

1 Main Street Station. Start your tour off in early-20th-century San Francisco . . . Vegas style, at this lovely property. As you stroll through, note the many Victorian decor elements, from the wrought-iron railings to the antique brass casino cages. Ask at the lobby for the casino's worthwhile self-guided tour of its lovely antiques collection. The males in your party should check out the men's room on the main casino floor—that slab of rock holding up the urinals is a genuine

piece of the Berlin wall. *200 N. Main St.* 800/465-0711 or 702/387-1896. www.mainstreetcasino.com.

2 Plaza Hotel & Casino. It opened in 1971 as the Union Plaza, its name an homage to the Union Pacific Railroad station that originally occupied this site. Though by no means the oldest hotel in the area, the Plaza's facade is so typically "Vegas" that it tends to pop up often in movies (*Back to the Future II, Cool World,* and *The Mexican,* among others) as a generic casino. *1 Main St.* ☎ *702/386-2110. www. plazahotelcasino.com.*

❸ The Golden Gate Hotel & Casino. This four-story building is Sin City's oldest hotel, dating back to 1906 (it opened as the Hotel Nevada), when room and board cost $1 a day. In one incarnation, it was the Sal Sagev (spell each word backward for the inside joke) hotel. Today, the exterior facade reflects the original building's roots. *1 Fremont St.* ☎ *702/382-3510. www.goldengate casino.net.*

The Plaza Hotel & Casino's ultra-Vegas exterior has been featured in many a cinematic production.

Vegas Vic, arguably the most famous neon sign in Las Vegas.

The 99¢ shrimp cocktail, *the* symbol of bargain Las Vegas, originated at the Golden Gate Hotel & Casino back in 1959 (well, it cost only 50¢ then), and by 1991 they'd served 25 million of them. The shrimp served today in the hotel's **❹ Bay City Diner** is just bay shrimp, but it's actually a pretty good snack, and a Vegas must. *In the Golden Gate Hotel & Casino, 1 Fremont St.* ☎ *702/382-3510. www.goldengate casino.net. $.*

❺ "Vegas Vic." This 40-foot-tall (12m) neon cowboy, one of the city's most recognized icons, went up for the first time in 1951 and has suffered many an indignity since. He lost his voice (he once offered up a "howdy partner" to visitors) when actor Lee Marvin (in town, to shoot *The Professionals*) complained in 1966 that he was too loud and had him silenced. His arm used to wave, and that doesn't work anymore either. Then his hat was partially cut off to make way for the canopy for the Fremont Street Experience in 1994. And that ever-present cigarette ain't too popular nowadays either. But he (and across-the-street neighbor "Sassy Sally"—you can't miss her) is one of the last bastions of Old Vegas, and you should tip your hat to him. *25 Fremont St.*

❻ Binion's Gambling Hall & Hotel. The former Horseshoe Casino dates back to 1951, when it was built on the site of the old Apache Hotel (some remnants of which are still visible) by legendary casino operator Benny Binion (1904–1989). One of the most venerable gambling establishments in Vegas, and up until a couple of years ago the home of the World

Series of Poker (which began life in 1970), Binion's is pretty desiccated, but is still where hard-line gamblers go to play. The place isn't nearly as dazzling as its lurid history (former owner Ted Binion's stripper girlfriend was tried for his murder in 1998, a story that includes a vault filled with treasure buried in the desert), but newish owners may at some point change that. *128 Fremont St.* ☎ *800/937-6537. www.binions.com.*

⑦ Golden Nugget Las Vegas. Its 1946 construction date makes this one of Vegas's oldest extant hotels; but a face-lift at press time had it looking quite good, and it's the indisputable star of Downtown. It's had its moments of fame, notably when it became casino magnate Steve Wynn's first local purchase in 1973, and then during its brief run in 2004 as the setting of a short-lived reality series called *The Casino,* which documented the

Hard-core gamblers still flock to Binion's, though the World Series of Poker is no longer played here.

Stop in at the Golden Nugget Las Vegas to rub the solid gold Hand of Faith for luck.

The Hand of Faith Nugget

antics of subsequent owners. But its biggest claim to fame nowadays resides in its lobby: The **Hand of Faith,** the world's largest gold nugget, was found in Australia and weighs in at nearly 62 pounds (28kg). *129 Fremont St.* ☎ *702/385-7111. www.goldennugget.com.*

⑧ Fremont Hotel & Casino. This 15-story hotel debuted in 1956 as Nevada's tallest building. It's also where Mr. Las Vegas, Wayne Newton, got his start in Sin City. For that alone it gets a *Danke schoen. 200 Fremont St.* ☎ *800/634-6182 or 702/385-3232. www.fremontcasino. com.*

⑨ Four Queens Hotel & Casino. Opened in 1966, this venerable property was named in homage to the original builder's four daughters. Today the 3.2-acre (1.3-hectare) giant property occupies an entire city block right in the heart of

Downtown, and is notable in that it's home to a half-price theater ticket booth that's usually not as crowded as the others in town. *202 Fremont St.* ☎ *702/38-4011. www.four queens.com.*

⓿ Fitzgerald's Casino & Hotel. A relative newcomer to Downtown (it first opened as the Sundance Hotel in 1979), this 34-story property is most noteworthy for its somewhat fading Irish theme, and its ownership—it's the only African American–owned casino in Las Vegas. *301 Fremont St.* ☎ *800/ 274-LUCK (274-5825) or 702/388-2400. www.fitzgeralds.com.*

⓫ El Cortez Hotel & Casino. When it opened in 1941 (at a then whopping cost of $245,000—gotta love inflation), this small hotel was Downtown's largest and most luxurious resort. So good was it that Bugsy Siegel bought it in 1946, but he later dumped it in order to finance his dream of the Strip. It's been renovated and gutted over the years, but you'll still spot some of the original's Spanish-flavored details. And wave to the top of the hotel tower while you're here; current hands-on owner Jackie Gaughan, a local legend, lives at the tippy top! *600 Fremont St.* ☎ *800/634-6703 or 702/385-5200. www.el cortezhotelcasino.com.*

⓬ Las Vegas Academy/ Old Las Vegas High School. And now for a rare bit of culture in Downtown. This beauty of a school building, built in 1930 and on the National Register of Historic Places, was the first high school built in Las Vegas and is the best Art Deco building in the city. Note the elaborate concrete and stucco friezes on the facade; they depict a number of species of animal, plants, and other figures of interest. It's now home to the city's school of performing arts. *315 E. 7th St.*

⓭ Neon Museum Gallery. Though Vegas is still all about the bright lights, the introduction of computer-generated signage has meant the slow death of a great art form, the city's iconic neon signs. These have been gradually phased out, condemned as hokey and old-fashioned, and would have been consigned to trash heaps had this nonprofit not stepped in. There are plans in the works for a permanent facility to display many of its recovered treasures, but in the meantime some have been erected around Fremont Street and other parts of Downtown. The **Hacienda's horse and rider** stands above the intersection of Fremont Street and Las Vegas Boulevard South, while the **Aladdin's glittery lamp** is at the northwest corner. *On Fremont St. (between Main St. & Las Vegas Blvd.). Free admission. Open 24 hr. Best viewed after dark.*

The old Hacienda's horse and rider is one of the most famous signs in the Neon Museum.

Fremont Street during the day: the canopy over the pedestrian zone helps protect shoppers and gamblers from the hot Nevada sun.

⓮ ★★ Fremont Street Experience. Sauntering down Fremont Street is the closest you can get these days to the archetypal Vegas (because buildings and corresponding lighted signs are set so much closer together), which may be why it was chosen as the setting for U2's "Still Haven't Found What I'm Looking For" video. Nowadays, most visitors come for the giant 90-foot-high (27m) canopy erected over the pedestrian mall, which displays a genuinely impressive light-and-sound show (the whole thing appropriately named "Viva Vision"). Several different shows play in rotation, including one based on aliens and Area 51. Good views are available just about anywhere on the mall, as all it requires is neck-craning, but if you want to get a little closer to the action, stand on a balcony at Fitzgerald's or in that hotel's branch of McDonald's. *Fremont St., between Main St. & Las Vegas Blvd. www.vegasexperience.com. Free admission. Shows nightly every hour, dusk to midnight.* ●

Fremont Street is best toured at night, when it's lit up in all of its neon- and laser-enhanced glory.

Shopping Best Bets

Best Place for **Tacky Vegas Souvenirs**
★★ Bonanza Gift and Souvenir Shop, *2460 Las Vegas Blvd. S.* (p 70)

Best **Classy but Naughty Underthings**
★★★ Agent Provocateur, *The Forum Shops at Caesars Palace, 3500 Las Vegas Blvd. S.* (p 67)

Best **Sweets & Pastries**
★★★ Jean-Philippe, *Bellagio, 3600 Las Vegas Blvd. S.* (p 69)

Best **Jewelry**
★★ Tiffany & Co., *Via Bellagio, 3600 Las Vegas Blvd. S.* (p 73)

Best **Place for a Showgirl Wig**
★★★ Serge's Showgirls Wigs, *953 E. Sahara Ave.* (p 66)

Best **Place for Wizard Paraphernalia**
Dragon's Lair, *The Realm Shops at Excalibur, 3850 Las Vegas Blvd. S.* (p 70)

Best **Place for Books on Gambling**
★ Gambler's Book Shop, *630 S. 11th St.* (p 66)

Best **Place to Buy the Makings for Your Own Casino**
★ Gambler's General Store, *800 S. Main St.* (p 71)

Best **Outlets**
★★★ Fashion Outlets Las Vegas, *32100 Las Vegas Blvd. S.* (p 69)

Best **Place to Feel Royal**
★★★ Truefitt & Hill, *The Forum Shops at Caesars Palace, 3500 Las Vegas Blvd. S.* (p 66)

Best **Vintage Clothes**
★ The Attic, *1018 S. Main St.* (p 67)

Best **Toys**
★ FAO Schwartz, *The Forum Shops at Caesars Palace, 3500 Las Vegas Blvd. S.* (p 74)

Best **Pret a Porter**
★★★ Prada, *Via Bellagio, 3600 Las Vegas Blvd. S.* (p 68)

Best **Museum Shop**
★★★ Atomic Testing Museum, *755 E. Flamingo Rd.* (p 70)

Best **Chocolates**
★★ Chocolate Swan, *Mandalay Place at Mandalay Bay, 3930 Las Vegas Blvd. S., Ste. 121B* (p 69)

Best **High-Fashion Casual**
★ Juicy Couture, *The Forum Shops at Caesars Palace, 3500 Las Vegas Blvd. S.* (p 68)

Best **Place for Antiques**
★ Antique Square, *2014–2034 E. Charleston Blvd.* (p 65)

For designer duds and accessories, it's hard to beat Prada.

Previous Page: A window display at Agent Provocateur, the city's best lingerie shop.

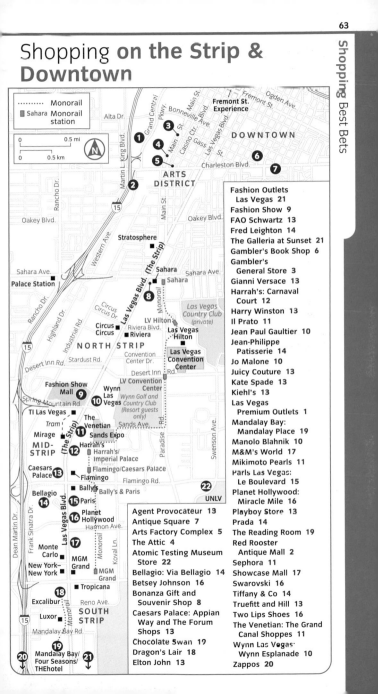

Shopping **on the Strip & Downtown**

Fashion Outlets Las Vegas 21
Fashion Show 9
FAO Schwartz 13
Fred Leighton 14
The Galleria at Sunset 21
Gambler's Book Shop 6
Gambler's General Store 3
Gianni Versace 13
Harrah's: Carnaval Court 12
Harry Winston 13
Il Prato 11
Jean Paul Gaultier 10
Jean-Philippe Patisserie 14
Jo Malone 10
Juicy Couture 13
Kate Spade 13
Kiehl's 13
Las Vegas Premium Outlets 1
Mandalay Bay: Mandalay Place 19
Manolo Blahnik 10
M&M's World 17
Mikimoto Pearls 11
Paris Las Vegas: Le Boulevard 15
Planet Hollywood: Miracle Mile 16
Playboy Store 13
Prada 14
The Reading Room 19
Red Rooster Antique Mall 2
Sephora 11
Showcase Mall 17
Swarovski 16
Tiffany & Co 14
Truefitt and Hill 13
Two Lips Shoes 16
The Venetian: The Grand Canal Shoppes 11
Wynn Las Vegas: Wynn Esplanade 10
Zappos 20

Agent Provocateur 13
Antique Square 7
Arts Factory Complex 5
The Attic 4
Atomic Testing Museum Store 22
Bellagio: Via Bellagio 14
Betsey Johnson 16
Bonanza Gift and Souvenir Shop 8
Caesars Palace: Appian Way and The Forum Shops 13
Chocolate Swan 19
Dragon's Lair 18
Elton John 13

Shopping **off the Strip**

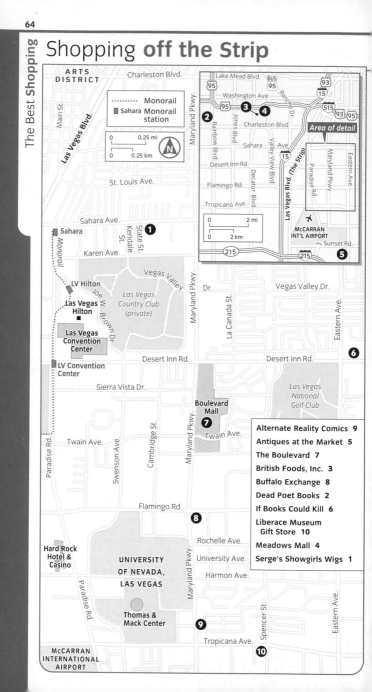

Location	#
Alternate Reality Comics	9
Antiques at the Market	5
The Boulevard	7
British Foods, Inc.	3
Buffalo Exchange	8
Dead Poet Books	2
If Books Could Kill	6
Liberace Museum Gift Store	10
Meadows Mall	4
Serge's Showgirls Wigs	1

Las Vegas Shopping A to Z

Antiques

★ Antiques at the Market

EAST OF STRIP   Sixty stalls of antiques, memorabilia, collectibles, vintage clothes, jewelry, and accessories. The selection and a close-to-the-airport location make this a convenient stop for voracious antiques shoppers on their way home with weekend winnings burning a hole in their pockets. *6665 S. Eastern Ave. (between Sunset Rd. & Warm Springs Rd.).* ☎ *702/307-3960. AE, MC, V. Map p 64.*

★ Antique Square DOWNTOWN

It's the smallest of the city's three antiques malls, but careful shoppers can uncover a plethora of treasures, including comics, vintage Las Vegas matchbooks, postcards, ashtrays, and other souvenirs of bygone casinos. *2014–2034 E. Charleston Blvd.* ☎ *702/471-6500. AE, MC, V. Map p 63.*

★ Red Rooster Antique Mall

DOWNTOWN   Think lots of stuff stuffed into 25,000 square feet (2,323 sq. m): Vegas memorabilia,

Kiehls is not as exclusive as it once was, but is still an excellent place to pick up cosmetics.

vintage jewelry, clothes, furnishings, and such collectibles as carnival glass. Plus the dealers are on hand to answer questions (not always a given elsewhere). *1109 Western Ave. (at Charleston Blvd. & I-15).* ☎ *702/382-5253. AE, MC, V. Map p 63.*

Beauty Products & Accessories

★★ Jo Malone NORTH STRIP

This London-based perfumer combines aromas such as pomegranate and pepper, and verbena and basil in her scents and candles for the home. Her fresh non-fussy personal care items include refreshingly light orange blossom and signature grapefruit eau de colognes. *Wynn Esplanade, 3131 Las Vegas Blvd. S.,* ☎ *702/770-3485 www.wynnlas vegas.com. AE, DISC, MC, V. Map p 63.*

★★★ Kiehl's MID-STRIP   This 150-year-old cosmetics line isn't quite as limited in access as it used to be, thanks to a buyout from a much larger cosmetics company. But the line's skin and hair products, particularly the popular Lip Balm #2, still make any store visit a treat. *In The*

Red Rooster Antique Mall is one of the largest in Las Vegas.

Forum Shops at Caesars Palace, 3500 Las Vegas Blvd. S. ☎ 702/784-0025. www.kiehls.com. AE, DC, MC, V. Map p 63.

★ **Sephora** MID-STRIP False eyelashes! Nail polish! Perfume! Lipstick! Toenail clippers! If you need a beauty item, you'll find it here. And if you want to wow them at the tables or get ready for a night of club hopping, have your face made up for free by a staff member. *In The Venetian Grand Canal Shoppes, 3355 Las Vegas Blvd. S.* ☎ 702/735-3896. www.sephora.com. AE, DISC, MC, V. Map p 63.

★★★ **Serge's Showgirls Wigs'** EAST OF STRIP The name says it all. What, you thought those long falls of luscious locks were real? Less of a commitment than extensions, but loaded with fantasy, wigs run the gamut from expensive to disposable. *953 E. Sahara Ave. 702/732-1015.* www.showgirlwigs.com. AE, DISC, MC, V. Map p 64.

★★★ **Truefitt & Hill** MID-STRIP In business for over 200 years and patronized by HRH the Duke of Edinburgh (that would be Queen Elizabeth II's husband, Prince Philip), this British outfit's high-end, luxurious men's shaving supplies and skin care products will make you feel like a king. Okay, a prince. But a very well groomed one. *In The Forum Shops at Caesars Palace, 3500 Las Vegas Blvd. S.* ☎ 702/735-7428. www.truefitt andhill.com. AE, DISC, MC, V. Map p 63.

Books & Stationery
★ **Alternate Reality Comics** EAST OF STRIP As the name suggests, the emphasis here is on underground comics, but the stock is comprehensive enough to include mainstream titles. *4800 S. Maryland Pkwy., Ste. D.* ☎ 702/736-3673. AE, DISC, MC, V. Map p 64.

★★ **Dead Poet Books** WEST OF STRIP Even in Vegas, I love a musty old bookstore, and the owners here are particularly literary types. *3874 W. Sahara Ave.* ☎ 702/227-4070. MC, V. Map p 64.

★ **Gambler's Book Shop** DOWNTOWN I keep telling you, you can't beat the system. And yet, this shop swears that you can. Or at least that one of their thousands of titles knows how and will tell all. *630 S. 11th St.* ☎ 702/382-7555. www.gamblersbook.com. AE, MC, V. Map p 63.

★ **If Books Could Kill** EAST OF STRIP Six thousand square feet (557 sq. m) of used books, and a shop that doesn't mind if you sit down and read one on the spot. *2466 E. Desert Inn Rd., Ste. G.* ☎ 702/792-9554. www.if-books-could-kill.com. AE, DISC, MC, V. Map p 64.

★★ **The Reading Room** SOUTH STRIP The only bookstore on—or even near—the Strip. It's small, but this nicely stocked shop provides an unexpected oasis in a hectic casino hotel shopping mall. *In Mandalay Place at Mandalay Bay, 3930 Las*

Literary lovers will find lots of good buys at Dead Poet Books.

The Attic is one of the best vintage shops in Las Vegas.

Vegas Blvd. S., Ste. 201A. ☎ *702/632-9374. AE, MC, V. Map p 63.*

Clothing & Shoes

★★★ Agent Provocateur

MID-STRIP   This British lingerie line, favored by Kate Moss and other slinky celebs, is for those who want some art and style in their seduction wear. The black silk satin Nikita line and the lacy Love styles definitely fit the bill; some of their stuff has to be seen to be believed. *The Forum Shops at Caesars Palace, 3500 Las Vegas Blvd. S.* ☎ *702/696-7174. www.agent provocateur.com. AE, MC, V. Map p 63.*

★ The Attic DOWNTOWN   In

addition to used clothing of varying vintages, this shop makes its own poodle skirts. *1018 S. Main St.* ☎ *702/388-4088. www.theatticlas vegas.com. AE, MC, V. Map p 63.*

Betsey Johnson MID-STRIP

Playful, sexy, strong, and boldly feminine fashions—flouncy dresses with bright floral prints, lacy tops, vibrant knits and velvet skirts, curve-displaying garments—have been Betsey Johnson's signature styles since the mid-1980s. *In Planet Hollywood's*

Miracle Mile, 3663 Las Vegas Blvd. S. ☎ *702/731-0286. AE, MC, V. Map p 63.*

★ Buffalo Exchange EAST OF

STRIP   This vintage chain store relies a lot on consignment, so selection will vary. The store's buyers have good taste, though the stock edges more toward recent decades rather than rare finds from the '40s. *4110 S. Maryland Pkwy. (at Flamingo Rd.).* ☎ *702/791-3960. www.buffalo exchange.com. MC, V. Map p 64.*

★★★ Gianni Versace MID-STRIP

This designer line, synonymous with opulent celebrity-endorsed high fashion, manages to be both cutting edge and classic, with attention paid to detail and fabric. *The Forum Shops at Caesars Palace, 3500 Las Vegas Blvd. S.* ☎ *702/796-7222. www. versace.com. AE, MC, V. Map p 63.*

★★★ Jean Paul Gaultier NORTH

STRIP   The first and only Gaultier store in the U.S. showcases the decadent designer's avant-garde *prêt-à-porter,* accessories, and scents for men and women. *In Wynn Esplanade, 3131 Las Vegas Blvd. S.,* ☎ *702/770-3490. AE, DC, DISC, MC, V. Map p 63.*

Two Lips Shoes is a great place to pick up fashion-forward footwear on the cheap.

★ Juicy Couture MID-STRIP
Single-handedly responsible for the ubiquity of velour sweat suits, not to mention the word "Juicy" along backsides. To be fair, the designers tapped into the casual wear zeitgeist by making some genuinely cute clothes. *In The Forum Shops at Caesars Palace, 3500 Las Vegas Blvd. S. ☎ 702/365-5600. www.juicy couture.com. AE, MC, V. Map p 63.*

★★★ Kate Spade MID-STRIP.
Bright colors and sleek styles with a modern vibe have made this line of handbags, luggage, stationery, and accessories hip from the Hamptons to Hollywood. *In The Forum Shops at Caesars Palace, 3500 Las Vegas Blvd. S. ☎ 702/515-6075. www.kate spade.com. AE, DISC, MC, V. Map p 63.*

★★★ Manolo Blahnik NORTH
STRIP Revealing just the right amount of "toe cleavage," this store's expensive, sexy, and strappy sandals and stiletto-heeled shoes were enshrined in pop culture by *Sex and the City. Wynn Esplanade, 3131 Las Vegas Blvd. S. ☎ 702/770-3477. AE, DC, DISC, MC, V. Map p 63.*

Playboy Store MID-STRIP
Because you'll want to wear something slinky from Playboy's fashion line on a visit to the only Playboy Club in existence (p 105). *In The Forum Shops at Caesars Palace, 3500 Las Vegas Blvd. S. ☎ 702/851-7470. AE, DISC, MC, V. Map p 63.*

★★★ Prada MID-STRIP
Its clothes are the opposite of Vegas: timeless, classy, and simple. Equally elegant are the shoes and accessories. *Via Bellagio, 3600 Las Vegas Blvd. S. ☎ 702/866-6886. www.prada.com. AE, DC, DISC, MC, V. Map p 63.*

★ Two Lips Shoes MID-STRIP
Cute flats and satin Mary Janes share space with hip high-heeled sandals and leather pumps—all fashion forward and reasonably priced. Some are even well padded enough to add comfort to your style. *In Planet Hollywood's Miracle Mile, 3663 Las Vegas Blvd. S. ☎ 702/737-0369. www.two lipsshoes.com. AE, DISC, MC, V. Map p 63.*

★ Zappos WEST OF THE STRIP.
This outlet of the popular online shoe retailer stocks a huge selection

At the Playboy Store, you'll find everything you need to bring out your inner Bunny.

Designer bargains abound at the Las Vegas Premium Outlets, but the outdoor venue can get too cold or hot to handle when Mother Nature isn't cooperative.

of name-brand shoes—from formal to athletic—as well as handbags and belts. *7770 S. Dean Martin Dr.* ☎ *702/943-7900. www.zappos.com. AE, DISC, MC, V. Map p 63.*

Factory Outlets

★★★ **Fashion Outlets Las Vegas** PRIMM   A 40-minute schlep from the city, but worth it for the inside shopping (air-conditioning!), plus Versace, Tommy Hilfiger, Williams Sonoma, and Banana Republic outlets, among others. *32100 S. Las Vegas Blvd.* ☎ *888/424-6898. www.fashionoutletlasvegas. com. AE, DISC, MC, V. Map p 63.*

Las Vegas Premium Outlets
DOWNTOWN   The high-end names here—Armani, Dolce & Gabbana, Calvin Klein—make this most conveniently located outlet center enticing for dedicated bargain hunters, but amateurs may not have the stamina to endure the open-air facility on hot days. *875 S. Grand Central Pkwy. (at I-15).* ☎ *702/474-7500. www.premiumoutlets.com. AE, DISC, MC, V. Map p 63.*

Food & Chocolate
★★ **British Foods, Inc.**   Britannia rules at this import grocer, which stocks more than 750 types of edibles (and a couple of trinkets) from all over Her Majesty's Commonwealth. Come here for a Cadbury fix (you can get options that you'll rarely find anywhere else in the U.S.), or to stock up on teas, biscuits, sausage rolls, jams, puddings, British bacon, pasties, and even haggis. *375 S. Decatur Blvd., #11. 702/579-7777. www.britishgrocer.com. Map p 64.*

★★ **Chocolate Swan** SOUTH STRIP   The handmade truffles and hand-dipped chocolates are rich and luxurious, but the cakes are the real winners—three layers of Vienna cream sandwiched between airy sponge cake, and then frosted with butter cream. It doesn't come cheap, but their exacting standards show. *In Mandalay Place at Mandalay Bay, 3930 Las Vegas Blvd. S., Ste. 121B.* ☎ *702/632-9366. www.chocolate swan.com. AE, DC, DISC, MC, V. Map p 63.*

★★★ **Jean-Philippe Patisserie** MID-STRIP   Come for the chocolate fountain, stay for the award-winning pastries (including a brioche-oozing *dulce de leche*) and maybe some authentic gelato, and then leave with a box full of expensive truffles. Repeat as necessary. *Bellagio, 3600 Las Vegas Blvd. S.* ☎ *702/693 8788. AE, DC, DISC, MC, V. Map p 63.*

Want to taste a gray M&M? Hot pink? Both? M&M's World is the place to do it.

★ **M&M's World** SOUTH STRIP Walls filled with tubes of unusually colored M&Ms and themed merchandise. It's totally gimmicky until you realize what an awesome assortment you can make by mixing hot pink with black. *In the Showcase Mall, 3785 Las Vegas Blvd. S. (just north of MGM Grand).* ☎ *702/736-7611. AE, DISC, MC, V. Map p 63.*

Gift Shops

★★ **Arts Factory Complex** DOWNTOWN You'll find more than neon cityscapes and desert scenes on display and for sale in this two-story complex (once a crematorium), where a number of painters, photographers, and sculptors maintain studios and galleries. *103 E. Charleston Blvd.* ☎ *702/382-3886. www.theartsfactory.com. AE, MC, V. Map p 63.*

★★★ **Atomic Testing Museum Store** MID-STRIP The museum is as serious as its subject matter, but its shop is where absurdity—atomic tests used to be tourist attractions—is allowed to sneak in, in the form of Albert Einstein action figures, Miss

Atomic Bomb magnets, and other bomb-and-blast–themed trinkets. *755 E. Flamingo Rd.* ☎ *702/794-5161. www.atomictestingmuseum. org. AE, DISC, MC, V. Map p 63.*

★★ **Bonanza Gift & Souvenir Shop** NORTH STRIP The self-proclaimed "world's largest gift shop." All I can say for sure is that it is indeed big, contains everything from dice earrings to pseudo "Indian" goods, and has never let me down when I'm looking for the perfect tacky souvenir. *2460 Las Vegas Blvd. S.* ☎ *702/384-0005. www.worldslargestgiftshop.com. AE, DISC, MC, V. Map p 63.*

Dragon's Lair SOUTH STRIP Crystal balls, magic wands, dragon figurines, and magically themed knickknacks to help bring out your inner wizard. *In the Realm Shops at Excalibur, 3850 Las Vegas Blvd. S.* ☎ *702/597-7850. AE, DISC, MC, V. Map p 63.*

★ **Elton John** MID-STRIP Few can resist the Elton John eyewear—

For the perfect tacky Vegas souvenir, look no further than the immense Bonanza Gift & Souvenir Shop.

Want a cool pair of fuzzy dice? Your own slot machine? If it's gambling related, then the Gambler's General Store has it.

replicas of ones he wore during the '70s and '80s—and other fabulously Captain Fantastic sparkly goodies available here. *The Appian Way at Caesars Palace, 3500 Las Vegas Blvd. S.* ☎ *702/365-5600. AE, DISC, MC, V. Map p 63.*

★ Gambler's General Store
DOWNTOWN   Eight thousand square feet (743 sq. m) filled with all manner of gambling-related merchandise. It's *the* place to purchase that most splendid of Vegas souvenirs, your very own antique (or current) slot machine. Or you could settle for a book on blackjack. *800 S. Main St.* ☎ *702/382-9903. www.gamblersgeneralstore.com. AE, DISC, MC, V. Map p 63.*

★ Il Prato   Need a mask for
Mardi Gras? A gown fit for Carnivale? This Venetian-themed gift shop stocks items ranging from beautiful masks and marionettes to detailed miniatures and fine stationery. The prices will make you wince, but the quality is there. *In The Grand Canal Shoppes, 3355 Las Vegas Blvd. S.* ☎ *702/733-1201. www.ilpratousa.com. AE, DC, DISC, MC, V. Map p 63.*

★★ Liberace Museum Gift Store   SOUTH STRIP   Not enough
bedazzled and bejeweled objects to suit my tastes, but if you need a refrigerator magnet with the honoree's mug on it—or even a mug with his face—here's the place. *1775 E. Tropicana Ave.* ☎ *702/798-5595. www.liberace.org. AE, MC, V. Map p 64.*

★ Swarovski   MID-STRIP   Crystals
(made by a company that has specialized in the finest of same for generations) adorn everything from purses to picture frames in this glittering shop. Costly? Yes. But the quality is there. *In Planet Hollywood's Miracle Mile, 3663 Las Vegas Blvd. S.* ☎ *702/732-7302. www.swarovski.com. AE, DISC, MC, V. Map p 63.*

Hotel Shopping Arcades
★★ Bellagio: Via Bellagio   MID-STRIP   I can't even afford the small
bit of oxygen it takes to walk this short, but high-priced, luxury shopping promenade, marked by such names as Armani, Hermès, and Chanel. But I sure do like pretending I can. *3600 Las Vegas Blvd. S. (at the corner of Flamingo Rd.).* ☎ *702/693-7111. AE, DC, DISC, MC, V. Map p 63.*

★★★ Caesars Palace: Appian Way & The Forum Shops

MID-STRIP Every bit as much an attraction as it is a shopping destination. Think Rodeo Drive—Christian Dior, Louis Vuitton, and so on—reimagined as the Via Veneto and some Italian cityscapes, plus some ridiculous talking statues. *3500 Las Vegas Blvd. S.* ☎ *702/731-7110. www.caesars.com. AE, DISC, MC, V. Map p 63.*

Harrah's: Carnaval Court

MID-STRIP Notable for being the only outdoor hotel shopping mall, to say nothing of being the only outdoor shopping on the Strip itself, this collection of stalls sells purses, hippie-style clothes, jewelry, and other inexpensive trinkets. *3475 Las Vegas Blvd. S.* ☎ *702/369-5000. www.harrahs.com. AE, DC, DISC, MC, V. Map p 63.*

Mandalay Bay: Mandalay Place

SOUTH STRIP In appearance, more like an actual indoor mall than a hotel shopping arcade, but in content it has neither the rarified atmosphere of Via Bellagio or the Wynn Promenade, nor the variety of The Forum Shops. But it does have a bookstore (a rare entry), a men's shop called The Art of Shaving, a great wine store, and a superior chocolatier. That may be just enough. *3930 Las Vegas Blvd. S. (between Luxor & Mandalay Bay).* ☎ *702/632-7777. AE, DC, DISC, MC, V. Map p 63.*

Paris Las Vegas: Le Boulevard

SOUTH STRIP Ooo-la-la! It's *le petit Paree,* complete with cobblestone streets, quaint lampposts, replicas of the Pont Alexandre III and the Eiffel Tower, shops carrying chic sunglasses and watches, French imports such as Yves Saint-Laurent and Christian Lacroix, and a boutique dedicated to that ubiquitous French invention—*le bikini. 3655 Las Vegas Blvd. S.* ☎ *702/946-7000. www.parislv.com. AE, DC, DISC, MC, V. Map p 63.*

Planet Hollywood: Miracle Mile

SOUTH STRIP Once upon a time this was a sumptuous, exotically themed bazaar of luxury goods named Desert Passage. Now it has been remodeled into a simulacrum of a modern upscale urban shopping district for mall goods. Check out the Jumbo-trons. *3667 Las*

Combine top-notch shopping and an Ancient Roman–theme with some tacky elements, and you get The Forum Shops, the quintessential Vegas shopping destination.

Vegas Blvd. S. ☎ 702/785-5555. www.desertpassage.com. www. canyouhandlethismuchshopping.com. AE, DC, DISC, MC, V. Map p 63.

★★ The Venetian: The Grand Canal Shoppes MID-STRIP Stroll through St. Mark's Square and wander along a faux Grand Canal replete with serenading gondoliers. *Trompe l'oeil* clouds float past the "roofs" of the 15th-century-style "houses" that are home to stores fit for the Doge, including Jimmy Choo, Mikimoto, Privilege, and Kenneth Cole. Performers who interact with shoppers while in period costume complete the experience. *3355 Las Vegas Blvd. S.* ☎ *702/414-4500. www. venetian.com. AE, DC, DISC, MC, V. Map p 63.*

Wynn Las Vegas: Wynn Esplanade NORTH STRIP Not as large as Via Bellagio, this marble-walled stroll features such dream-and-drool-inducing retailers as Cartier, Judith Leiber, and Oscar de la Renta. *In Wynn Las Vegas, 3131 Las Vegas Blvd. S.* ☎ *702/770-7000. www.wynnlasvegas.com. AE, DC, DISC, MC, V. Map p 63.*

Jewelry
★★★ Fred Leighton MID-STRIP Specializing in period estate jewelry—including expensive turn-of-the-20th-century and Art Deco baubles dripping with emeralds, sapphires, rubies, and other precious and semiprecious stones—this boutique showcases one-of-a-kind envy-and swoon-inducing works of art. This is where I would blow all my jackpots. *In Via Bellagio, 3600 Las Vegas Blvd. S.* ☎ *702/693-7050. AE, DC, MC, V. Map p 63.*

★★ Harry Winston MID-STRIP *The* diamond dealer for haute couture consumers. Winston's stones shine as brightly as the stars who

Won a slot jackpot and want some bling to celebrate the victory? Harry Winston is the place...but it better have been a big jackpot.

wear them on red carpets. *In The Forum Shops at Caesars Palace, 3500 Las Vegas Blvd. S.* ☎ *702/933-7370. www.harrywinston.com. AE, DC, MC, V. Map p 63.*

★ Mikimoto Pearls MID-STRIP The originator of cultured pearls, Mikimoto has been creating the famous smooth white Akoyo pearl since 1893. The store also carries cultured South Sea pearls in shades of gray, pink, and cream. *In The Venetian Grand Canal Shoppes, 3355 Las Vegas Blvd. S.* ☎ *702/735-3896.* ☎ *702/414-3900. www.mikimoto america.com. AE, DC, DISC, MC, V. Map p 63.*

★★ Tiffany & Co. MID-STRIP There may be some who are unmoved by the power of Tiffany, even after Truman Capote and Miss Hepburn explained it to all, but I am not one of them. Even just a simple diamond seems to sparkle more brightly in a Tiffany setting. *In Via Bellagio, 3600 Las Vegas Blvd. S.* ☎ *702/697-5400. AE, DC, DISC, MC, V. Map p 63.*

Malls

The Boulevard EAST OF THE STRIP
Dillard's, Macy's, Sears, and JCPenney
are the anchors at this mall, which
has 140 retail stores, including Foot
Locker, Radio Shack, and Brookstone.
Out-of-state visitors can visit the
Customer Service Center for special
offers. *3528 S. Maryland Pkwy.
(between Twain Ave. & Desert Inn
Rd.).* ☎ *702/732-8949. www.blvdmall.
com. AE, DISC, MC, V. Map p 64.*

★★ Fashion Show MID-STRIP
One of the strangest design elements
ever seen in a shopping center—or
anywhere else for that matter—is the
giant twisted steel sculpture called
The Cloud, which hovers above the
entrance as part of a multimedia display featuring LED screens, flashing
lights, and music. During the winter,
fake snow drifts down on shoppers
visiting the 240 shops, including
Neiman Marcus, Macy's, Blooming-
dale's, and Nevada's only branch of
Nordstrom. It's so very Vegas. *3200
Las Vegas Blvd. S.* ☎ *702/369-0704.
www.thefashionshow.com. AE, DISC,
MC, V. Map p 63.*

★ The Galleria at Sunset WEST
OF STRIP   Along with Macy's, Dillard's, and JCPenney, this immense
and well-stocked suburban mall is
home to a Sanrio store (home of
Hello Kitty and friends), Lane Bryant,
and a slew of other mall standards.
*1300 W. Sunset Rd. (at Stephanie St.,
just off I-15), Henderson.* ☎ *702/434-
0202. www.galleriaatsunset.com.
AE, DISC, MC, V. Map p 63.*

★ Meadows Mall WEST OF STRIP
This ultramodern mall combines a
wide range of traditional mall shops,
such as Victoria's Secret, GNC, Bor-
ders Express, and Foot Locker, with
an anchor lineup of Macy's, Dillard's,
Sears, and JCPenney. *4300 Meadows
Lane.* ☎ *702/878-3331. www.
meadowsmall.com. AE, DISC, MC, V.
Map p 64.*

★ Showcase Mall SOUTH STRIP
If one store dedicated to Coca-Cola,
another to M&Ms, and a huge below-
ground arcade with state-of-the-art
games designed by Steven Spielberg
aren't enough to make your eyes
pop, the mall's Grand Canyon Experience gift shop has a man-made thun-
derstorm every 20 minutes. *3785 Las
Vegas Blvd. S. (right next to MGM
Grand).* ☎ *702/597-3122. AE, DISC,
MC, V. Map p 63.*

Toys

★ FAO Schwartz MID-STRIP   An
animatronic two-story Trojan horse
will bid you welcome and a warm
farewell as you leave bearing gifts
from this landmark toy store, which
sells its own line of stuffed animals,
plus trains, dolls, action figures, and
so forth. Check out the treehouse,
which can be rented for birthday
parties. *In The Forum Shops at Caesars Palace, 3500 Las Vegas Blvd. S.*
☎ *702/796-6500. www.fao.com. AE,
DISC, MC, V. Map p 63.* ●

*Guarded by an animatronic Trojan horse
that wows shoppers, FAO Schwartz is
Vegas's top toy store.*

The Best **Casinos**

Casino Best Bets

The casino at the MGM Grand is arguably the largest in the world—you'll get lost at least once.

Most **Glamorous**
Bellagio, *3600 Las Vegas Blvd. S.
(p 79)*

Most **Visually Stimulating**
New York–New York, *3790 Las Vegas Blvd. S. (p 81)*

Best **Casino for Budget Gamblers**
Main Street Station, *200. N. Main St. (p 81)*

Best **Layout**
Red Rock Resort, *10973 W. Charleston Rd. (p 82)*

Least **Smoky**
Mandalay Bay, *3930 Las Vegas Blvd. S. (p 81)*

Most **Comfortable Chairs**
Wynn Las Vegas, *3131 Las Vegas Blvd. S. (p 82)*

Most **Airy**
Luxor, *3900 Las Vegas Blvd. S. (p 81)*

Most **Likely to Get Lost In**
MGM Grand, *3799 Las Vegas Blvd. S. (p 81)*

Best **Smoke-Free Poker Rooms**
Bellagio, *3600 Las Vegas Blvd. S. (p 79)*; or Mirage, *3400 Las Vegas Blvd. S. (p 81)*

Best **Fake Sky**
Paris, *3655 Las Vegas Blvd. S. (p 82)*

Most **Confusing to Navigate**
Caesars Palace, *3500 Las Vegas Blvd. S. (p 79)*

Most **Rock 'n' Roll**
Hard Rock, *4455 Paradise Rd. (p 80)*

Best **Classic Casino**
Binion's Horseshoe, *128 E. Fremont St. (p 79)*

Friendliest **Poker Tables**
MGM Grand, *3799 Las Vegas Blvd. S. (p 81)*

Most **Distracting**
Circus Circus, *2880 Las Vegas Blvd. S. (p 79)*

Best **Lit**
Gold Coast, *4000 W. Flamingo Rd. (p 79)*

Previous Page: The casino floor at the Rio All-Suite Hotel & Casino.

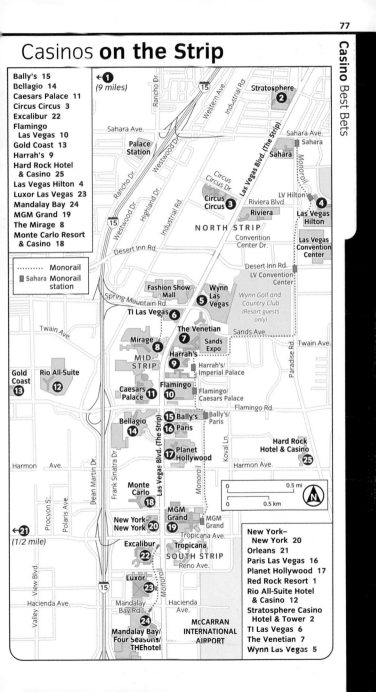

Casinos **on the Strip**

Bally's 15
Bellagio 14
Caesars Palace 11
Circus Circus 3
Excalibur 22
Flamingo
  Las Vegas 10
Gold Coast 13
Harrah's 9
Hard Rock Hotel
  & Casino 25
Las Vegas Hilton 4
Luxor Las Vegas 23
Mandalay Bay 24
MGM Grand 19
The Mirage 8
Monte Carlo Resort
  & Casino 18

.... Monorail
▌ Sahara Monorail
  station

New York–
  New York 20
Orleans 21
Paris Las Vegas 16
Planet Hollywood 17
Red Rock Resort 1
Rio All-Suite Hotel
  & Casino 12
Stratosphere Casino
  Hotel & Tower 2
TI Las Vegas 6
The Venetian 7
Wynn Las Vegas 5

Downtown Casinos

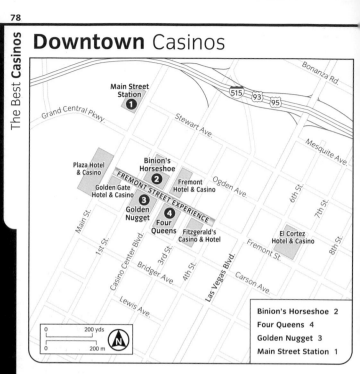

Main Street Station ❶

Plaza Hotel & Casino

Binion's Horseshoe ❷

Golden Gate Hotel & Casino

FREMONT STREET EXPERIENCE

Golden Nugget ❸

Four Queens ❹

Fitzgerald's Casino & Hotel

Fremont Hotel & Casino

El Cortez Hotel & Casino

Grand Central Pkwy.

Stewart Ave.

Ogden Ave.

Fremont St.

Bridger Ave.

Carson Ave.

Lewis Ave.

Main St.

1st St.

Casino Center Blvd.

3rd St.

4th St.

Las Vegas Blvd.

6th St.

7th St.

8th St.

Mesquite Ave.

Bonanza Rd.

515 93 95

0 200 yds
0 200 m

Binion's Horseshoe 2
Four Queens 4
Golden Nugget 3
Main Street Station 1

Casinos A to Z

Rating Alert

When it comes to casinos, the general rule is "you love where you win, you hate where you lose." A casino could be stunning and you'll still loathe it if you lose a bundle there. Because luck is so annoyingly unpredictable and casino choice so personal a selection, you won't find star ratings in this chapter. I hope you end up loving all of them.

Bally's MID-STRIP   Once the height of casino-dom, Bally's is now pretty much an afterthought. Which is too bad; there's nothing wrong here, and much to like. Ceilings are high and machines are well spaced,

so it doesn't feel crowded. Because it has less of a profile, the casino seems to try harder, and that results in a pleasant place to gamble. *3645 Las Vegas Blvd. S.* ☎ *702/739-4111. www.ballyslv.com. Map p 77.*

For a big thrill—if not the largest jackpot—visit one of the casinos and play a giant slot machine like this one in Bally's.

Bellagio MID-STRIP   The fancy-pants casino in town, complete with colorful canopies over the gaming area. It's just a tiny bit intimidating for some, but sophisticated and grown-up for others. It gets big points for the grid layout (including color-coordinated rugs to help guide you), which makes navigating this place less of a chaotic experience. *3600 Las Vegas Blvd. S.* ☎ *702/693-7111. www.bellagio.com. Map p 77.*

Binion's Horseshoe DOWNTOWN   The former home of the World Series of Poker (now moved to the Rio), Binion's is still the place serious gamblers go about their business, which isn't to say it's not fun, but rather a particular kind of fun. Thanks to the colorful ups and downs of a long string of owners, the place has seen better days, though improvements (by yet another new owner) are on the horizon. Lower table limits are another attraction. *128 E. Fremont St.* ☎ *702/382-1600. www.binions.com. Map p 78.*

Caesars Palace MID-STRIP   A great big rambling mess of a casino, but despite the sprawl this is still an oh-so-Vegas place to gamble. Glitzy chandeliers, toga-clad waitresses, gianormous "Roman" statues—it's exactly what I want from this city. Some parts of the casino are lighter and more airy than others. The huge sports book has cushy chairs, but is placed somewhat awkwardly in the line of traffic. Weekend nights bring the Pussycat Dolls Pit, where go-go girls gyrate above burlesque-clad dealer girls at pink-colored tables with very high limits. *3570 Las Vegas Blvd. S.* ☎ *702/731-7110. www. caesars.com. Map p 77.*

Circus Circus NORTH STRIP   Surely the most gimmick-laden casino in town, where the main action is covered by a Big Top in which various highflying circus performers do their thing virtually around the clock. Obviously, this is meant as a way to entertain the kids—many of whom pass through the area, making it exceedingly noisy and crowded—while adults spend their college tuition funds. No one has fallen onto the tables from up above (that I know of), but I still fret. *2880 Las Vegas Blvd. S.* ☎ *702/734-0410. www.circus circus.com. Map p 77.*

Excalibur SOUTH STRIP   It's adorned with suits of armor, stained-glass panels, heraldic banners, impressively massively iron chandeliers, and other castle-ready accouterments. Unfortunately, the atmosphere is more cluttered than cool. *3850 Las Vegas Blvd. S.* ☎ *702/597-7700. www.excalibur. com. Map p 77.*

Flamingo Las Vegas MID-STRIP   Not much in the way of style—renovations haven't ditched its pretty high claustrophobia rating—but its central location and lack of pretense make this a good choice for basic play. *3555 Las Vegas Blvd. S.* ☎ *702/ 733-3111. www.flamingolv.com. Map p 77.*

Four Queens DOWNTOWN   Sweetly anachronistic, the Four Queens is just the sort of Downtown casino—low limits and unintimidating crowds—that makes you wonder why you bothered with the behemoths on the Strip in the first place. *202 Fremont St.* ☎ *702/385-4011. www.fourqueens.com. Map p 78.*

Gold Coast WEST OF STRIP   I like this locals favorite—set right next to the Rio—because it's totally unique in Vegas: It has windows! It also has high ceilings, and a relatively high number of video-poker machines (and some of those may actually have odds favorable to you . . . another rarity). *4000 W. Flamingo Rd.* ☎ *702/367-7111. www.goldcoast casino.com. Map p 77.*

Golden Nugget DOWNTOWN Downtown's classiest casino is all the better thanks to serious renovations by its latest owner. In looks and feel, it's the closest thing in the area to a Strip casino, though its table minimums thankfully don't ascend that far. *129 E. Fremont St.* ☎ *702/385-7111. www.goldennugget.com. Map p 78.*

Hard Rock Hotel & Casino EAST OF STRIP An admirable work of Boomer marketing, where rock music blares, and gamers play on tables designed like piano keyboards with chips emblazoned with musicians' faces. You drop change into Jimi Hendrix–brand slots or kick back in the sports book's reclining leather chairs. Too loud for some, it's the only place to gamble for others. *4455 Paradise Rd.* ☎ *702/693-5000. www.hardrock hotel.com. Map p 77.*

Harrah's MID-STRIP It's too crowded, smoky, and dated to make it a first-choice casino, but the Party Pits—where music blares and dealers cavort—are a draw. *3475 Las Vegas Blvd. S.* ☎ *702/369-5000. www.harrahs.com. Map p 77.*

Some of the best bets in town are available inside casino sports books, where you can usually sit down and watch the race you've wagered on.

Las Vegas Hilton EAST OF STRIP The classy, main casino is polished, but come here for the fun space-themed portion, which is designed to look like a spaceport, and where you'll find futuristic slot machines— just pass your hand through a light beam to activate them. The enormous sports book is the world's largest and has a video wall that's second in size only to NASA's. *3000 Paradise Rd.* ☎ *702/732-7111. www.lvhilton.com. Map p 77.*

Learning the Ropes

Hitting up a one-armed bandit (that's a slot machine in gaming lingo) isn't exactly brain surgery, but ignorance won't likely result in bliss if you sit at a poker or craps table when you don't know what you're doing. For a rundown of the major games in town, complete with basic strategy tips, check out "The Savvy Gambler." If you prefer hands-on instruction, many casinos offer free gambling lessons (ask a dealer to find out if lessons are offered in a particular casino) to those interested in the major table games. If you're merely curious instead of highly interested, these will more than satisfy your casino cravings. Not only will you avoid losing money, but you'll probably have some fun, too. And if the lesson proves instructive, some casinos offer low-stakes games following their gambling lessons, so your initial indulgence won't prove as costly. Note that most lessons are given on weekdays, so if you're in town for the weekend, you'll be out of luck.

Luxor Las Vegas SOUTH STRIP
The tallest casino ceiling on the Strip makes for the least claustrophobic gambling situation, and that's even before the cool Egyptian theme kicks in. A genuinely fun place to drop some dough. *3900 Las Vegas Blvd. S.* ☎ *702/262-4000. www.luxor.com. Map p 77.*

Main Street Station DOWNTOWN
Calling this casino "cute" isn't meant to suggest there is a puppy and kitten theme. Instead, it's turn-of-the-last-century San Francisco, with old-fashioned fans dropping down from a Victorian tin ceiling. The atmosphere, combined with lower-than-Strip limits, makes it a winner. *200 N. Main St.* ☎ *702/387-1896. www.mainstreet casino.com. Map p 78.*

Mandalay Bay SOUTH STRIP
Thanks to the higher-than-average ceiling and an attempt to create an elegant atmosphere, this is an appealing place to play. Its extreme southern location means it's often not overwhelmingly crowded, but if there is an event at the hotel's arena or the House of Blues, expect a massive influx of additional players. *3950 Las Vegas Blvd. S.* ☎ *702/632-7000. www.mandalaybay.com. Map p 77.*

MGM Grand SOUTH STRIP
The biggest of the big, 171,500 square feet (15,933 sq. m) of gaming space is divided into four areas in an attempt to reduce it to a manageable size. It doesn't help. But big doesn't mean impersonal, and some of the friendliest poker tables are found here. *3799 Las Vegas Blvd. S.* ☎ *702/891-7777. www.mgmgrand.com. Map p 77.*

The Mirage MID-STRIP
It's been revamped from its original tropical decor into Asian sleek, which only makes me like it more. The old-school tortuous layout makes navigating a little difficult, but the vibe is good. *3400 Las Vegas Blvd. S.* ☎ *702/791-7111. www.mirage.com. Map p 77.*

Monte Carlo Resort & Casino
SOUTH STRIP This place tries to evoke gambling in Monaco, and though the decor shows lots of attention, it's a little bit busy on both the eyes and the ears. That said, the smoke factor is pretty low and it's definitely one of the best-smelling casinos in town. *3770 Las Vegas Blvd. S.* ☎ *702/730-7777. www.monte carlo.com. Map p 77.*

New York–New York SOUTH
STRIP Hilarious and hectic, because the designers attempted to cram all the highlights of Manhattan into one massive gaming place. As much fun to look at as to play in, though some justifiably find it too hectic, crowded, and distracting. *3970 Las Vegas Blvd. S.* ☎ *702/740-6969. www.nynyhotel casino.com. Map p 77.*

Orleans WEST OF STRIP
A low claustrophobia level, good video-poker options, and cheaper table minimums lure locals and tourists seeking better odds than those available on the Strip. The Cajun and zydeco music they occasionally play on the sound system makes it that much more fun. *4500 W. Tropicana Ave.* ☎ *702/365-7111. www.orleans casino.com. Map p 77.*

The steady ring of a slot machine is one of the signature sounds of a casino.

Paris Las Vegas Casino MID-STRIP   Oddly sweet, as it's set beneath a ceiling painted like an April day in Paris and is partly under the feet of the hotel's Eiffel Tower re-creation. The 83,000-square-foot (7,710-sq.-m) gaming area is ringed by Disneyesque European facades. *3655 Las Vegas Blvd. S.* ☎ *702/946-7000. www.parislv.com. Map p 77.*

Planet Hollywood SOUTH STRIP   An impressive interior showcases classic Hollywood glamour, and all the usual gambling suspects have been rounded up for your betting pleasure. It's not exactly serene, but the casino floor is now way calmer than it was during its Aladdin days. *3667 Las Vegas Blvd. S.* ☎ *702/736-0111. www.aladdincasino.com. Map p 77.*

Red Rock Resort WEST OF STRIP   For sheer, nontheme design, this is the best-looking casino in town, utilizing natural woods, glass ornaments, and stone. Like the rest of the resort, it's a stunner. It's also a convivial place to play. *10973 W. Charleston Blvd.* ☎ *702/797-7625. www.redrockstation.com. Map p 77.*

Rio All-Suite Hotel & Casino MID-STRIP   The 85,000-square-foot (7,900-sq.-m) main casino is dark and claustrophobic; stick to the section in the Masquerade Village area, which has much higher ceilings and is way more pleasant. And don't get distracted by those scantily costumed waitresses . . . who might break into song and dance every now and then. *3700 W. Flamingo Rd.* ☎ *702/252-7777. www.harrahs.com. Map p 77.*

Stratosphere Casino Hotel & Tower NORTH STRIP   You'll get more bang for your buck at this low-limit haven, which is often less crowded than many of its Strip cohorts. It's especially good for video poker aficionados. *2000 Las Vegas Blvd. S.* ☎ *702/380-7777. www. stratospherehotel.com. Map p 77.*

TI Las Vegas MID-STRIP   They've completely obliterated the dripping-with-plunder pirate theme that used to make this place fun, and all that remains is a nice casino. For most of you, that will be enough. *3300 Las Vegas Blvd. S.* ☎ *702/894-7111. www.treasureisland.com. Map p 77.*

The Venetian MID-STRIP   I miss the old tacky Vegas casinos, which this classy joint—check out the Venetian art on the ceilings!—is most definitely not. It's hard to navigate; but because the smoke factor is very low and I hit it big here once, I love it. *3355 Las Vegas Blvd. S.* ☎ *702/414-1000. www.venetian.com. Map p 77.*

Wynn Las Vegas NORTH STRIP   A large but simple layout and the overall classy gestalt are pluses, but on the minus side, table limits are expensive here. No matter; the machines (tight as they may be) run from nickels on up, so park yourself in the most comfortable slot seats in town and save the tables for Downtown. *3131 Las Vegas Blvd. S.* ☎ *702/770-7100. www.wynnlasvegas.com. Map p 77.* ●

Blackjack is the most popular table game in most Las Vegas casinos; for tips on playing it, see p. 148.

Dining Best Bets

Best **Diner**
★★ Triple George Grill $$ 201 N. 3rd St. (p 98)

Best **Burger**
★ Burger Bar $ Mandalay Place, 3930 Las Vegas Blvd. S. (p 89)

Best **Bakery**
★★ Freed's $ 4780 S. Eastern Ave. (p 92)

Best **Sushi**
★★★ Shibuya $$$ MGM Grand, 3799 Las Vegas Blvd. S. (p 97)

Best **Place to Blow All Your Jackpot Winnings**
★★★ L'Atlier Joël Robuchon $$$$ MGM Grand, 3799 Las Vegas Blvd. S. (p 94)

Best **Thai**
★★★ Lotus of Siam $ The Commercial Center, 953 E. Sahara Ave. (p 94)

Best **In-House Celebrity-Chef Meal**
★★★ Picasso $$$$ Bellagio, 3600 Las Vegas Blvd. S. (p 95)

Best **View**
★★★ Alizé $$$ Palms Casino Resort, 4321 W. Flamingo Rd. (p 87)

Best **Breakfast**
★★ Hash House a Go Go $ 6800 W. Sahara Ave. (p 93)

Best **Local Celebrity Chef**
★★★ Rosemary's $$$ 8125 W. Sahara Ave. (p 97)

Best **Italian**
★★★ Corsa Cucina $$$ Wynn Las Vegas, 3131 Las Vegas Blvd. S. (p 90)

Best **Steak**
★★ Austins Steakhouse $$ Texas Station, 2101 Texas Star Lane (p 88)

Previous Page: A gourmet dish from the highly regarded kitchen of L'Atlier Joël Robuchon.

Most **Romantic**
★★★ Alizé $$$ Palms Casino Resort, 4321 W. Flamingo Rd. (p 87)

Best **Buffet**
★★★ Wynn Las Vegas Buffet $$ Wynn Las Vegas, 3131 Las Vegas Blvd. S. (p 98)

Best **Bistro**
★★★ Bouchon $$ The Venetian, 3355 Las Vegas Blvd. S. (p 89)

Best **Inexpensive Meal**
★★★ Capriotti's $ 324 W. Sahara Ave. (p 90)

Best **Mexican**
★★ Border Grill $$ Mandalay Bay, 3950 Las Vegas Blvd. S. (p 89)

Best **Place to Eat Like Liberace**
★★ Carluccio's Tivoli Gardens $$ 1775 E. Tropicana Blvd. (p 90)

Best **Food Court**
★★ Cypress Street Marketplace $ Caesars Palace, 3570 Las Vegas Blvd. S. (p 90)

Rosemary's is a local favorite with especially superb seafood.

South Strip Restaurants

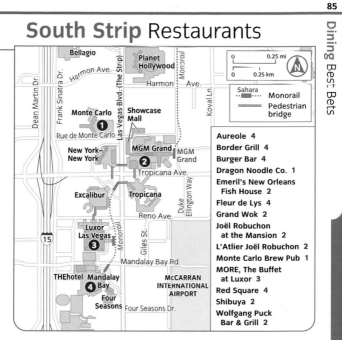

Aureole 4
Border Grill 4
Burger Bar 4
Dragon Noodle Co. 1
Emeril's New Orleans
  Fish House 2
Fleur de Lys 4
Grand Wok 2
Joël Robuchon
  at the Mansion 2
L'Atlier Joël Robuchon 2
Monte Carlo Brew Pub 1
MORE, The Buffet
  at Luxor 3
Red Square 4
Shibuya 2
Wolfgang Puck
  Bar & Grill 2

Mid-Strip Restaurants

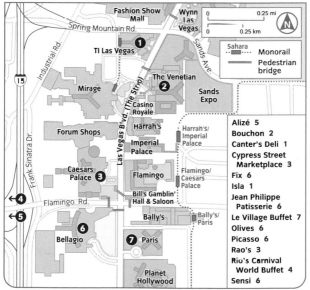

Alizé 5
Bouchon 2
Canter's Deli 1
Cypress Street
  Marketplace 3
Fix 6
Isla 1
Jean Philippe
  Patisserie 6
Le Village Buffet 7
Olives 6
Picasso 6
Rao's 3
Rio's Carnival
  World Buffet 4
Sensi 6

Las Vegas Restaurants

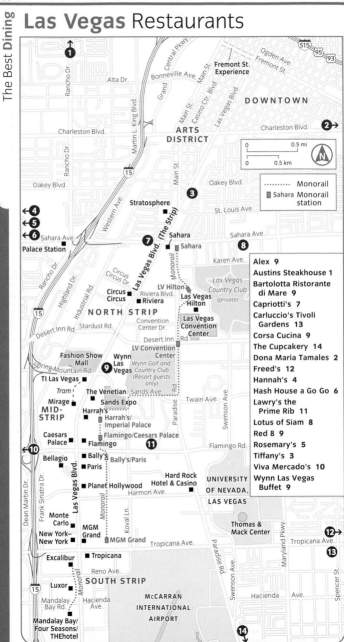

Alex **9**
Austins Steakhouse **1**
Bartolotta Ristorante
di Mare **9**
Capriotti's **7**
Carluccio's Tivoli
Gardens **13**
Corsa Cucina **9**
The Cupcakery **14**
Dona Maria Tamales **2**
Freed's **12**
Hannah's **4**
Hash House a Go Go **6**
Lawry's the
Prime Rib **11**
Lotus of Siam **8**
Red 8 **9**
Rosemary's **5**
Tiffany's **3**
Viva Mercado's **10**
Wynn Las Vegas
Buffet **9**

Downtown Restaurants

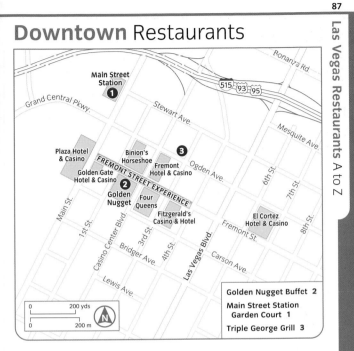

Main Street Station ❶

Plaza Hotel & Casino

Binion's Horseshoe

Golden Gate Hotel & Casino

FREMONT STREET EXPERIENCE

Golden Nugget ❷

Four Queens

Fremont Hotel & Casino ❸

Fitzgerald's Casino & Hotel

El Cortez Hotel & Casino

Grand Central Pkwy.

Stewart Ave.

Ogden Ave.

Bonanza Rd.

Mesquite Ave.

515 93 95

6th St.

7th St.

8th St.

Main St.

1st St.

Casino Center Blvd.

3rd St.

4th St.

Bridger Ave.

Lewis Ave.

Las Vegas Blvd.

Fremont St.

Carson Ave.

0   200 yds
0   200 m

Golden Nugget Buffet **2**

Main Street Station Garden Court **1**

Triple George Grill **3**

Las Vegas Restaurants A to Z

★★★ **Alex** NORTH STRIP *CONTI-NENTAL* Chef-owner Alex Strada did a stint as "Iron Chef America," and though his prix-fixe menus don't come cheap, the complex dishes are thoughtfully put together and don't ignore delicate touches, such as tiny vegetables cooked to the right crunch. The service is equally superb. *In Wynn Las Vegas, 3131 Las Vegas Blvd. S.* ☎ *888/352-DINE or 702/248-DINE. Reservations strongly suggested. Jacket recommended. 3-course prix-fixe menu $145; 7-course tasting menu $195. AE, DC, DISC, MC, V. Tues–Sun dinner. Map p 85.*

★★★ **Alizé** MID-STRIP *FRENCH* Perhaps the most dazzling space in Vegas, in that the space itself is simple, but the setting—floating above Vegas and the desert at the top of

the Palms—is not. Sit next to one of the floor-to-ceiling windows, and bask. The food is just as ethereal, though the fish is sometimes dry; stick to meat and you'll be happy. *In Palms Casino Resort, 4321 W. Flamingo Rd.* ☎ *702/951-7000. www.alizelv.com. Reservations*

The French cuisine at Alizé is more than a match for its superb views.

strongly recommended. Food minimum $45 per person. Main courses $30–$52; 5-course tasting menu $95; 7-course tasting menu $125. AE, MC, V. Dinner nightly. Map p 85.

★★ **Aureole** SOUTH STRIP *NOUVELLE AMERICAN* The food here is American regional haute, but many also come for the height—the four-story glass wine tower, where bottles are fetched by enticing cat-suited "wine goddesses" in harnesses. It's a Vegas-style gimmick, but the cuisine (served via prix-fixe menus) is strong enough to stand on its own. *In Mandalay Bay, 3950 Las Vegas Blvd. S.* ☎ *877/632-1766 or 702/632-7401. www.aureolelv.com. Reservations required. Prix-fixe dinner $75; tasting menu $95. AE, MC, V. Dinner daily. Map p 85.*

★★ **Austins Steakhouse** WEST OF STRIP *STEAK* Vegas hotel steakhouses are often pretty interchangeable. The more expensive ones are on the Strip, which is one reason to trek to this longtime local favorite. The other is the 24-ounce

The magnificent decor at Bartolotta Ristorante di Mare serves as a proper backdrop to its equally delectable Italian cuisine.

rib-eye—plenty big enough to share—a massive chunk of meat with a smoky, garlicky flavor that earns raves from pretty much everyone. *In Texas Station, 2101 Texas Star Lane.* ☎ *702/631-1033. Reservations recommended. Main courses $15–$50. AE, DC, DISC, MC, V. Dinner nightly. Map p 86.*

Dining Tips

Vegas is no longer the bastion of low-priced dining that many travelers imagine it is. You can eat well or you can eat cheap, but it's not often that you can do both (though I do give you a number of options in this chapter that fit the bill). Even the vaunted buffet doesn't offer as much bang for the buck as it used to if you want food that is more than forgettable. So if you want to please your palate without emptying your wallet, here are a couple of options:

1. **Hit the primo restaurants at lunch.** Prices in this chapter, unless otherwise specified, are for main courses at dinner. Prices at lunch are often discounted 20% to 50%.

2. **Get off the Strip.** Restaurants that don't have to shell out big bucks for the real estate they sit on tend to have lower prices. Plus, restaurants that depend on locals are more invested in keeping their quality up and their prices from reaching the height of the stratosphere.

★★★ Bartolotta Ristorante di Mare NORTH STRIP *ITALIAN*

Award-winning chef Paul Bartolotta gets his fish flown in daily from the Mediterranean, and then cooks it simply, classically, and divinely. You can choose from a variety that may well include species hitherto unfamiliar to you, or have an excellent pasta dish instead. The restaurant also has a rare outdoor dining area, complete with modern art. *In Wynn Las Vegas, 3131 Las Vegas Blvd. S.* ☎ *888/352-DINE or 702/248-DINE. Reservations recommended. Main courses dinner $24–$55; family-style tasting $135 per person; Grand Seafood Feast $155 per person. AE, DC, DISC, MC, V. Lunch & dinner daily. Map p 86.*

★★ Border Grill SOUTH STRIP *MEXICAN*

The Food Network's Two Hot Tamales, Mary Sue and Susan, learned Mexican home-style cooking south of the border, and put their own twist on traditional dishes. It's not the place to go for plain old tacos—though you can, if you like—and you should skip the often bland fish dishes. *In Mandalay Bay, 3950 Las Vegas Blvd. S.* ☎ *702/632-7403. www.bordergrill.com. Reservations recommended. Main courses*

Border Grill is renowned for its twists on traditional Mexican cuisine.

You can't do much better for bistro cooking in Vegas than Thomas Keller's Bouchon.

$15–$28. AE, DC, DISC, MC, V. Lunch & dinner daily. Map p 85.

★★★ Bouchon MID-STRIP *BISTRO*

You won't find famed owner-chef Thomas Keller in the kitchen, but you also won't be disappointed. There's a deep satisfaction that comes from consuming this superlative bistro's regional French cooking in all its deserved glory. *In The Venetian, 3355 Las Vegas Blvd. S.* ☎ *702/414-6200. Reservations strongly recommended. Main courses $8–$45. Oyster bar $15–$99. AE, DC, MC, V. Breakfast & dinner daily. Map p 85.*

★ Burger Bar SOUTH STRIP *DINER*

A little costly for "just" a burger; but diners get to build their own custom creation from a menu containing dozens of topping options, so the markup is nearly worth it. It can be fun and creative (though I think there is no good reason to have truffles *and* lobster on your burger). Skip the Kobe beef—it's too much money for a meat that doesn't make a good patty anyway. *In Mandalay Bay, 3930 Las Vegas Blvd. S.* ☎ *702/632-9364. Main courses $8–$24. AE, DISC, MC, V. Lunch & dinner daily. Map p 85.*

★★ **Canter's Deli** MID-STRIP *DELI*
A semireplica of a Los Angeles institution, though minus the ageless waitstaff and with a menu only one-fifth the size of the original's. Still, the pastrami is authentic and so is the brisket, and it smells like a real deli. Plus, black-and-white cookies! *In TI Las Vegas, 3300 Las Vegas Blvd. S.* ☎ *702/894-7111. AE, DISC, MC, V. Main courses $10–$20. Lunch & dinner daily. Map p 85.*

★★★ **Capriotti's** NORTH STRIP *DELI* A rare combination for Vegas: something affordable and delicious. Capriotti's makes enormous submarine sandwiches that inspire such loyalty that many an out-of-town customer has planned their entrance and exit from Vegas around a stop here. Try the Slaw B. Joe, the Bobby, or design your own; opt for the "large" of anything and you can easily feed two. *324 W. Sahara Ave.* ☎ *702/474-0229. www.capriottis.com. Most sandwiches under $10. No credit cards. Lunch daily. Map p 86.*

★★ **Carluccio's Tivoli Gardens**
EAST OF STRIP *ITALIAN* Liberace owned and designed this place, and

You can watch the chefs in the open kitchen at Corsa Cucina prepare fresh Italian favorites.

the interior still look likes it. Need I say more? Okay, it's classic (and very satisfying) American-Italian comfort food: heavy pastas, heavy red sauce, lots of butter. It's hard to go wrong with a menu where everything is so right. *1775 E. Tropicana Blvd. (next to Liberace Museum).* ☎ *702/795-3236. Reservations recommended. Main courses $8–$18. AE, DC, DISC, MC, V. Dinner Tues–Sun. Map p 86.*

★★★ **Corsa Cucina** NORTH STRIP *ITALIAN* A superb venture from deeply talented chef Stephen Kalt, who takes Italian classics and puts his own stamp on them. Regional favorites, such as tissue-thin veal carpaccio, remind me that Italian food is hardly confined to red sauce. The chef is usually accessible in the open kitchen, so ask him what you should eat that night. *In Wynn Las Vegas, 3131 Las Vegas Blvd. S.* ☎ *888/352-DINE or 702/352-DINE. Reservations recommended. Main courses $25–$48. AE, DC, DISC, MC, V. Lunch Sun–Wed; dinner daily. Map p 86.*

★ **The Cupcakery** EAST OF STRIP *BAKERY* Cupcakes are all the rage these days and this is Vegas's only outlet for the trendy dessert. It's a good one. Try the Grasshopper, a rich chocolate topped with minty-strong green frosting; or the ganache, which is stuffed with fudge. *9860 S. Eastern Ave., Ste. 100* ☎ *702/207-CAKE (2253). www.thecupcakery.com. Most cupcakes $2.50. AE, DISC, MC, V. Open daily. Map p 86.*

★★ kids **Cypress Street Marketplace** MID-STRIP *FOOD COURT* A better-than-average food court, with an array of unexpected dishes, including North Carolina pulled pork, Vietnamese noodles, and more. Customers are given cards on which their purchases are swiped at each booth, and the total is billed at the cash register. It's an excellent choice for

The classic Mexican cuisine at Dona Maria Tamales is beloved by young and old alike.

families with a wide array of dietary desires. *In Caesars Palace, 3570 Las Vegas Blvd. S.* ☎ *702/731-7110. Most items under $15. AE, DC, DISC, MC, V. Lunch & dinner daily. Map p 85.*

★★ **Dona Maria Tamales** NORTH STRIP *MEXICAN* Classic Mexican food that's heavy on the lard, heavy on the sauces, heavy on the crowds (especially at lunch), and light on the wallet. You definitely want to try the tamales, but the enchiladas and chiles rellenos are excellent, too. *910 Las Vegas Blvd. S.* ☎ *702/382-6538. www.donamariatamales.com. Main courses $6–$13. AE, DC, DISC, MC, V.*

Breakfast, lunch & dinner daily. Map p 86.

★★ **Dragon Noodle Co.** SOUTH STRIP *CHINESE* One of the better Chinese restaurants in town, and a strong choice for a reasonably priced meal. The very fresh food is prepared in an open kitchen and served family style (it's great for large groups). And they have a sushi bar! *In Monte Carlo Resort & Casino, 3770 Las Vegas Blvd. S.* ☎ *702/730-7965. www.dragon noodleco.com. Main courses $5.50– $17. AE, DC, DISC, MC, V. Lunch & dinner daily. Map p 85.*

Getting a Table

The growing reputation of Vegas as a foodie haven means that getting a table at the best spots is a lot harder than it used to be. If you can, make reservations in advance or you may find that spot you had your hearts set on totally booked throughout your stay. And note that at places that don't take reservations (especially in the casino hotels), you may find yourself standing in line for a while to get inside (unless you gamble enough to get a pass that will get you in faster—see p 146 for details on players clubs and comps).

★ Emeril's New Orleans Fish House SOUTH STRIP *CREOLE*

Not as reliable as the original in New Orleans, and the fish dishes are often the least impressive. But a Creole-spiced rib-eye has Emeril's infamous kick, and the decadent lobster cheesecake is like nothing you've ever tried before. *In MGM Grand, 3799 Las Vegas Blvd. S. ☎ 702/891-7374. www.emerils.com. Reservations required. Main courses $25–$45 (more for lobster). AE, DC, DISC, MC, V. Lunch & dinner daily. Map p 85.*

★★ Fix MID-STRIP *AMERICAN*

Silly presentation rules here. Call it stunt food, or food as entertainment. "Forks," for example, is smoked salmon and caviar (served on the eponymous utensil, tines in the air). Given the range of small plates, hamburgers, desserts, and steaks, coupled with later-night hours, this is a good backup choice for fancy but not too froufrou dining. *In Bellagio, 3600 Las Vegas Blvd. S. ☎ 877/234-6358 or 702/693-8400. www.fixlasvegas. com. Reservations recommended. Main courses $29–$48. AE, MC, V. Dinner nightly. Map p 85.*

The food at Fix is not only delicious, but inventively presented, too.

★★★ Fleur de Lys SOUTH STRIP *FRENCH*

From celebrity chef Hubert Keller you get a sexy, sophisticated setting where you dine on cunningly designed seasonal creations in multi-course tasting menus priced better than many peers in town. From the scallops served with smoked salmon and sour cream ravioli to the artfully constructed desserts to the wonderful service, you won't go wrong here. *In Mandalay Place, 3930 Las Vegas Blvd. S. ☎ 702/632-9400. Reservations recommended. Jacket recommended. 3- to 5-course menu $74–$94. AE, DC, DISC, MC, V. Dinner daily. Map p 85.*

★★ Freed's EAST OF STRIP *BAKERY*

An old-fashioned bakery in a new-fashioned town. It sells creamy cakes, buttery cookies, and sugary and gooey everything. Much of it is made with incredibly fresh ingredients; all of it works for those of us with a sweet tooth. *4780 S. Eastern Ave. ☎ 702/456-7762. www.freedsbakery.com. Most pastries under $6. AE, DISC, MC, V. Open daily. Map p 86.*

★★ Golden Nugget Buffet

DOWNTOWN *BUFFET* Downtown is one of the last holdouts for bargains; you'd pay least $2 to $3 more for a buffet of this quality on the Strip. Most of the seating is in plush booths, and the tables are laden with an extensive salad bar, delicious fruit, fresh seafood, and marvelous desserts. Most lavish is the all-day Sunday champagne brunch. *In the Golden Nugget, 129 E. Fremont St. ☎ 702/385-7111. Breakfast $9; lunch $10; dinner $17; Sat brunch $16; Sun brunch $17; Fri–Sun Seafood & More Buffet $20. AE, DC, DISC, MC, V. Breakfast, lunch & dinner daily. Map p 87.*

★★ Grand Wok SOUTH STRIP *PAN ASIAN*

The pan-Asian (mostly limited to Chinese and Japanese) menu means options ranging from soup

Hannah's is justifiably renowned for its Asian-American offerings.

(bowls big enough to serve four light appetites) to sushi. It's a fine place for a good and inexpensive lunch. *In MGM Grand, 3799 Las Vegas Blvd. S. ☎ 702/891-7777. Reservations not accepted. Main courses $9–$19; sushi rolls & pieces $4.50–$15. AE, DC, DISC, MC, V. Lunch & dinner daily. Map p 85.*

★★★ Hannah's WEST OF STRIP
ASIAN It's rare for Vegas to have a homegrown restaurant of note, which is why it's worth driving here. With its culinary roots in Vietnam, Hannah's offers superb Asian-American food that has generated a strong local following. The Shaken Beef is a justly popular dish that pops up on nouveau Vietnamese menus. *1050 S. Rampart Blvd. S. ☎ 702/932-9399. www.hannahslv.com. Reservations recommended. Main courses $15–$42; sushi rolls $4–$35. AE, DC, DISC, MC, V. Lunch & dinner daily; brunch Sun. Map p 86.*

★★★ Hash House a Go Go WEST
OF STRIP *BREAKFAST* A suitably goofy concept restaurant, where breakfast is taken to the limit as

salmon and cream cheese are worked into the hash, the pancakes are the size of a large pizza, and the waffles have bacon baked right into them. Dinner brings other excellent options, but you want to make the drive here for breakfast. Prices aren't dirt-cheap, but everything is meant to be shared. *6800 W. Sahara Ave. ☎ 702/804-4646. www.hashhouse agogo.com. Main courses $9–$20. AE, MC, V. Breakfast, lunch & dinner daily. Map p 86.*

★★ Isla MID-STRIP *MEXICAN*
"Modern Mexican cuisine" means you don't come here for the burritos, but instead for guacamole that contains lobster and passion fruit or such goody desserts as a churro fondue tower. Or perhaps you come for the largest tequila collection in Vegas. *In TI Las Vegas, 3300 Las Vegas Blvd. S. ☎ 866/286-3809 or 702/894-7223. Main courses $12–$30. AE, DC, DISC, MC, V. Dinner daily. Map p 85.*

★★★ Jean Philippe Patisserie
MID-STRIP *CAFÉ/BAKERY* The product of an award-winning pastry chef, the Patisserie first attracted notice for its immense chocolate fountain, and then inspired deep devotion with such fare as a *dulce de leche*–stuffed brioche, serious gourmet chocolates, authentic gelato, and much more. It also serves sandwiches and crepes both savory and sweet, making this a perfect spot for a light meal. *In Bella- gio, 3600 Las Vegas Blvd. S.*

One of the divine pastries sold at Jean Phillipe Patisserie: Each is worth every calorie.

☎ 702/693-8788. *All items $2–$12. AE, DC, DISC, MC, V. Open daily. Map p 85.*

★★★ Joël Robuchon at the Mansion SOUTH STRIP *FRENCH*

Knowledgeable foodies worldwide were all atwitter when much-lauded master chef Robuchon was coaxed out of early retirement and into this lush fine-dining venture. It will be a pricey experience, but you shouldn't expect to pay less for great art—and that's what Robuchon offers, masterpieces on a plate, all served with multi-Michelin-starred level attention and care. *In MGM Grand, 3799 Las Vegas Blvd. S. 702/891-7925. 6-course tasting menu $225, 16-course tasting menu $360. AE, DC, DISC, MC, V. Sun–Thurs 5:30–10pm, Fri–Sat 5:30–10:30pm. Map p 85.*

★★★ L'Atlier Joël Robuchon

SOUTH STRIP *FRENCH* This is the casual, counter-seating version of the formal restaurant run by legendary chef Joël Robuchon. Prices here are lower, the vibe is lively rather than reverent, and the food not only is just as good as over at the main facility, but is some of the finest French food in the world. Plan enough time and appetite to sample as many of the delicate, playful, fanciful creations as you can. *In MGM Grand, 3799 Las Vegas Blvd. S. ☎ 702/891-7358. Reservations strongly recommended. Average check $125 per person. AE, DC, DISC, MC, V. Dinner daily. Map p 85.*

★★★ Kids Lawry's the Prime Rib EAST OF STRIP *STEAK* You will

find no better prime rib in town than at this branch of the Los Angeles institution. The ritual is half the fun: The staff takes your order for side dishes only, and then you select a cut from large gleaming metal carts that are wheeled to your table. Plus, you get spinning salad bowls! It's a good choice for carnivores and families.

For masterful French cuisine in an equally inspired setting, look no further than Joël Robuchon at the Mansion.

4043 Howard Hughes Pkwy. ☎ 702/893-2223. www.lawrysonline.com. *Reservations recommended. Main courses $29–$44. AE, DC, DISC, MC, V. Dinner daily. Map p 86.*

★★★ Le Village Buffet MID-STRIP

BUFFET Not just a cute buffet, set amid French village facades, but a clever one, wherein the stations are named after regions of France and the food therein more or less reflects the influence of same. Don't expect the most convincing versions of French countryside food, but it makes an excellent change of pace from regular buffets, and for the cost is a good option for a more interesting meal. *In Paris Las Vegas, 3655 Las Vegas Blvd. S. ☎ 888/266-5687. Breakfast $14; lunch $19; dinner $25; Sun brunch $25. AE, DC, DISC, MC, V. Breakfast, lunch & dinner daily. Map p 85.*

★★★ Lotus of Siam EAST OF

STRIP *THAI* Its legend rests on its coronation, some years ago, by *Gourmet* magazine as the best Thai food in North America. Really? I haven't tried them all, but I have journeyed to this strip mall hole-in-the-wall restaurant, and was glad.

Be sure to ask for the special-items menu to get the full effect of the authenticity. *In the Commercial Center, 953 E. Sahara Ave.* ☎ *702/735-3033. www.saipinchutima.com. Reservations strongly recommended for dinner. Lunch buffet $9; main courses $9–$18. AE, DISC, MC, V. Lunch Mon–Fri; dinner daily. Map p 86.*

★★★ kids Main Street Station Garden Court DOWNTOWN

BUFFET Like pretty much everything else in Vegas, the classic buffet—and by that I mean mounds of food for budget prices—is gradually getting edged out in favor of flashy-looking high-cost places. This place has found the sweet spot of value, serving really quite good buffet staples for value prices. *In the Main Street Station, 200 N. Main St.* ☎ *702/387-1896. Breakfast $6; lunch $9; dinner $11–$17; weekend champagne brunch $11. Free for children 3 & under. AE, DC, DISC, MC, V. Breakfast, lunch & dinner daily. Map p 87.*

★★ kids Monte Carlo Brew Pub

SOUTH STRIP *PUB FARE* This rustic-looking microbrewery serves hearty, not-so-high-falutin' food in a noisy but cheerful atmosphere (its 40 TVs yield a lot of decibels). Combine the general high quality, generous portions, and decent prices and this may be a better deal than most buffets. *In Monte Carlo Resort & Casino, 3770 Las Vegas Blvd. S.* ☎ *702/730-7777. Main courses $6–$15. AE, DC, DISC, MC, V. Lunch & dinner daily. Map p 85.*

★★ kids MORE, The Buffet at Luxor SOUTH STRIP *BUFFET* In a move to de-Egypt a hotel set in a pyramid (as if!), what used to be a fun, themed buffet is now *neato* modern classy. I want my mummies back! That said, the food is the best in its price range and the offerings are satisfyingly diverse. The desserts

are notable only for the pretty large selection of diabetic-friendly options. *In Luxor, 3900 Las Vegas Blvd. S.* ☎ *702/262-4000. Breakfast $12; lunch $14; dinner $20; Sunday brunch $18. AE, DC, DISC, MC, V. Breakfast, lunch & dinner daily. Map p 85.*

★★ Olives MID-STRIP *ITALIAN/MEDITERRANEAN* Celebrity chef

Todd English's moderately priced cafe, no longer as impressive—or as economical—as it once was, is still a fine place for a light lunch. Sample one of the flatbreads, perhaps topped with fig, Gorgonzola, and prosciutto, along with a salad, or give a simple pasta a go. *In Bellagio, 3600 Las Vegas Blvd. S.* ☎ *702/693-7223. www.toddenglish.com. Reservations recommended. Main courses $20–$38, flatbreads $10–$15. AE, DC, DISC, MC, V. Lunch & dinner daily. Map p 85.*

★★★ Picasso MID-STRIP *FRENCH*

Julian Serrano is one of the few celebrity chefs in town who actually works in his own kitchen. Meals are multicourse tasting menus, which rotate regularly, but for your sake, I hope it includes the Maine lobster with corn trio, including a corn flan

Dine on excellent French cuisine while surrounded by millions of dollars worth of art at Picasso.

The Soviet theme at Red Square may cause a double take, but nobody complains about the Russian cuisine—or the world-class collection of vodkas.

that is like consuming sunshine. It's hard to compete with the many Picassos hanging on the walls, but Serrano manages it. *In Bellagio, 3600 Las Vegas Blvd. S. ☎ 877/234-6358 or 702/693-8105. Reservations recommended. Fixed-price 4-course dinner $105; 5-course degustation $115. AE, DC, DISC, MC, V. Dinner Wed–Mon. Map p 85.*

★★ **Rao's** MID-STRIP *ITALIAN*   The legendary New York eatery is notorious for the impossibility of actually eating there because of its small size. So thank Caesars for increasing the odds of getting a seat at this Vegas branch by re-creating the interior twice over, plus adding a new patio area. They've also imported the menu untouched, so you can try the famous lemon chicken, baseball-sized meatballs, or any of the other Italian home-cooked items that have made Rao's name. *In Caesars Palace, 3570 Las Vegas Blvd. S. ☎ 877/346-4642. Reservations recommended. Main courses $23–$45. AE, DC, DISC, MC, V. Lunch & dinner daily. Map p 85.*

★★ **Red 8** NORTH STRIP *ASIAN*
A pan-Asian cafe that serves credible dim sum, rice (including porridge), noodle dishes, Korean barbecue, and Mongolian beef. Avoid the "market price" specials and you should be able to get out of here with a moderately priced bill, a relief in the otherwise costly Wynn. *In Wynn Las Vegas, 3131 Las Vegas Blvd. S. ☎ 888/352-DINE or 702/248-DINE. Main courses $14–$28. AE, DISC, MC, V. Lunch & dinner daily. Map p 86.*

★★ **Red Square** SOUTH STRIP *CONTINENTAL/RUSSIAN*   When I think of this restaurant, it's usually because of the hilarity of its over-the-top interior—a post-Communist Party riot of Bolshevik and Soviet-era gewgaws. Then I think of the ice bar and the impressive vodka selection, one of the largest in the world. Then I remember that the food, especially the Roquefort-crusted filet mignon, is really quite good. And I wonder why I don't think of that first. Then I remember the headless statue of Lenin out front and get distracted all over again. *In Mandalay Bay, 3950 Las Vegas Blvd. S. ☎ 702/632-7407. Reservations recommended. Main courses $17–$36. AE, DC, MC, V. Dinner daily. Map p 85.*

★★ Rio's Carnival World Buffet

MID-STRIP *BUFFET* Locals have long voted this the best in Vegas; I say that, qualitywise, it's probably better than ever, if not the best. The cuisines offered are pretty global (Mexican, Chinese, Brazilian, Italian, and more), and there's even a diner setup for burgers, fries, and milkshakes. Best of all, the desserts (usually disappointing at Vegas buffets) are worth blowing your diet on. *In Rio All-Suite Hotel & Casino, 3700 W. Flamingo Rd. ☎ 702/252-7777. Breakfast $14; lunch $17; dinner $24; Sat–Sun champagne brunch $24. AE, DC, MC, V. Breakfast, lunch & dinner daily. Map p 85.*

★★★ Rosemary's WEST OF STRIP

NOUVELLE AMERICAN Locals long ago realized what a treasure this is, and you should follow their example

Sensi's bento box is a popular and tasty lunch option.

and take the admittedly lengthy drive from the Strip to sample chefowners Michael and Wendy Jordan's cross section of American regional specialties. One of the few places in town where I can heartily recommend trying any fish dish, especially those with a New Orleans twist. *8125 W. Sahara Ave. ☎ 702/869-2251. www.rosemarysrestaurant. com. Reservations strongly recommended. Main courses $24–$39. AE, MC, V. Lunch Mon–Fri; dinner daily. Map p 86.*

★★ Sensi MID-STRIP *ECLECTIC*

Usually a place with "a little of this, a little of that" is an example of the adage "jack of all trades and master of none." But despite featuring Italian, American, grilled, and Asian-influenced dishes, Sensi is successful across the entirety of its eclectic menu. The lunchtime bento box is a popular item. *In Bellagio, 3600 Las Vegas Blvd. S. ☎ 877/234-6358. Main courses $14–$22 lunch; $22–$44 dinner. AE, MC, V. Lunch & dinner daily. Map p 85.*

★★★ Shibuya SOUTH STRIP

ASIAN/SUSHI A must for sushi fans and sake connoisseurs alike. Rejoice over such signature dishes as *toro tartare* and wild miso salmon, or order the divine tasting menu. The sommelier will gladly pair each course with sake by the glass (the list is the largest in the U.S., and much of it is exclusive to Shibuya) to complete the experience. *In MGM Grand, 3799 Las Vegas Blvd. S. ☎ 702/891-3001. Reservations highly recommended. Average dinner $75 per person. AE, DC, DISC, MC, V. Map p 85.*

★★ Tiffany's NORTH STRIP *DINER*

This unflashy, 60-year-old coffee shop was Las Vegas's first 24-hour restaurant. Plunk down at the counter and gorge yourself on basic American comfort food; the best bet is the ⅓-pound burger and "thick, creamy shake"—both for around $6! Note, however, that the surrounding neighborhood can be rough. *1700 Las Vegas Blvd. S. (at East Oakey Blvd.).* ☎ *702/444-4459. Most items under $8. No credit cards. Daily 24 hr. Map p 86.*

★★ **Triple George Grill** DOWNTOWN *DINER* Replicating the interior of San Francisco's 150-year-old Taditch Grill is an odd homage even for a city that re-creates Venice, but because the restaurant also tries to replicate the menu, it's hard to complain. The culinary focus is a bit scattered—from blackened catfish to corned beef hash—but the "George's favorites," priced under $15, is a good budget option. *201 N. 3rd St.* ☎ *702/384-2761. www.triple georgegrill.com. Main courses $18–$35. AE, MC, V. Lunch & dinner daily. Map p 87.*

★★ **Viva Mercado's** WEST OF THE STRIP *MEXICAN* Locals justifiably claim the food at Viva Mercado's as the best Mexican cuisine in town. The restaurant's health-conscious attitude (no dish is prepared in any kind of animal fat), amazing seafood options, and friendly staff make it worth the drive from the Strip. It's also great for vegetarians. *3553 S. Rainbow Rd. (at Spring Mountain Rd.).* ☎ *702/871-8826. www.vivamercadoslv.com. Main courses $10–$20. AE, DISC, MC, V. Lunch & dinner daily. Map p 86.*

★★ **Wolfgang Puck Bar & Grill** SOUTH STRIP *CALIFORNIA* Get your Puck fix at this moderately priced establishment, where there is nothing surprising on the menu (except maybe the potato chips drizzled with truffle oil and blue cheese) and the wine list is quite solid. *In MGM Grand, 3799 Las Vegas Blvd. S.* ☎ *702/891-3019. www.wolfgangpuck.com. Reservations recommended. Main courses $28–$38. AE, DC, DISC, MC, V. Lunch & dinner daily. Map p 85.*

★★★ **Wynn Las Vegas Buffet** NORTH STRIP *BUFFET* It may be the most expensive buffet in town, but it's also the best. Hands down. After all, there is Indian food, Kansas City-style barbecue, Southern specialties, ceviche, jerk chicken, and a dessert station that for once isn't a waste of calories. *In Wynn Las Vegas, 3131 Las Vegas Blvd. S.* ☎ *702/770-3463. Breakfast $18; lunch $22; dinner $38; Sat–Sun brunch $28–$32. AE, DC, DISC, MC, V. Breakfast, lunch & dinner Mon–Fri; brunch & dinner Sat–Sun. Map p 86.* ●

Sushi fans and sake lovers are catered to at Shibuya, where the general Asian cuisine is nothing to sneeze at; see p 97.

Nightlife Best Bets

Best Cocktail Lounge
★★ Petrossian, *Bellagio, 3600 Las Vegas Blvd. S. (p 104)*

Best Retro Scene
★ Peppermill's Fireside Lounge, *2985 Las Vegas Blvd. S. (p 104)*

Best Places to Celebrity Watch
★★★ Tao, *The Venetian, 3355 Las Vegas Blvd. S. (p 108)* or ★★★ PURE, *Caesars Palace, 3570 Las Vegas Blvd. S. (p 107)*

Best Gay Bar
★★ Krave, *Planet Hollywood Hotel & Casino, 3667 Las Vegas Blvd. S. (p 109)*

Best Place to Make a Fool of Yourself
★ Coyote Ugly, *New York–New York, 3790 Las Vegas Blvd. S. (p 103)*

Best View
★★ ghostbar, *Palms Resort & Casino, 4321 W. Flamingo Rd. (p 104)*

Previous Page: Ivan Kane's Forty Deuce is home to Sin City's top burlesque show.

Best Blues
Sand Dollar Blues Lounge, *3355 Spring Mountain Rd. (p 105)*

Best Microbrews
★ Triple 7 Brew Pub, *Main Street Station, 200 N. Main St. (p 105)*

Best Burlesque
★★★ Ivan Kane's Forty Deuce, *Mandalay Bay, 2950 Las Vegas Blvd. S. (p 104)*

Friendliest Club on the Strip
★ Tabu, *MGM Grand, 3799 Las Vegas Blvd. S. (p 108)*

Friendliest Club off the Strip
★★★ Cherry, *Red Rock, 11011 W. Charleston Rd. (p 106)*

Best Piano Bar
★★ The Bar at Times Square, *New York–New York, 3790 Las Vegas Blvd. S. (p 103)*

Best Strip Club
★★★ Treasures, *2801 Westwood Dr. (p 110)*

It's a tourist trap, but Coyote Ugly is packed every night by visitors eager to see its bar-dancing waitresses.

Las Vegas Nightlife

The Bank 7
The Bar at Times Square 11
Body English 15
Caramel 14
Champagnes Café 14
Cleopatra's Barge 5
Coyote Ugly 11
Dispensary Lounge 19
Double Down Saloon 17
Eiffel Tower Bar 8
ghostbar 7
Gipsy 16
Good Times 18

Ivan Kane's Forty Deuce 13
Jet 3
Krave 9
Moon 6
Playboy Club 6
Petrossian 7
PURE 5
Pussycat Dolls Lounge 5
Rain Nightclub 6
rumjung'e 13
Seamless 12
Tabu 10
Tangerine 1
Tao Nightclub 2
Toby Keith's I Love This Bar & Grill 4
Whiskey Sky 20

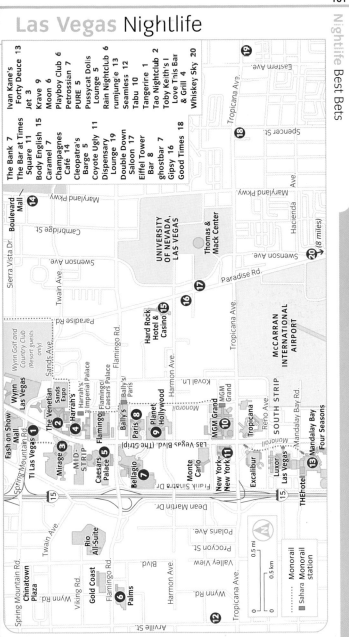

Nightlife Off the Strip

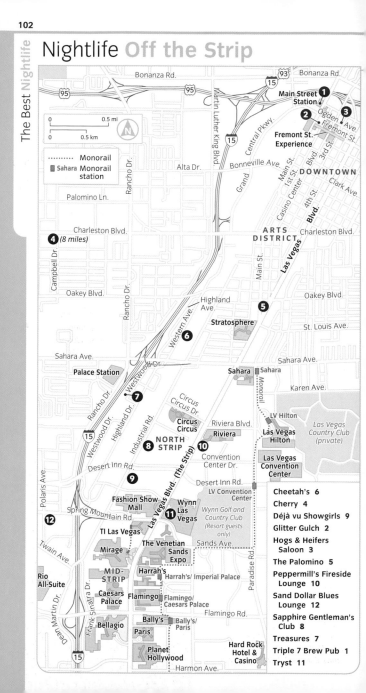

Cheetah's **6**

Cherry **4**

Déjà vu Showgirls **9**

Glitter Gulch **2**

Hogs & Heifers Saloon **3**

The Palomino **5**

Peppermill's Fireside Lounge **10**

Sand Dollar Blues Lounge **12**

Sapphire Gentleman's Club **8**

Treasures **7**

Triple 7 Brew Pub **1**

Tryst **11**

Las Vegas Nightlife A to Z

Bars

★★ The Bar at Times Square

SOUTH STRIP If one piano is good, two must be better. Dueling pianos rule this lively lounge, smack in the middle of Vegas's homage to the Big Apple. If you make requests, try to give the poor performers more to do than just play Billy Joel. *New York–New York, 3790 Las Vegas Blvd. S.* ☎ *702/740-6969. $10 cover after 8pm Fri–Sat. Map p 101.*

★★ Caramel

MID-STRIP Warm, comfortable, and classy but not stodgy, thanks to a mix of contemporary music and novelty drinks. True cocktail aficionados will sniff at any place that mixes alcohol and dessert (in the same drink!) as recklessly as they do here, but for the rest of us, it's all part of the fun. *Bellagio, 3600 Las Vegas Blvd. S.* ☎ *702/693-7111. Map p 101.*

★★ Champagnes Café

EAST OF STRIP Every time I despair the loss of old Vegas—and I mean sleazy Vegas, not finger-snapping Rat Pack Vegas—I find a little corner of it still holding on. A little dark, a little seedy, and completely ossified—except for the DJ and the karaoke night. *3557 S. Maryland Pkwy. (between Twain Ave. & Desert Inn Rd.).* ☎ *702/737-1699. Map p 101.*

★ Coyote Ugly

SOUTH STRIP Part tourist trap, part genuinely good fun (as if that combo doesn't describe the whole city). You know the gimmick: The waitresses get up on the bar and dance around. A little frat boy, or even pedestrian-guy-trying-for-naughty-thrills, sure, but no less fun for all that. *New York–New York, 3790 Las Vegas Blvd. S. (at Tropicana Ave.).*

☎ *702/740-6969. www.coyoteuglysaloon.com. Cover varies, but it's usually $10 & up on weekends. Map p 101.*

★ Dispensary Lounge

EAST OF STRIP The 1970s idea of cool, but not a retro re-creation—this is the real thing, complete with ferns and a water wheel. You just know Quentin Tarantino hangs out here when he's in town. *2451 E. Tropicana Ave. (at Eastern Ave.).* ☎ *702/458-6343. Map p 101.*

★★★ Double Down Saloon

EAST OF STRIP Local iconoclasts (from Manic Panic punks to strippers to even some famous faces) love this perfect dump, where the jukebox has selections ranging from Zappa to Rev. Horton Heat, the bartenders push something called Ass Juice, and signs remind patrons that "you puke, you pay." *4640 Paradise Rd. (at Naples Dr.).* ☎ *702/791-5775. www.doubledownsaloon.com. Map p 101.*

The Double Down Saloon is the best dive bar in Vegas.

If you're feeling daring, add your own bra to the collection that hangs above the bar at the boisterous Hogs & Heifers.

★ **Eiffel Tower Bar** SOUTH STRIP Look down on everyone (just like a real Parisian—I'm kidding . . . mostly) from this chic and elegant room on the 11th floor of the Eiffel Tower. Drop by this date-impressing bar for a sophisticated and relatively affordable drink if your attire meets the business-casual dress code. *In Paris Las Vegas, 3655 Las Vegas Blvd. S. ☎ 702/948-6937. Map p 101.*

★★ **ghostbar** WEST OF STRIP Hovering over the city, this beautifully designed space age bar boasts a stunning setting and some of the most superb views around. It's usually crammed with beautiful people paying absurd prices for drinks. If you've had one shot too many or generally suffer from vertigo, avoid the glass floor that's set over the pool area many stories below. *Palms Resort & Casino, 4321 W. Flamingo Rd. (just west of the Strip). ☎ 702/942-7778. Cover varies, usually $10 & up. Map p 101.*

★ **Hogs & Heifers Saloon** DOWNTOWN That's "hogs" as in bikes. The movie *Coyote Ugly* was actually based on the original NYC Hogs & Heifers, and for a copy, this works pretty well. The most boisterous and partying place in Downtown.

201 N. 3rd St. (between Ogden & Stewart aves.). ☎ 702/676-1457. Map p 102.

★★★ **Ivan Kane's Forty Deuce** SOUTH STRIP One of the most rip-snorting places in Vegas, thanks to the twice-nightly strip and teasing burlesque shows. The talented dancers just add to the '20s speak-easy vibe. Beautifully designed and executed, it's packed to the gills pretty much all the time. *Mandalay Bay, 2950 Las Vegas Blvd. S. ☎ 702/632-7000. www.fortydeuce.com. Cover varies. Map p 101.*

★ **Peppermill's Fireside Lounge** NORTH STRIP Hilariously wrong and wonderful, this bar is a mélange of '80s fuchsia fluorescent lights, a '70s fire pit (the star attraction), and fake bougainvillea. Cozy up in the cushy pit or get a snack at the adjoining coffee shop. The enormous-sized drinks just add to the fun. *2985 Las Vegas Blvd. S. ☎ 702/735-7635. Map p 102.*

★★ **Petrossian** MID-STRIP Located right off the Bellagio lobby, and thus taking advantage of that space's impressive beauty, Petrossian is visually one of the prettiest places to drink in the city. Its cocktails don't

Cozy up to a fire pit at Peppermill's Fireside Lounge, where the interior wows . . . as do the large drinks.

come cheap, but they come with much knowledge—bartenders are required to attend continuing education classes—and are made with the finest ingredients; and thus true cocktailians will tell you it's better to pay somewhat more for something so very right. *Bellagio, 3600 Las Vegas Blvd. S. ☎ 702/693-7111. Map p 101.*

★ **Playboy Club** WEST OF STRIP It was a sad day for an entire generation when the last Playboy Club shuttered its doors. It was a happy day for swingers, ironically retro and deadly serious alike, when a new one opened again. There's expensive gambling, there are vintage magazine covers rotating on video screens, there's not nearly the bastion of cool that it once so proudly bore, but it's still kind of swell to see the Bunnies again. Even if they do make lousy dealers. *In the Palms, 4321 W. Flamingo Rd. ☎ 702/942-7777. Cover varies & includes admission to Moon nightclub. Map p 101.*

Pussycat Dolls Lounge MID-STRIP A Los Angeles club act turned major international act, but don't expect to see the recording stars perform in this lounge just off the PURE nightclub. Still, the local gals strut their stuff (a couple of times an hour) well enough that you probably won't mind. *In Caesars Palace, 3570 Las Vegas Blvd. S. ☎ 702/731-7873. Cover varies. Map p 101.*

Sand Dollar Blues Lounge WEST OF STRIP No longer quite the shabby biker bar it has been for the last 20 years or so; a lick of paint has cleaned the place up, though the blues (and jazz) are still as down and dirty as ever. In a town full of prefab places (House of Blues, anyone?), something genuine is to be celebrated. *3355 Spring Mountain Rd. (at Polaris Ave.). ☎ 702/871-6651. www.sanddollarblues.com.*

Cover varies, but it is usually no more than a few bucks. Map p 102.

★ **Tangerine** MID-STRIP Another chance to get your go-go-girl burlesque fix (though vastly inferior to Ivan Kane's Forty Deuce, p 104). The smallish size of this citrus-shaded club—it's atmospheric when the colored lights warm up the fabric draping the walls—does make for a sexy, intimate atmosphere. *In TI at The Mirage, 3300 Las Vegas Blvd. S. ☎ 702/894-7111. Cover varies. Map p 101.*

★ **Triple 7 Brew Pub** DOWNTOWN Its first demographic appeal is to microbrew buffs, though anyone longing to drink somewhere in Downtown that isn't smoky and noisy will find this something of a haven; glass walls separate it from the casino, cutting out much of that chaos. They also serve solid bar food. *In Main Street Station, 200 N. Main St. ☎ 702/387-1896. Map p 102.*

★★ **Whiskey Sky** EAST OF STRIP A bit of a trek, but a great place to play, given all its perfect elements: Rande Gerber (Mr. Cindy Crawford, to you) interior design, check; go-go dancers, check; pounding beats,

Hit Downtown's Triple 7 Brew Pub for a microbrew and a chance to drink in relatively peaceful surroundings.

Dance the night away in memorable surroundings at Red Rock Station's Cherry.

check; sultry outdoor area complete with mattress and cabanas for lounging and canoodling, check; the Strip in the distance for an excellent view, check. *In the Green Valley Resort, 2300 Paseo Verde Pkwy., Henderson.* ☎ *702/617-7560. Cover varies, usually $10 & up. Map p 101.*

Dance Clubs

★★ **The Bank** MID-STRIP The replacement for the classy Light, because they just had to tinker with a winner to attract a "discerning audience with higher sensibilities." That translates as rich, exclusive, and uppity. You can bank on it being packed every night, but I think this trend is a bust. *In Bellagio, 3600 Las Vegas Blvd. S.* ☎ *702/693-8300. www.lightgroup.com. Cover varies, usually $25. Map p 101.*

★★ **Body English** EAST OF STRIP The brainchild of L.A. clubmeister Brent Bolthouse, this is the kind of Gothic wonder Anne Rice's Lestat would have enjoyed in his rock-star days. If you don't have *Rolling Stone* and *Spin* covers to your credit, expect to deal with some absurd velvet-rope attitude and waits. It's that kind of exclusive. *In the Hard Rock Hotel, 4455 Paradise Rd.* ☎ *702/693-5000. www.bodyenglish.com. Cover varies. Map p 101.*

★★★ **Cherry** WEST OF STRIP A fantastically designed space—thank Rande Gerber again—that echoes the red of Red Rock Canyon and the titular fruit. The enveloping tunnel entrance just starts the experience. A circular bar and raised dance floor dominate the interior, while outside the decadent action takes in the pool area, which is home to a fire pit and rotating beds. Don't miss the bathrooms—I don't want to give anything away, but there are several surprises waiting. *In Red Rock Resort, 11011 W. Charleston Rd.* ☎ *702/423-3112. Cover varies. Map p 102.*

★ **Cleopatra's Barge** MID-STRIP It was such a big deal when this bar/club opened because the boat setting—yes, it looks like an Egyptian barge and actually floats on water—was just a novelty and wonder. Oh, more innocent times indeed, but the place is still a landmark and it's still kind of a kick. *In Caesars Palace,*

The very hot Jet caters to a hip crowd with three separate dance floors and a state-of-the-art sound system.

3570 Las Vegas Blvd. S. ☎ 702/731-7110. *2-drink minimum. Map p 101.*

★★ **Jet** MID-STRIP A technical wonder of a vast nightclub, it's composed of three different rooms, each with its own distinct vibe (and usually different music). The main room features a dance floor that is usually steaming. It's much more successful than other, similar ventures in town. *In the Mirage, 3400 Las Vegas Blvd. S.* ☎ 702/632-7600. *Cover varies, usually $20 & up. Map p 101.*

★ **Moon** WEST OF STRIP Another basic trendy nightclub—dance floor, smoke machines, house music—but not nearly as inviting as Jet or Rain, its closest competitors. On the plus side, your cover will get you in here and into the Playboy Club (p 105) just above it. *In Palms Resort & Casino, 4321 W. Flamingo Rd.* ☎ 702/492-3960. *Cover varies. Map p 101.*

★★★ **PURE** MID-STRIP At this writing, the hottest club in town. It's two stories and 36,000 square feet (3,345 sq. m.) of white/ivory/silver design, intense crowding, hot sounds, and pure madness. Lines to get in are long; tales of celebrity embarrassment within are even longer. This is the place where Christina Aguilera holds her after-show parties and

If you can stomach the lines to get in, PURE is the hottest club in Vegas and a major celeb hangout.

Brittany Spears collapses on New Year's Eve. *In Caesars Palace, 3570 Las Vegas Blvd. S.* ☎ 702/731-7110. *Cover varies. Map p 101.*

★★ **Rain Nightclub** MID-STRIP Though the beat is eardrum shatteringly loud, one has to admit they sure know how to do a nightclub right. Assuming you can get inside (the lines start early and stay long), you should maneuver the multi-levels, check out all the electronic gee-whiz gizmos (a serious lighting system, for starters) that add even more to the experience, and wonder at how little body fat is inside. *In Palms Resort & Casino, 4321 W. Flamingo Rd.* ☎ 702/940-7246. *$20 cover. Map p 101.*

Getting in the Door

Club hopping in Vegas isn't a very practical affair, given the number of hours you may spend in line to get past the velvet rope guarding the entrance to the top nightspots. You're best off picking a club and then sticking around for the evening. To help increase the amount of time you spend on the dance floor, be sure to dress appropriately (see "You Are What You Wear," on p 110), be on time if you've made a reservation, and try to have at least one woman in your party (ladies rule on club lines). Ask your hotel concierge if he can get you onto the club's guest list, or call the club yourself. If all else fails, you can try a discreet tip ($20 or more) to the doorman.

Don't let the Zen decor fool you—the hip don't wait to get into Tao Nightclub for peace and quiet, but for its pounding dance music.

★ **rumjungle** SOUTH STRIP
Too many of the clubs in Vegas are interchangeable, so rumjungle's distinctive elements are refreshing. From the fire-lined wall of water to the bottles illuminated with laser beams to the largest collection of rum in Vegas to the food on skewers, it's a scene not like any other. *In Mandalay Bay, 3950 Las Vegas Blvd. S.* ☎ *702/632-7408. $10–$20 cover. Map p 101.*

★★ **Seamless** WEST OF STRIP
By day—and most of the night—this is a strip club, but around 4am the girls leave the stage, and tables and chairs are cleared for a dance floor that is the site of the most intense after-hours action in Vegas. The party goes on until everyone gives up, which can be as late as noon the next day, whereupon the girls reappear and their clothes again disappear. *4740 S. Arville St.* ☎ *702/227-5200. $20 cover. Map p 101.*

★ **Tabu** SOUTH STRIP   You'll hear the phrase "ultra lounge" a lot in Vegas. All it means is "fancier than a bar, smaller than a nightclub." This is probably the best of an admittedly choice (if often interchangeable) lot. Which might sound like I'm damning it with faint praise, but it really is smooth. *In MGM Grand, 3799 Las Vegas Blvd. S.* ☎ *702/891-7183.*

www.tabulv.com. Cover varies, but about $10 for men & free for women. Map p 101.

★★★ **Tao Nightclub** MID-STRIP
A gorgeously designed space that seems to span forever, encompassing an ultra lounge, restaurant, and nightclub—all of which covers a couple of floors. The decor is Zen-Asian, which is absurd, because thanks to the anxious crowds hoping to gain entrance, the flashing lights, and the pounding music, it's anything but peaceful. *In The Venetian, 3355 Las Vegas Blvd. S.* ☎ *702/388-8588. Cover varies. Map p 101.*

Seamless is half dance club, half strip club, and the best club for after-hours partying in Vegas.

★ Toby Keith's I Love This Bar & Grill MID-STRIP
Country, convivial, and crowded, especially when its music-star owner turns up to play a set or two. No, really, he does. Try the deep-fried Twinkies. *In Harrah's, 3475 Las Vegas Blvd. S. ☎ 702/369-5084. Map p 101.*

★★ Tryst NORTH STRIP
One of the most likely places to catch a celebrity doing something that someone will take a photo of with their cellphone and put on the Web. (This is where Brittany and Paris hung out during their brief BFF phase.) It is a pretty sexy space, notable also for the 90-foot (27m) waterfall and the patio that opens over a lagoon; it's rare to have a shot at fresh air in a Vegas club. *In Wynn Las Vegas, 3131 Las Vegas Blvd. S. ☎ 702/770-3375. Cover varies. Map p 102.*

Tryst is popular with celebs, who like to hang out beneath the sexy club's waterfall.

Gay Bars

★★ Gipsy EAST OF STRIP
A longtime staple of the local gay scene, Gipsy continues to be the most popular. The sunken dance floor, the excellent location, and costly renovations help keep it fresh. Look for gimmicks, including the occasional stripper, and a pretty young crowd. *4605 Paradise Rd. (at Naples Dr.). ☎ 702/731-1919. www.gipsylv.net. Cover varies but is usually $5 & up on weekends, less or even free on weekdays. Map p 101.*

★ Good Times EAST OF STRIP
Favored by locals, this is a good cross between neighborhood gay bar and dance club. It's laid out so that you can actually talk if you don't want to just strut your stuff on the dance floor. *In the Liberace Plaza, 1775 E. Tropicana Ave. (at Spencer St.). ☎ 702/736-9494. www.good timeslv.com. Map p 101.*

★★ Krave MID-STRIP
The first gay club on the Strip, but open enough to attract a mixed crowd—unlike most other joints, its go-go dancers come in both genders. That's probably the key; the club wants to promote itself more as "alternative" than anything sexuality specific, but the result is a fine place to party regardless of your goals. *In Planet Hollywood Hotel & Casino, 3667 Las Vegas Blvd. S. (entrance on Harmon). ☎ 702/836-0830. www.kravelas vegas.com. Cover varies. Map p 101.*

Strip Clubs

★ Cheetah's WEST OF STRIP
Here's your classic sporty frat boy strip-club vibe, small and cheesy but

Technically, Krave is the first gay club on the Strip, but it's a popular party place with people of all orientations.

You Are What You Wear

We may all be taught not to judge a book by its cover, but that's what pretty much every nightclub (and even the strip clubs) in town is going to do. Most of the clubs have precise dress codes, banning the obvious gang attire, but also, in some cases, collarless shirts, sneakers, baseball caps, shorts, jeans, sandals, and more. When in doubt, call ahead, but you might want to pack something fashionable and metrosexual just to be sure.

also friendly. Not as up-to-the-minute wow as newer places, but a lot less pressure because of it. *2121 Western Ave.* ☎ *702/384-0074. Topless. $20 cover after 8pm until early morning. Map p 102.*

★★ **Déjà vu Showgirls** NORTH STRIP   In addition to the "totally nude" draw, dancers here tend to do actual routines rather than just languidly stroll about the stage. *3247 Industrial Rd.* ☎ *702/894-4167. Unescorted women allowed. Totally nude. Cover $25. Map p 102.*

★ **Glitter Gulch** DOWNTOWN   An expensive renovation has made this dingy old-timer catch up with the new kids in town. *20 Fremont St.* ☎ *702/385-4774. Topless. 2-drink minimum (drinks $7 & up). Map p 102.*

★ **The Palomino** NORTH STRIP   Smart owners gave this aging all-nude facility a minor face-lift (farewell, red flocked wallpaper; hello, flatscreen monitors) on weekends, and then turned the upstairs over to male strippers. (Yes, they get totally naked as well.) Expect a very gender-mixed crowd with an urban vibe. *1848 Las Vegas Blvd. N.* ☎ *702/642-2984. Totally nude. $15–$30 cover. Map p 102.*

★★★ **Sapphire Gentleman's Club** NORTH STRIP   Billed as the largest strip club in the world, it's hard to see where a dance club like,

say, Rain (p 107) leaves off and the "Gentleman's Club" takes over. The girls are less clad than the Strip's ubiquitous go-go dancers, but really just by a scant degree. *3025 S. Industrial.* ☎ *702/796-0000. Unescorted women allowed. Topless. $20 cover after 6pm. Map p 102.*

★★★ **Seamless** WEST OF STRIP   Here's where the already blurred line between dance club and strip club disappears—at 4am, to be precise. Prior to that, this is a high-tech strip club, with a futuristic interior that would fit right in with some of the new nightclubs in town. When the clock strikes four, the strippers turn into regular go-go dancers (p 108). The transition is indeed "seamless," and it does make for one-stop nightlife shopping. *4740 S. Arville St.* ☎ *702/227-5200. $20 cover. Map p 101.*

★★★ **Treasures** WEST OF STRIP   A mélange of Victorian sporting house—the way a real "gentlemen's club" should look, if you ask me—and high-tech accouterments (look at the effects on the stage, including the neon stripper pole). You pay for this comfort and style, but its class also makes it a comfortable first-time strip-club experience. *2801 Westwood Dr.* ☎ *702/257-3030. No unescorted women. Topless. Cover $45 & up (includes drinks). Map p 102.* ●

8 The Best Arts, Entertainment & Weddings

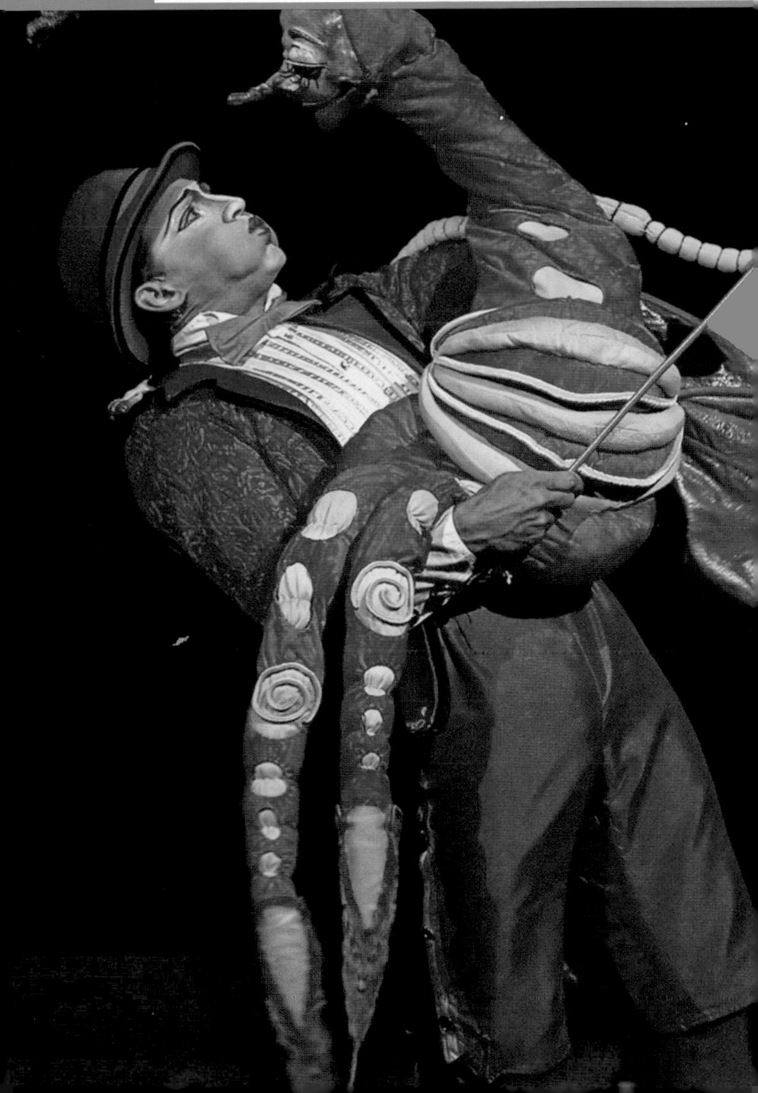

Arts, Entertainment & Weddings Best Bets

Best **Cirque Production**
★★★ *KÀ*, MGM Grand, 3799 Las Vegas Blvd. S. (p 115)

Best **Cirque Production Set on Water**
★★★ *O*, Bellagio, 3600 Las Vegas Blvd. S. (p 116)

Best **Cirque Bargain**
★★★ *Mystère*, TI Las Vegas, 3300 Las Vegas Blvd. S. (p 117)

Best **Classy Nudie Show**
★★ MGM Grand's *Crazy Horse Paris*, MGM Grand, 3799 Las Vegas Blvd. S. (p 117)

Smartest Show in Town
★★★ *Penn & Teller*, the Rio, 3700 W. Flamingo Rd. (p 118)

Best **Comedy Club**
★★★ *The Second City*, Flamingo Las Vegas, 3555 Las Vegas Blvd. S. (p 114)

Best **High-Tech Performance Art**
★★★ *Blue Man Group*, The Venetian, 3355 Las Vegas Blvd. S. (p 115)

Best **Traditional Magic**
★★★ *Lance Burton: Master Magician*, Monte Carlo Resort & Casino, 3770 Las Vegas Blvd. S. (p 117)

Best **Beefcake**
★★★ *Thunder from Down Under*, Excalibur, 3850 Las Vegas Blvd. S. (p 118)

Funniest Show
★★ *Rita Rudner*, Harrah's, 3475 Las Vegas Blvd. S. (p 118)

Best **Afternoon Show**
★★★ *Mac King*, Harrah's, 3475 Las Vegas Blvd. S. (p 117)

When you just can't wait to get down the aisle, head for the 24-hour drive-up window at the Little White Wedding Chapel.

Best **Comeback**
★★ *Barry Manilow*, Las Vegas Hilton, 3000 Paradise Rd. (p 115)

Best **Really Expensive Ticket**
★★ *Elton John*, Caesars Palace, 3570 Las Vegas Blvd. S. (p 116)

Best **Old-Fashioned Vegas Revue**
★★★ *Jubilee!*, Bally's Las Vegas, 3645 Las Vegas Blvd. S. (p 116)

Best Chapel for **Kitsch**
Little White Wedding Chapel, *1301 Las Vegas Blvd. S. (p 120)*

Best Place to **be Married by an Elvis Impersonator**
★ *Graceland Wedding Chapel*, 619 Las Vegas Blvd. S. (p 119)

Best for a **Traditional Wedding**
★ *A Special Memory Wedding Chapel*, 800 S. 4th St. (p 120)

Previous Page: Cirque du Soleil has become a Vegas entertainment juggernaut, and its very first show in town, Mystère, is still going strong.

A&E on the Strip

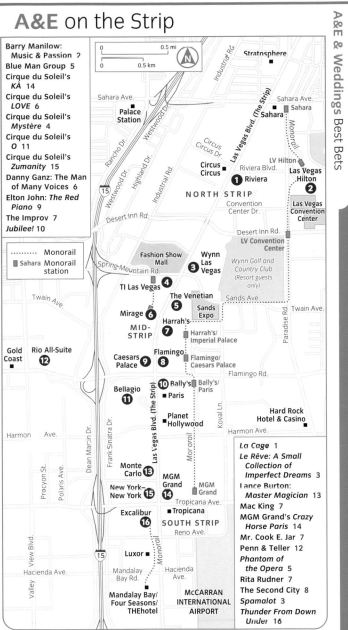

Barry Manilow: Music & Passion ?
Blue Man Group 5
Cirque du Soleil's KÀ 14
Cirque du Soleil's LOVE 6
Cirque du Soleil's Mystère 4
Cirque du Soleil's O 11
Cirque du Soleil's Zumanity 15
Danny Ganz: The Man of Many Voices 6
Elton John: The Red Piano 9
The Improv 7
Jubilee! 10

Monorail
Sahara Monorail station

La Cage 1
Le Rêve: A Small Collection of Imperfect Dreams 3
Lance Burton: Master Magician 13
Mac King 7
MGM Grand's *Crazy Horse Paris* 14
Mr. Cook E. Jar 7
Penn & Teller 12
Phantom of the Opera 5
Rita Rudner 7
The Second City 8
Spamalot 3
Thunder From Down Under 16

Las Vegas A&E A to Z

Comedy Clubs

★★ The Improv MID-STRIP
One of the many U.S. offspring of the famed NYC comic institution (which opened in 1963). The top comics on the circuit usually cycle through here. You might see the next Robin Williams or Jerry Seinfeld, who both worked their way up through the Improv. *In Harrah's Las Vegas, 3475 Las Vegas Blvd. S.* ☎ *800/392-9002 or 702/369-5111. Tickets $25. Map p 113.*

★★★ The Second City MID-STRIP   A branch of the famous-name generator in Chicago (*Saturday Night Live* would be nowhere without it as a training ground). Shows here take the form of improv work, with themes and subjects suggested by the audience. It's high-quality stuff; but any given night depends on the material the performers are given to work with, so come at your creative best. *In Flamingo Las Vegas, 3555 Las Vegas Blvd. S.* ☎ *800/221-7299 or 702/733-3333. www.secondcity.com. Tickets $40. Map p 113.*

The Blue Man Group didn't start out in Vegas, but their performance art antics have found a welcome home here.

It's not the best of the Cirque du Soleil gang, but LOVE *might tickle the fancy of Fab Four fans.*

Live Shows

★★ Barry Manilow: Music & Passion EAST OF STRIP   Mock him all you want, but the man puts on a hell of a show, new hips and all. Music, dancing, a classic all-around entertainer, timeless songs, and Fanilows. What Vegas shows used to be about. *In the Las Vegas Hilton, 3000 Paradise Rd.* ☎ *800/222-5361. www.lvhilton.com. Tickets $85–$145. Map p 113.*

★★★ kids Blue Man Group MID-STRIP   Three men coated in blue paint play with more paint, marshmallows, and musical instruments made out of PVC pipe while the audience howls. It's middlebrow performance art, and no less enjoyable for all that. *In The Venetian, 3355 Las Vegas Blvd. S.* ☎ *877/833-6423. www.venetian.com. Tickets $85–$110. Map p 113.*

★★★ kids Cirque du Soleil's KÀ SOUTH STRIP   Factor in the actual story line (separated royal siblings battle various forces in their efforts to reunite), the special effects, the incredible moving stage, and the overall artistry of Cirque, and this is probably the best show in the city. *In MGM Grand, 3799 Las Vegas Blvd. S.* ☎ *866/774-7117 or 702/531-2000. www.cirquedusoleil.com. Tickets $99–$150. Map p 113.*

★ **Cirque du Soleil's *LOVE*** MID-STRIP   Largely just a bunch of interpretive dances set to remixed Beatles tunes, with the usual Cirque arty and weird set design floating through. It's pretty, but even Beatles fans might be disappointed at the lack of substance. *In The Mirage, 3400 Las Vegas Blvd. S.* ☎ *800/963-9637 or 702/792-7777. www.beatles.com. Tickets $69–$150. Map p 113.*

★★★ **kids** **Cirque du Soleil's *Mystère*** MID-STRIP   The first big Cirque production in Vegas and still one of the best. Don't come looking for a story line; just settle back and let the imagery and acrobatics wash over you. *In TI Las Vegas, 3300 Las Vegas Blvd. S.* ☎ *800/963-9634 or 702/796-9999. www.cirquedusoleil. com. Tickets $60–$95 (plus tax). Map p 113.*

★★★ **Cirque du Soleil's *O*** MID-STRIP   The action in this dreamy and moving piece takes place in, around, and above a 1.5-million-gallon pool. It's as if Dali and Magritte collaborated on an Esther Williams show. So beautiful, it might make you cry. *In Bellagio, 3600 Las Vegas Blvd. S.* ☎ *888/488-7111 or 702/693-7722. www.cirquedusoleil.com. Tickets $99–$150. Map p 113.*

Cirque du Soleil's *Zumanity* SOUTH STRIP   This ode to sexuality is a rare near-total miss by the otherwise reliable Cirque brand. Not so much erotic as it is trying too hard. *In New York–New York, 3790 Las Vegas Blvd. S.* ☎ *866/606-7111 or 702/740-6815. www.zumanity.com.*

These rubber-jointed contortionists are only one of the many delights found in Cirque du Soleil's sublime O.

Age 18 & over only. Tickets $125 (sofas), $85–$99 (theater seats), $69 (cabaret stools, partial views), $129 per person (duo sofas, sold in pairs). Map p 113.

★★ **Danny Ganz: The Man of Many Voices** MID-STRIP   Ganz's talent is an old-fashioned one, and his vocal flexibility is somewhat uneven; some of his impersonations are eerily accurate, while others are just barely in the ballpark. The show changes nightly depending on his mood and whim, but I sure hope you get the George Burns doing MC Hammer bit. *In The Mirage, 3400 Las Vegas Blvd. S.* ☎ *800/963-9634 or 702/792-7777. www.mirage.com. Tickets $100. Map p 113.*

★★ **Elton John: *The Red Piano*** MID-STRIP   A terrifically realized theatrical showcase for an enduring artist. Expect all the hits, plus set pieces that continue John's long tradition of wacky spectacle. A video featuring Justin Timberlake as young Elton is a particular highlight. Too bad Sir Elton performs only about 75 nights a year. *In Caesars Palace, 3570*

Legendary performer Elton John has found a fabulous showcase for his skills in The Red Piano *at Caesars Palace.*

Las Vegas Blvd. S. ☎ *888/4ELTONJ (435-8665). www.ticketmaster.com. Tickets $110–$275. Map p 113.*

★★★ *Jubilee!* MID-STRIP   The best of a sadly dying breed, the Vegas topless revue. Thanks to terrific production values, which include the story of Samson and Delilah and the sinking of the *Titanic* (no, I'm not making this up, and yes, the topless parts don't make sense—as if you really care), not to mention enormous Bob Mackie wigs, this is camp perfection. *In Bally's Las Vegas, 3645 Las Vegas Blvd. S.* ☎ *800/237-7469 or 702/739-4567. www.ballys.com. Tickets $65–$82. Map p 113.*

La Cage NORTH STRIP   This long-running female impersonator show is both completely stupid and oddly appealing. Men dressed as various famous women lip-sync to said women's hits. It works intermittently and is right on the edge of being quite good. *In the Riviera Hotel & Casino, 2901 Las Vegas Blvd. S.* ☎ *877/892-7469 or 702/794-9433. www.rivierahotel.com. 18 & over only. Tickets $55. Map p 113.*

★★★ kids **Lance Burton:** *Master Magician* SOUTH STRIP   Burton's folksy demeanor and sardonic wit are fine accompaniments to his genuine magic skills. Forget the big splashy sequences and focus on the close-up magic that is Burton's specialty. His comedy juggler, Michael Goudeau, is the town's most valuable supporting player. *In the Monte Carlo Resort & Casino.* ☎ *877/386-8224 or 702/730-7160, 3770 Las Vegas Blvd. S. www.montecarlo.com. Tickets $60–$73. Map p 113.*

★ *Le Rêve: A Small Collection of Imperfect Dreams* NORTH STRIP   Basically a Cirque rip-off, including utilizing a tank of water for a set. By the time you read this, a redo by choreographer Moses Pendleton should have helped provide its own identity. *In Wynn Las Vegas, 3131 Las Vegas Blvd. S.* ☎ *888/320-110. www.wynnlasvegas.com. Ages 13 & older. Tickets $100–$121 (online discounts available). Map p 113.*

★★★ kids **Mac King** MID-STRIP   Given Vegas's sky-high ticket prices, this is possibly the best value in town. The affable King adroitly mixes comedy and magic (of the mind-blowing, close-up variety), and is a good choice for an afternoon break. *In Harrah's, 3475 Las Vegas Blvd. S.*

The topless Vegas revue may be dying, but Jubliee!, *with its signature showgirls, lives on.*

The performers in MGM Grand's Crazy Horse Paris *tease as they artfully take it all off.*

☎ 800/427-7247. www.harrahs.com. Tickets $20. Discount coupons are almost always available in local magazines & handouts. Map p 113.

★★★ MGM Grand's *Crazy Horse Paris* SOUTH STRIP

Inspired by the Parisian institution, this erotic burlesque nudie show is artfully done, as beautifully proportioned performers gracefully doff their clothes in clever ways. It's what "adult entertainment" ought to be, and puts *Zumanity* to shame. *In MGM Grand, 3799 Las Vegas Blvd. S.* ☎ 877/880-0880. www.mgmgrand.com. 18 & over only. Business casual attire required. Tickets $59 (plus tax). Map p 113.

Mr. Cook E. Jar MID-STRIP

Lounge singers are a dying breed, but Cook isn't going down without a fight. He's so terrible, he's good; he's actually pretty good, with a startlingly flexible voice to go along with his stage posturing. A must-do Vegas experience. *In Harrah's Carnaval Court Lounge, 3475 Las Vegas Blvd. S.* ☎ 702/369-5222. www.harrahs.com. Free admission. Map p 113.

★★★ **Penn & Teller** MID-STRIP

The smartest show in town, as the famous duo gleefully skewer the very magician tradition they happen to excel at. *In the Rio Hotel, 3700 W. Flamingo Rd.* ☎ 888/746-7784. www.playrio.com. Ages 5 & over only. Tickets $60–$75. Map p 113.

★ *Phantom of the Opera*

MID-STRIP An abridged version (90 min., no intermission) of the famous Andrew Lloyd Webber musical, with even more special effects. *In The Venetian, 3355 Las Vegas Blvd. S.* ☎ 866/641-7469 or 702/414-7469. www.venetian.com. Tickets $82–$157. Map p 113.

★★ **Rita Rudner** MID-STRIP The

stand-up comedienne comes off as Every Woman, not to mention the audience's Best Friend Forever, as she wryly and dryly tosses out one-liners that cut to the heart of gender relations. And she's funny as heck doing it. *In Harrah's, 3475 Las Vegas Blvd. S.* ☎ 702/369-5222. www.harrahs.com. Tickets $54–$105. Map p 113.

★★ *Spamalot* NORTH STRIP Eric

Idle's Tony-award-winning musical adaptation of *Monty Python and the Holy Grail*, this is clearly a can't-miss

The famous magical duo of Penn & Teller show off their skills and sense of humor at the Rio.

for fans, but even the uninitiated will find its goofiness a delight. *In Wynn Las Vegas, 3131 Las Vegas Blvd. S. ☎ 888/320-9966. www.wynnlasvegas. com. Tickets $49–$99. Map p 113.*

★★★ Thunder from Down Under

SOUTH STRIP Something for the women (and the gay men), as hunky Aussies of great charm and taut pecs pose, preen, and parade. Yes, they take it off. But not all off. *In Excalibur, 3850 Las Vegas Blvd. S. ☎ 702/597-7600. www.thunder fromdownunder.com. Ages 18 & older; guests 18–20 must be accompanied by adult. Gentlemen welcome. Tickets $40–$50. Map p 113.*

Making it Legal

Going to the chapel in Vegas isn't hard, but even spur-of-the-moment nuptials require Uncle Sam's approval. For details on getting a marriage license in Vegas, see p 28, bullet **6**.

Enjoy Phantom of the Opera *in a custom-built theater at The Venetian.*

Getting Discount Tickets

Las Vegas ticket prices keep on climbing every year. The good news is that Vegas has two discounters to shop from (though you must purchase tickets in person).

Tickets2Nite (☎ 888/TIX2NITE; www.tickets2nite.com) puts any unsold seats for that evening on sale. It's located in the Showplace Mall right next to the MGM Grand, and is open from noon to 9pm. Its rival, **Tix 4 Tonight** (☎ 877/849-4868; www.tix4tonight.com), also offers day-of-show discounts from 11am to 8pm. It has four locations scattered throughout the city, the most convenient being the Downtown branch in the Four Queens Hotel, and the Strip location in front of the Fashion Show Mall. It also will sometimes offer a sneak peek of tickets available on its website.

Discounts from both services can range from 10% to as high as 50% on between 35 and 50 performances daily (shows that I've seen sold include *Phantom of the Opera, Blue Man Group,* and *Zumanity.* Note that tickets are released for sale throughout the day, so getting there early won't necessarily net you a better selection.

119

Wedding Chapels A to Z

Best Wedding Chapels

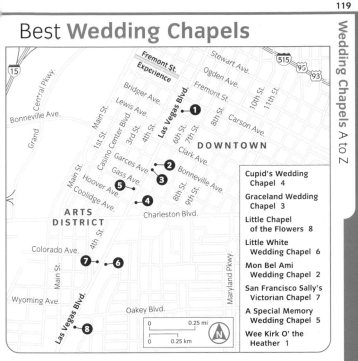

Cupid's Wedding Chapel 4

Graceland Wedding Chapel 3

Little Chapel of the Flowers 8

Little White Wedding Chapel 6

Mon Bel Ami Wedding Chapel 2

San Francisco Sally's Victorian Chapel 7

A Special Memory Wedding Chapel 5

Wee Kirk O' the Heather 1

Wedding Chapels A to Z

★ kids **Cupid's Wedding Chapel**
The self-described "little chapel with the big heart" lives up to its rep, and not only because it doesn't churn out ceremonies quite as fast as the other places in town (weddings are by appointment only). It also rolls out the red carpet to couples blending preexisting families, making it a great option for those with kids. *827 Las Vegas Blvd. S. (between Gass & Hoover aves.).* ☎ *800/543-2933 or 702/598-4444. www.cupidswedding. com. Map p 119.*

★ **Graceland Wedding Chapel**
Elvis never slept here and he didn't get married here, but this mom-and-pop joint has catered to a number of rock stars over the years (and you can get an Elvis impersonator if you want

the King to officiate). It's not the nicest in town, but the tiny chapel (only 33 seats) is a pretty friendly place to get hitched. *619 Las Vegas Blvd. S. (at E. Bonneville Ave.).* ☎ *800/ 824-5732 or 702/382-0091. www. gracelandchapel.com. Map p 119.*

Cupid's Wedding Chapel is a great option for those blending families.

Many a path to wedded bliss has crossed the Little Chapel of the Flowers.

★ Little Chapel of the Flowers

This slick 24-hour operation is a good bet for a traditional wedding (though no rice or confetti throwing—bummer!). Choose among the friendly complex's five chapels (I like the Victorian best), use the drivethrough, or opt for an outdoor ceremony. *1717 Las Vegas Blvd. S. (at E. Oakey Blvd.).* ☎ *800/843-2410 or 702/735-4331. www.littlechapel.com. Map p 119.*

Little White Wedding Chapel

Are there better and friendlier places in town to tie the knot? Yes. But for pure Vegas kitsch, you can't beat this 24-hour wedding factory, which is little, is white, and has a really famous drive-through window, where many a celeb has embarked on a path to 48 hours of wedded bliss. Just avoid the noisy gazebo. *1301 Las Vegas Blvd. S. (between E. Oakey & Charleston blvds.).* ☎ *800/545-8111 or 702/382-5943. www.alittlewhitechapel.com. Map p 119.*

★ Mon Bel Ami Wedding Chapel

This pretty church-style building does frilly and fancy ceremonies (though you can still get Elvis if you want him). Weddings aren't of the rushed variety, making it less popular with the walk-in set and better for those who like to plan ahead. *607 Las Vegas Blvd. S. (at E. Bonneville Ave.).* ☎ *866/503-4400 or 702/388-4445. www.monbelami.com. Map p 119.*

★ San Francisco Sally's Victorian Chapel

Forget a large wedding at this tiny Victorian chapel (six people is pushing it), but if you want a little fantasy in your nuptials (of the dress-up variety—think Scarlett O'Hara or some other period get-up), then this is the place. The motherly attention from the staff makes it that much better. *1304 Las Vegas Blvd. S. (between E. Oakey & Charleston blvds.).* ☎ *800/658-8677 or 702/385-7777. Map p 119.*

★ A Special Memory Wedding Chapel

Want a traditional, nontacky, big-production wedding? Here's the place. The pretty interior of the main New England–style chapel actually looks like a church, it seats 110, and there's even a cool staircase from which a bride can make a grand entrance. Of course, if you want that drive-through option, it's still there (this is Vegas). *800 S. 4th St. (at Gass Ave.).* ☎ *800/962-7798 or 702/384-2211. www.aspecialmemory.com. Map p 119.*

★ Wee Kirk O' the Heather

Though it's the oldest wedding chapel in Vegas (opened in 1940), the decor at this veteran is fresh, the service is warm, and the whole package strikes just the right balance between kitsch and classic. *231 Las Vegas Blvd. S. (between Bridger & Carson aves.).* ☎ *800/843-2566 or 702/382-9830. www.weekirk.com. Map p 119.* ●

Hotel Best Bets

Most **Luxurious**
★★★ Four Seasons $$$$ 3960
Las Vegas Blvd. S. (p 128)

Best **Business Hotel**
★★ Las Vegas Hilton $$ 3000
Paradise Rd. (p 129)

Best **Views**
★★ Palms Casino Resort $$$
4321 W. Flamingo Rd. (p 131)

Best **Room on the Strip**
★★★ THEhotel at Mandalay Bay
$$$ 3950 Las Vegas Blvd. S. (p 134)

Best **Classic Vegas Hotel**
★★ Caesars Palace $$$ 3570
Las Vegas Blvd. S. (p 126)

Best **Use of Wacky Theme**
★★ New York–New York Hotel &
Casino $$ 3790 Las Vegas Blvd. S.
(p 131)

Best **Moderately Priced Strip Rooms**
★★ Luxor Las Vegas $$ 3900
Las Vegas Blvd. S. (p 129)

Most **Improved Rooms**
★ The Flamingo Las Vegas $$
3555 Las Vegas Blvd. S. (p 127)

Best **for Families**
★ Circus Circus $ 2880 Las Vegas
Blvd. S. (p 126)

Best **Bathrooms**
★★ The Venetian $$$ 3355 Las
Vegas Blvd. S. (p 135)

Best **Downtown Bargain**
★★ Main Street Station $ 200 N.
Main St. (p 130)

Best **Gym**
★★ The Venetian $$$ 3355 Las
Vegas Blvd. S. (p 135)

Best **Swimming Pool**
★★ The Mirage $$ 3400 Las Vegas
Blvd. S. (p 130)

Previous Page: The lobby of the Red Rock
Resort.

Best **Resort**
★★★ Red Rock Resort $$$ 10973
W. Charleston Rd., Summerlin (p 132)

Best **Getaway**
★★★ Ritz-Carlton, Lake Las Vegas
$$$ 1610 Lake Las Vegas Pkwy.,
Henderson (p 133)

Best **Lobby**
★★ New York–New York $$ 3790
Las Vegas Blvd. S. (p 131)

Best **Beds**
★★★ Red Rock Resort $$$ 10973
W. Charleston Rd., Summerlin (p 132)

Best **Rock 'N' Roll Hotel**
★★ Hard Rock Hotel & Casino $$$
4455 Paradise Rd. (p 128)

Best **Strip Bargain**
★ Stratosphere Las Vegas Hotel &
Casino $ 2000 Las Vegas Blvd. S.
(p 134)

Best **Non-Casino Hotel**
★★★ Ritz-Carlton $$$$ 1610 Lake
Las Vegas Pkwy., Henderson (p 133)

Best **"Locals" Hotel**
★★ South Point $$ 9777 Las Vegas
Blvd. S. (p 134)

The Venetian has the best bathrooms
in Vegas.

South Strip Hotels

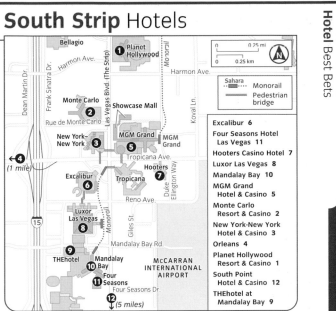

Excalibur 6

Four Seasons Hotel Las Vegas 11

Hooters Casino Hotel 7

Luxor Las Vegas 8

Mandalay Bay 10

MGM Grand Hotel & Casino 5

Monte Carlo Resort & Casino 2

New York-New York Hotel & Casino 3

Orleans 4

Planet Hollywood Resort & Casino 1

South Point Hotel & Casino 12

THEhotel at Mandalay Bay 9

Mid-Strip Hotels

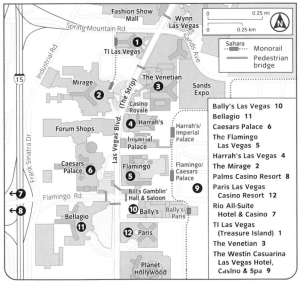

Bally's Las Vegas 10

Bellagio 11

Caesars Palace 6

The Flamingo Las Vegas 5

Harrah's Las Vegas 4

The Mirage 2

Palms Casino Resort 8

Paris Las Vegas Casino Resort 12

Rio All-Suite Hotel & Casino 7

TI Las Vegas (Treasure Island) 1

The Venetian 3

The Westin Casuarina Las Vegas Hotel, Casino & Spa 9

Las Vegas Hotels

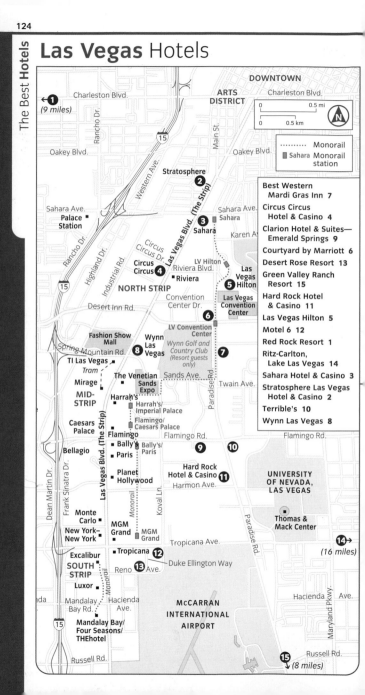

Downtown Hotels

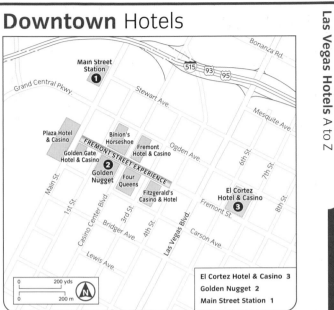

El Cortez Hotel & Casino 3
Golden Nugget 2
Main Street Station 1

Las Vegas Hotels A to Z

★ **Bally's Las Vegas** MID-STRIP Bally's has one of the best locations on the Strip (dead center, and on the monorail line), but not much of a wow factor in a city where that means a lot. Still, you can get a large, very comfy, and modern room for a ridiculously low rate. It's a very pleasant place to stay for value seekers. *3645 Las Vegas Blvd. S. (at Flamingo Rd.).* ☎ *800/634-3434 or 702/739-4111. www.ballyslv.com. 2,814 units. Doubles $99 & up. AE, DC, MC, V. Map p 123.*

★★ **Bellagio** MID-STRIP The first of the "luxury resort"–style Vegas casino hotels, which in this case means posher versions of the rooms one will find at the Mirage, a classy Euro-style pool area, and access to some of the best restaurants in town. Accommodations feel a little small compared to some of the even newer resorts, but they are still handsome. Though the size can be daunting—guests will be comfortable anywhere, but those in the new tower have a very long trek to the spa and pool—the grown-up atmosphere makes up for it. *3600 Las Vegas Blvd. S. (at the*

One of Bellagio's posh guest rooms; some rooms overlook the hotel's famous fountains.

corner of Flamingo Rd.). ☎ 888/987-6667 or 702/693-7111. www.bellagio.com. 3,933 units. Doubles $149 & up. AE, DC, DISC, MC, V. Map p 123.

Best Western Mardi Gras Inn EAST OF STRIP This well-run little casino hotel is popular with budget-minded Europeans, is only a block from the Convention Center, and has well-landscaped grounds. The spacious minisuites are of the midlevel motel variety—well tended, if not luxurious—but all have minikitchens. 3500 Paradise Rd. (between Sands Ave. & Desert Inn Rd.). ☎ 800/634-6501 or 702/731-2020. www.mardigrasinn.com. 314 units. Doubles $59 & up. AE, DC, DISC, MC, V. Map p 124.

★★ Caesars Palace MID-STRIP Though they've toned down the cheese factor, and upped this veteran to a ridiculous and often impossible-to-navigate size, there is still something particularly Vegas about Caesars. Rooms vary from tower to tower in terms of size, and no longer have that goofy romance that once characterized the place, but all are generically handsome and comfortable. The new spa, Qua, is a sybaritic stunner. Thanks to the Forum Shops, its hot club PURE, and a variety of

A petite suite in the Augustus Tower at Caesars Palace.

The rooms at Circus Circus may not be much to write home about, but the resort is still a great place to stay if you're traveling with kids.

bars and excellent restaurants, leaving here isn't necessary—which is good, because it's so hard to find the door. 3570 Las Vegas Blvd. S. (just north of Flamingo Rd.). ☎ 877/427-7243 or 702/731-7110. www.caesars.com. 3,348 units. Doubles $129 & up; suites $549 & up. AE, DC, DISC, MC, V. Map p 123.

★ kids Circus Circus Hotel & Casino NORTH STRIP The circus acts still fly above the casino action and families still stay here, but its days as an attraction hotel are long gone. Now it's the place to come for cheap rooms, though note that those Manor rooms are a bargain (or should be) for a reason. A dump-your-bags-and-head-to-more-interesting-climes location. 2880 Las Vegas Blvd. S. (between Circus Circus & Convention Center drives). ☎ 877/434-9175 or 702/734-0410. www.circuscircus.com. 3,774 units. Doubles $59 & up. AE, DC, DISC, MC, V. Map p 124.

★ kids Clarion Hotel & Suites—Emerald Springs EAST OF STRIP Housed in three peach-stucco buildings, the Emerald Springs offers a friendly, low-key alternative to the usual glitz and glitter of Vegas accommodations, though it's only 3 blocks from the Strip. Public areas and rooms here are notably clean and spiffy, and even the smallest accommodations (studios) offer small sofas, desks, and armchairs with hassocks. *325 E. Flamingo Rd. (between Koval Lane & Paradise Rd.).* ☎ *800/732-7889 or 702/732-9100. www.clarionlasvegas. com. 150 units. Suites $99 & up. AE, DC, DISC, MC, V. Map p 124.*

★ Courtyard by Marriott

EAST OF STRIP   A good-looking hotel (in a chain-establishment kind of way), this complex of three-story buildings in an attractively landscaped setting has pleasant-looking rooms (all with balconies or patios) and a location right across the street from a monorail station. *3275 Paradise Rd. (between Convention Center Dr. & Desert Inn Rd.).* ☎ *800/321-2211 or 702/791-3600. www.courtyard.com. 149 units. Rooms $109 & up (for up to 4 people). AE, DC, DISC, MC, V. Map p 124.*

★★ kids Desert Rose Resort

EAST OF STRIP   The suites here are bland, but they come with full kitchens and balconies (a rarity in Vegas, where windows rarely open). It's really a lifesaver for families looking for a comfortable place that is not too far off the beaten path (it's a block from the Strip) and won't break the bank. *5051 Duke Ellington Way.* ☎ *800/811-2450 or 702/739-7000. www.desertroseresort.com. 278 units. Suites $99 & up, including breakfast. AE, DC, DISC, MC, V. Map p 124.*

★★ El Cortez Hotel & Casino

DOWNTOWN   This Downtown veteran has been renovated into a cool old Vegas hotel of the variety that doesn't exist anymore. And it's ultra-affordable, too. The public areas are designed in a contemporary fashion you don't see that often in Downtown, and the traditionally furnished rooms (some quite large) have some useful modern features (minifridges, flat-panel TVs, and so on). *600 Fremont St. (between 6th & 7th sts.).* ☎ *800/634-6703 or 702/ 385-5200. www.elcortezhotelcasino. com. 428 units. Doubles $35 & up. AE, DISC, MC, V. Map p 125.*

★ kids Excalibur SOUTH STRIP

No longer the sword-and-sorcery fantasy escape hotel it once promised to be, this is the place to go either if you simply must stay in an oversized cartoonish castle and/or if you must stay on the Strip and need a bargain room. Said room will be anonymous and dull, but the upgraded pool area might help make the stay feel a little more special. *3850 Las Vegas Blvd. S. (at Tropicana Ave.).* ☎ *800/937-7777 or 702/597-7700. www.excalibur.com. 4,008 units. Doubles $49 & up. AE, DC, DISC, MC, V. Map p 123.*

★ kids The Flamingo Las Vegas MID-STRIP   Gradually

undergoing yet another redo, this Strip veteran is turning what were rather forgettable rooms into snazzy, kinda-now, kinda-wow eye-poppers. Thanks to hot pink walls

A suite at the Flamingo Las Vegas, whose pool is still one of the best in the city.

and accents, black-and-white photos of its heyday as Bugsy Siegel's hangout, and TVs embedded in the bathroom mirrors, you clearly want to stay in the new rooms. The rest of the hotel is a bit dated, though the pool area, complete with live birds, is one of the city's best. Good for families who cover an age range. *3555 Las Vegas Blvd. S. (between Sands Ave. & Flamingo Rd.).* ☎ *800/732-2111 or 702/733-3111. www.harrahs.com. 3,999 units. Doubles $79 & up. AE, DC, DISC, MC, V. Map p 123.*

★★★ **kids** **Four Seasons Hotel Las Vegas** SOUTH STRIP Situated at the top of Mandalay Bay, and accessed through its own entrance, this is your home away from Vegas (though the Strip action is right at your door if you need a fix). This grown-up oasis (though kids are warmly welcomed) has posh yet quietly tasteful accommodations, plus the service the Four Seasons is renowned for. And unlike at most of the other big-name hotels, there are no extra charges for such amenities as gym use. *3960 Las Vegas Blvd. S.* ☎ *877/632-5000 or 702/632-5000. www.fourseasons.com. 424 units.*

The first-rate pool area at the plush Green Valley Resort is great for lounging.

Doubles $200 & up. AE, DC, DISC, MC, V. Map p 123.

★★ **Golden Nugget** DOWNTOWN The finest hotel in Downtown, though one that has seen some ups and downs in the days since Steve Wynn ran it so well. It's currently on an upswing, with public areas sporting a fresh, fancy look. Rooms are consistent in size and decor with those at The Mirage, which is why they are by far the best in this area. Still, nothing down here can compete with the Strip, so just think of it as a bargain for the price, which by comparison it is. *129 E. Fremont St. (at Casino Center Blvd.).* ☎ *800/846-5336 or 702/385-7111. www.golden nugget.com. 1,907 units. Doubles $59 & up. AE, DC, DISC, MC, V. Map p 125.*

★★ **Green Valley Ranch Resort** HENDERSON Mash the Ritz-Carlton and W styles together and you have this greatly appealing resort. Its spacious rooms have supremely plush beds. The modern pool area, complete with sandy "beach" and mattresses for serious lounging, plus a boccie ball court, is terrific. The casino is small and a bit of a walk from the main hotel action, but the trendy Whiskey Beach bar is a nighttime draw. The long drive from the Strip and the none-too-low prices are the only detriments. *2300 Paseo Verde Pkwy. (at I-215).* ☎ *866/782-9487 or 702/617-7777. www.greenvalleyranchresort.com. 200 units. Doubles $129 & up. AE, DC, DISC, MC, V. Map p 124.*

★★ **Hard Rock Hotel & Casino** EAST OF STRIP Still the place to stay if you sport tattoos or Pamela Anderson on your arm, but its hipster cred has been somewhat eclipsed by newer kids in town. The beach-party pool area remains a happening hangout, but the rooms

The pool at the Hard Rock Hotel is one of the city's biggest hangouts.

try so hard for style that they sometimes forget comfort. Expanding and transitioning may help the latter, and rock 'n' roll is always here to stay—but you shouldn't stay here if you need to ask, "Who was Kurt Cobain and why is there a glass case of his stuff over there?" *4455 Paradise Rd. (at Harmon Ave.).* ☎ *800/HRD-ROCK (473-7625) or 702/ 693-5544. www.hardrockhotel.com. 657 units. Doubles $119 & up. AE, DC, MC, V. Map p 124.*

★ **Harrah's Las Vegas** MID-STRIP A dated, but adequate facility, best occupied if you can get a good rate, and ultimately acceptable because of its superconvenient mid-Strip location. Upgrades are improving the pedestrian rooms with better-quality beds and the like. *3475 Las Vegas Blvd. S. (between Flamingo & Spring Mountain roads).* ☎ *800/HARRAHS (427-7247) or 702/369-5000. www. harrahs.com. 2,579 units. Doubles $99 & up. AE, DC, DISC, MC, V. Map p 123.*

★ **Hooters Casino Hotel** SOUTH STRIP A South Florida theme and "party all the time" atmosphere pervades the famous (or is that infamous?) restaurant chain's

first-ever hotel, housed in the old San Remo building. The public areas are crammed with things to see (yes, there are Hooter Girls) and do, but are somewhat claustrophobia inducing. The rooms, though smaller and less luxurious than the modern Vegas norm, are still fun and comfortable. *115 E. Tropicana Ave.* ☎ *866/584-6687 or 702/739-9000. www.hooterscasinohotel.com. 696 units. Doubles $99 & up. AE, DC, DISC, MC, V. Map p 123.*

★★ **Las Vegas Hilton** EAST OF STRIP Still the first choice for the businessperson, because, unlike most other hotels in town, this one is more about business than pleasure. Rooms are somewhat more geared to working customers than playing customers, though the smallish casino is a good retreat, to say nothing of the Star Trek attraction (p 36)! There is plenty of on-site recreation, but the hotel's main draw is its proximity to the Convention Center. It's also a good fallback during nonconvention times, when prices can be pretty low. *3000 Paradise Rd. (at Riviera Blvd.).* ☎ *888/ 732-7117 or 702/732-5111. www.lv hilton.com. 3,174 units. Doubles $49 & up. AE, DC, DISC, MC, V. Map p 124.*

★★ **kids** **Luxor Las Vegas** SOUTH STRIP Deliciously goofy, thanks to its Egyptian homage. Rooms inside the pyramid are small and shower-only, but the slanted glass walls and the thrill of riding the "inclinator" (elevators on a slant) up there can make it worthwhile. Best of all are the corner rooms, where they plant a Jacuzzi tub right where those slanted windows meet. Tower rooms have more Egyptian and Art Deco style (and better bathrooms), but some rooms on the lower floors might be darkly claustrophobic. *3900 Las Vegas Blvd. S. (between*

Reno & Hacienda aves.). ☎ 888/777-0188 or 702/262-4444. www.luxor.com. 4,400 units. Doubles $59 & up. AE, DC, DISC, MC, V. Map p 123.

★★ **Main Street Station** DOWNTOWN One of the best deals in town, this hotel is clean, comfortable, and even kind of sweet, with a late-Victorian San Francisco style. Superior air circulation makes the public areas much less smoky than those at its counterparts. Rooms are unexpectedly stylish and cozy, though the location next to the freeway means that noise can be an issue for some. It's only a couple of blocks from the action on Fremont Street. *200 N. Main St. (between Fremont St. & I-95).* ☎ 800/465-0711 or 702/387-1896. www.mainstreetcasino.com. 406 units. Doubles $59 & up. AE, DC, DISC, MC, V. Map p 125.

★★ **kids Mandalay Bay** SOUTH STRIP It doesn't really live up to its South Asian theme, but this beauty is oddly kid-friendly, thanks to the big rooms and bathrooms (dig those marble bathtubs), the famously

One of the handsome guest rooms inside the huge MGM Grand, one of the largest hotels in the world.

well-equipped pool area (including beach, wave pool, and lazy river), and the ability to access your room without traversing the casino. An excellent and playful restaurant row, and a good shopping mall, plus various clubs and bars please the adults, thus rounding out the demographic appeal. *3950 Las Vegas Blvd. S. (at hacienda Ave.).* ☎ 877/632-7800 or 702/632-7777. www.mandalaybay.com. 3,309 units. Doubles $99 & up. AE, DC, DISC, MC, V. Map p 123.

★★ **kids MGM Grand Hotel & Casino** SOUTH STRIP Dauntingly big (it's the largest hotel in the U.S.), but with handsome rooms (complete with black-and-white photos of old movie stars) that escape the increasingly generic feel of others on the Strip. MGM also has a variety of restaurant options and the largest pool area apart from Mandalay Bay, complete with a lazy river. The West Wing rooms are smaller but have a hip flair and comfort that give them their own significant style, though ground-floor ones can be a bit dark. *3799 Las Vegas Blvd. S. (at Tropicana Ave.).* ☎ 800/880-0880 or 702/891-7777. www.mgmgrand.com. 5,034 units. Doubles $99 & up. AE, DC, DISC, MC, V. Map p 123.

★★ **The Mirage** MID-STRIP While its pretty but ordinary rooms are running a bit behind similar-sized ones on the Strip (the beds are stiff, and the bathrooms small), the rest of the hotel has been renovated from tropical tired to chic and sleek. The rainforest entrance is still one of the most impressive hotel welcomes in town, and the pool area is a tropical marvel complete with water slide. Good restaurants, terrific bars, and hot clubs complete the mix. *3400 Las Vegas Blvd. S. (between Flamingo Rd. & Spring Mountain Rd.).* ☎ 800/374-9000 or 702/791-7111.

The pretty rooms inside The Mirage are small, but the hotel itself impresses thanks to a vast array of amenities.

www.mirage.com. 3,044 units. Doubles $119 & up. AE, DC, DISC, MC, V. Map p 123.

★ Monte Carlo Resort & Casino SOUTH STRIP
Though its name evokes classic and classy, beyond the crystal chandelier–filled lobby this is a fairly generic hotel, much in need of a stylistic shake-up. Rooms are merely average, with small bathrooms, though the pool area has gotten fresh landscaping to make it more frolicsome fun. Affordable rates and a great location may make the lack of sparkle unimportant. *3770 Las Vegas Blvd. S. (between Flamingo Rd. & Tropicana Ave.).* ☎ 800/529-4828 or 702/730-7777. www.montecarlo.com. 3,002 units. Doubles $99 & up. AE, DC, DISC, MC, V. Map p 123.

Motel 6 EAST OF STRIP
The biggest Motel 6 in the country is a great budget choice and quite close to major Strip casino hotels (the MGM is nearby). The rooms are clean and attractively decorated (though some have shower-only bathrooms). *195 E. Tropicana Ave. (at Koval Lane).* ☎ 800/4-MOTEL-6 (466-8356) or 702/798-0728. www.motel6.com. 607 units. Doubles $51 & up. AE, DC, DISC, MC, V. Map p 124.

★★ kids New York–New York Hotel & Casino SOUTH STRIP
A bit chaotic, thanks to the massive amount of stuff crammed into its public areas—rather like Manhattan itself—but unless you need focus, the pleasures outweigh the inconveniences. Too bad the delirious theme run amok downstairs doesn't translate into as much fun for the guest rooms. They are middlebrow sophisticated, but nothing startling, and can vary dramatically in size and shape; they're also overpriced when compared with what you get at other spots on the Strip. *3790 Las Vegas Blvd. S. (at Tropicana Ave.).* ☎ 800/689-1797 or 702/740-6969. www.nynyhotelcasino.com. 2,023 units. Doubles $79 & up. AE, DC, DISC, MC, V. Map p 123.

★ kids Orleans SOUTH STRIP
Easily overlooked because it's just far enough away from the Strip, the Orleans is also not near anything else, and has no fancy reputation to help draw attention. It's still worth considering because you can often find some decent rates on the surprisingly roomy accommodations, which sport the occasional sweet Victorian touch. Free shuttle services to the Strip help with the isolation, as do the 70-lane bowling alley (open really late) and 18-screen multiplex. *4500 W. Tropicana Ave. (west of the Strip & I-15).* ☎ 800/ ORLEANS (675-3267) or 702/365-7111. www.orleanscasino.com. 1,886 units. Doubles $39 & up. AE, DC, DISC, MC, V. Map p 123.

★★ kids Palms Casino Resort
MID-STRIP Still one of the hipper hotels, and a bit daunting because of that. But look past the zero-body-fat types lining up to get into one of the many happening clubs and bars,

and you will find a good, cheap food court; a multiplex; and a fine child-care facility. It's not the first place I would suggest for a family, but those elements might sway you. Rooms have especially comfortable beds and lots of pizazz. Try to get a high-level unit for some of the best views of the city. *4321 W. Flamingo Rd. (just west of I-15).* ☎ *866/942-7777 or 702/942-7777. www.palms. com. 664 units. Doubles $99 & up. AE, DC, DISC, MC, V. Map p 123.*

★ **Paris Las Vegas Casino Resort** MID-STRIP   Rooms are a little generically pretty (though the bathtubs are satisfyingly deep), but the rest of the hotel is so dedicated to its theme—an element of Vegas that is vanishing, to my despair—and it's so well located on the Strip, that it hardly matters. *3655 Las Vegas Blvd. S.* ☎ *888/BONJOUR (266-5687) or 702/946-7000. www. parislv.com. 2,916 units. Doubles $119 & up; suites $350 & up. AE, DC, DISC, MC, V. Map p 123.*

★ **Planet Hollywood Resort & Casino** SOUTH STRIP   The many lives of the famous Aladdin continue on in its newest incarnation. At press time, the hotel was set to undergo a massive redo whose intention was to rid the interior of all of its "Genie in the Bottle" imagery and replace it with Hollywood glamour, however that actually translates. Figure on at least a few glass booths with dubious celebrity "memorabilia" inside. The rooms still won't be more than generic, but the bathrooms should be fairly large. *3667 Las Vegas Blvd. S.* ☎ *877/333-WISH (9474) or 702/ 785-5555. www.aladdincasino.com. 2,567 units. Doubles $99 & up. AE, DC, DISC, MC, V. Map p 123.*

★★★ **Red Rock Resort** SUMMERLIN   A fantastic resort—right across from the eponymous red rocks themselves—that's not that many minutes from the Strip, giving you both privacy and ready access. It's one of the best settings in

The Vegas Hotel Experience

Vegas hotels are not your average hotel experience. Most hotels are content to be located near attractions. Vegas hotels *are* the attraction. Or they bring the attractions into the hotel. Or both. Expect access to all kinds of unusual goodies, from happening nightclubs to roller coasters to, oh yes, casinos. But hotel size brings its own issues; 3,000-room (or more) resorts simply do not have the kind of service one expects at a true resort. Personal attention can be spotty, maintenance can be a bit slow (that stain on the carpet will likely stay there for some time), and it's highly likely you will hear plumbing and other noises emanating from nearby rooms. The final caveat is the hidden price. Most hotels charge extra for almost everything beyond bed and bath, including gym use, Wi-Fi use, pool cabana use—it all adds up. In the case of the Red Rock Resort, they audaciously automatically add that charge in as a mandatory "resort fee." Only true resorts such as the Four Seasons or Ritz-Carlton have inclusive room prices. Factor that in when making your decision.

Vegas. Rooms are striking, the comfy beds will make you disinclined to get up (especially with the big flatscreen TV in front of you), and the bathrooms are positively sprawling. The pool attracts celebrities pretending they want to keep a low profile. The gym and spa are not worth the mandatory additional price. *10973 W. Charleston Rd.* ☎ *866/767-7773 or 702/797-7625. www.redrockstation.com. 800 units. Rooms $139 & up (up to 4 people). AE, DC, DISC, MC, V. Map p 124.*

★ **Rio All-Suite Hotel & Casino** MID-STRIP   Still some of the largest rooms in Vegas, though no more "suites" than at the Venetian (you just get a living/sitting area along with your bedroom area) and outstripped in style by so many others. Because the place is also hectic—it feels like spring break all the time—and located off the Strip, it's not a first-choice venue. *3700 Las Vegas Blvd. S. (just west of I-15).* ☎ *888/752-9746 or 702/777-7777. www.playrio.com. 2,582 units. Doubles $99 & up. AE, DC, DISC, MC, V. Map p 123.*

A palazzo bedroom at the Rio, whose accommodations are among the largest in Vegas.

It's a schlep from the Strip, but the first-class rooms and amenities at the Ritz-Carlton Lake Las Vegas make it worth the journey.

★★★ **kids Ritz-Carlton, Lake Las Vegas** HENDERSON   Its distance from Vegas is the only thing that prevents the Ritz-Carlton from being an ideal resort, but even that is negated by what is gained—a splendid setting at Lake Las Vegas, fringed by desert mountains. Classy understated rooms of great comfort, plus terrific service and options for all sorts of outdoor activities (fishing, hiking, and so on) make this one of my favorite places in and around the city. Pay the extra fee to stay on the club level and be sure to ask for a lakeview room. *1610 Lake Las Vegas Pkwy.* ☎ *800/241-3333 or 702/567-4700. www.ritzcarlton.com. 349 units. Doubles $199 & up. AE, DC, DISC, MC, V. Map p 124.*

★ **Sahara Hotel & Casino** NORTH STRIP   One of the few venerable old casino hotels still standing in Vegas (it opened in 1952), the Sahara announced plans for an overhaul at press time, but at the moment it has a solid Moroccan theme, a roller coaster (though it mystifyingly discourages children), and budget-friendly rates. Rooms are motel bland (though windows actually open!), but if all you're looking for is four walls and a mattress, this isn't a bad choice at all. *2535 Las Vegas Blvd. S. (at E. Sahara Ave.).* ☎ *888/696-2121 or 702/737-2111. www.saharavegas.com. 1,720 units. Doubles $45 & up. AE, DC, DISC, MC, V. Map p 124.*

★★ **kids** **South Point Hotel & Casino** SOUTH STRIP This "locals" joint is lower profile and south of the Strip. But given the size of the rooms here, the frills (squishy beds, flatscreen TVs), and the access to plenty of on-site entertainment (movie theaters, bowling alley, a first-rate equestrian center, budget food choices)—all for a much lower price than its on-the-Strip competition—the (rather minor) distance from the main action hardly matters. *9777 Las Vegas Blvd. S.* ☎ *866/796-7111 or 702/796-7111. www.southpointcasino.com. 650 units. Doubles $59 & up. AE, DC, DISC, MC, V. Map p 123.*

One of the sleek suites at THEhotel at Mandalay Bay, arguably the best place to stay in Las Vegas.

★ **Stratosphere Las Vegas Hotel & Casino** NORTH STRIP Think of this place as a motel, with prices to match, and the difference between its humble yet adequate rooms and the much more lavish numbers down the Strip won't bother you a bit. You will need a car if you stay here because it's much too far to walk to the main Strip action or to Downtown. *2000 Las Vegas Blvd. S. (between St. Louis & Baltimore aves.).* ☎ *800/99-TOWER (998-6937) or 702/380-7777. www.stratospherehotel.com. 2,444 units. Doubles $39 & up. AE, DC, DISC, MC, V. Map p 124.*

★ **Terrible's** EAST OF STRIP This unexpected bargain isn't terrible at all (its owner is convenience store and gas station magnate Ed "Terrible" Herbst). And it's near the Strip! Rooms are as basic as can be, though accommodations in the newest hotel tower have fresh furnishings and flatscreen TVs. The pool area is particularly nice for a budget operation. *4100 Paradise Rd. (at Flamingo Rd.).* ☎ *800/640-9777 or 702/733-7000. www.terribleherbst.com. 325 units. Doubles $39 & up. AE, DC, DISC, MC, V. Map p 124.*

★★★ **THEhotel at Mandalay Bay** SOUTH STRIP Quite possibly the best hotel on the Strip. It's certainly the most sophisticated, with its Manhattan-style sleekly contemporary lobby; and it certainly has the largest rooms, each a dark-wood and gleaming black one-bedroom suite, complete with two flatscreen TVs and a deep soaking tub. Its separate-from-but-attached-to Mandalay Bay location means you can have your getaway and gamble too. *3950 Las Vegas Blvd. S.* ☎ *877/632-7800 or 702/632-7777. www.hotelatmandalaybay.com. 1,120 units. Suites $189. AE, DC, DISC, MC, V. Map p 123.*

The huge guest rooms inside The Venetian are among the best in the city.

★★ TI Las Vegas (Treasure Island) MID-STRIP

Strip away the theme (pirates and treasure, in this case) it had when it was known as Treasure Island, and what you have left is a very nice, all-too-easily-forgettable hotel. Good-sized rooms with some unexpected careful details (including decent art on the walls and large soaking tub in the bathroom) are superior to those at its Mirage sibling, even if that hotel is much more interesting overall. *3300 Las Vegas Blvd. S. (at Spring Mountain Rd.).* ☎ *800/288-7206 or 702/894-7111. www.treasureisland. com. 2,885 units. Doubles $89 & up. AE, DC, DISC, MC, V. Map p 123.*

★★ The Venetian MID-STRIP

Some of the largest and best rooms on the Strip, though not precisely the "suites" they advertise. Instead, it's one big space encompassing both bedroom and sunken living room, with plenty of stately touches and marble bathrooms with double sinks. The additional Venezia tower has its own entrance and more of a Ritz-Carlton vibe. The immense property can be hard to navigate. *3355 Las Vegas Blvd. S.* ☎ *877/883-6423 or 702/414-1000. 4,029 units. Doubles $149 & up. AE, DC, DISC, MC, V. Map p 123.*

★ The Westin Casuarina Las Vegas Hotel, Casino & Spa

MID-STRIP   Brand-name reliability means those Westin Heavenly Beds—though, oddly, not the best beds in town—and various features that make this more business traveler–friendly than pleasure seeker–appropriate. The gym is free, the casino kind of a fizzle. It has more pizazz than other chain hotels in town, but so much less than the powerhouse hotels that the prices seem a bit of a cheat. *160 E. Flamingo Rd.* ☎ *866/837-4215 or 702/836-9775. www. starwoodhotels.com. 825 units. Doubles $139 & up. AE, DC, DISC, MC, V. Map p 123.*

The Westin Casuarina's lack of pizazz makes it a somewhat bland option, but the "heavenly beds" do make for a good night's sleep.

Playing the Hotel Rate Game

Hotel rates in Las Vegas fluctuate more wildly than the stock market, and can be just as hard to predict. Rates in this chapter are the listed minimum rack rates (without the 9%–10% hotel tax included), but the same room at the same hotel can range from $50 to $300 to a lot more, depending on when you book. You will, for example, always pay top dollar around New Year's, on weekends, and when a major convention is in town. Take the prices I list with a grain of salt and always do your homework. Check out the going rates on the major hotel booking sites (Expedia.com, Travelocity.com, Travelaxe.com) and always check the websites of the hotels themselves for available discount packages and rates.

Also note that rates listed here are for double occupancy only; most Vegas hotels usually charge extra (sometimes as much as $35 per person, per night) for another person in the room, even if the extra guest happens to be your child. If you're bringing kids along, always ask about the hotel's policy when booking.

★★ **Wynn Las Vegas** NORTH STRIP   An adult luxury resort on steroids. While the enormous rooms are full of nifty touches—high-thread-count linens, Warhol silk-screens, curtains that operate with a push button, long tubs in the bathroom, fancy amenities—the overall experience is just too big to offer the kind of service one can get from an actual resort in the area. For these prices, you can do better. *3131 Las Vegas Blvd. S. (at the corner of Sands Ave.).* ☎ *888/320-9966 or 702/770-7100. www.wynnlas vegas.com. 3,933 units. Doubles $249 & up. AE, DC, DISC, MC, V. Map p 124.* ●

The nifty rooms inside the Wynn Las Vegas come with all sorts of bells and whistles, but they're also very pricey for what you get.

10 The Best Day Trips & Excursions

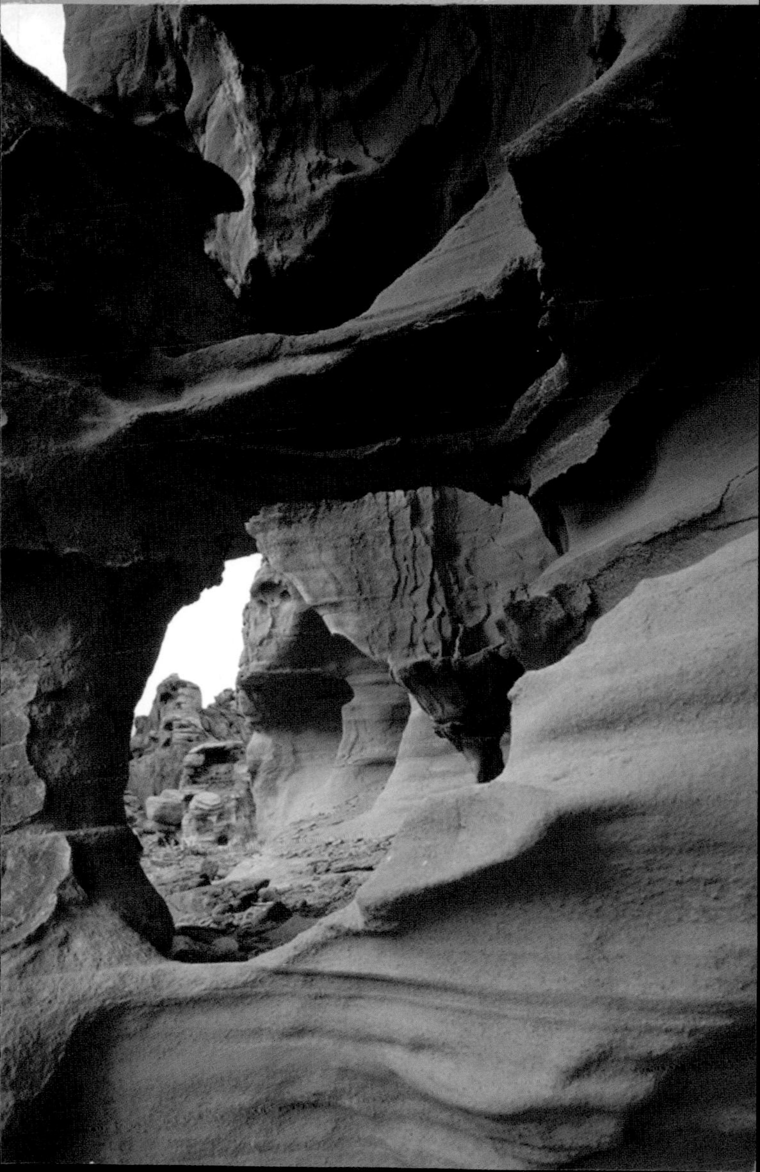

Hoover Dam & Lake Mead

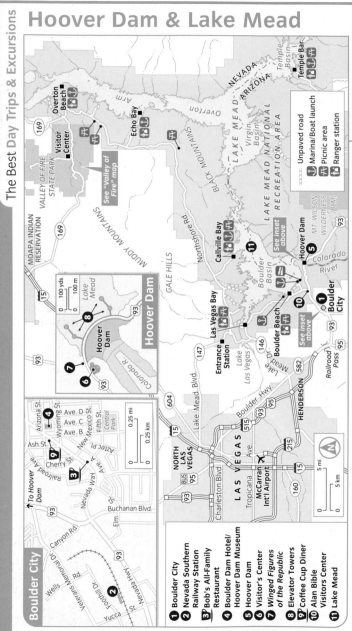

Legend:
- Unpaved road
- Marina/Boat launch
- Picnic area
- Ranger station

See "Valley of Fire" map

See inset above

Hoover Dam

Boulder City

❶ Boulder City
❷ Nevada Southern Railway Station
❸ Bob's All-Family Restaurant
❹ Boulder Dam Hotel/ Hoover Dam Museum
❺ Hoover Dam
❻ Visitor's Center
❼ Winged Figures of the Republic
❽ Elevator Towers
❾ Coffee Cup Diner
❿ Alan Bible Visitors Center
⓫ Lake Mead

Previous Page: One of the magnificent rock formations found in the Valley of Fire.

The architectural and engineering marvel that is Hoover Dam is probably the major reason there is a Vegas today (those lights on the Strip need lots of power). It's one of the world's major electrical-generating plants, but it's also a wonder of Art Deco design and a remarkable combination of beauty and function. It's also responsible for the creation of the 110-mile-wide (177km) Lake Mead, an unexpected recreational oasis smack in the middle of the desert. **START: From Las Vegas, take U.S. 93 South. U.S. 93 becomes U.S. 93/95 South, which then becomes Nevada Highway.**

① ★★ Boulder City. This charming small town (originally built by the Bureau of Reclamation to house the workers building Hoover Dam, originally called Boulder Dam) is all the more unexpected because it's only 20 miles (32km) from Vegas. It doesn't hurt that this is the only place in Nevada where it's not legal to gamble. Wander through the adorable downtown area (construction and growth are strictly regulated to maintain its character) as a Mayberry antidote to the "bright lights, big city" atmosphere which, despite its proximity, seems another lifetime away. ⏱ *30 min. Off Nevada Hwy. www.bouldercity.com.*

② ★ kids Nevada Southern Railway Station. This seasonal train ride offers visitors the chance to take a 3-mile (4.8km) journey along a historic train route (built in 1931 as a supply route for the Hoover Dam) aboard refurbished 1911 Pullman cars. A can't-miss for train buffs and a sweet outing for everyone else. ⏱ *45 min. Reservations are unnecessary, but allow 20 min. before departure time to buy tickets & choose a seat. 601 Yucca St., Boulder City. ☎ 702/486-5933. http://dmla.clan.lib.nv.us/docs/museums/BoulderCity/rr.htm. Admission $8 adults, $7 seniors 65 & up, $4 kids 11 years & under. Trains depart 10am, 11:30am, 1pm & 2:30pm from Boulder City Sat–Sun Sept–June.*

Want more proof Boulder City is frozen in time? Take a peek at **③ Bob's All-Family Restaurant**'s classic neon sign while you chow down on standard diner fare. *679 Nevada Hwy., Boulder City. ☎ 702/294-2627. $$.*

④ Boulder Dam Hotel/Hoover Dam Museum. This still-active hotel is set in a Dutch-colonial-style building built to house VIPs visiting the Dam construction. The structure also holds a museum that neatly explains why the dam and related construction projects represented virtually the only economic possibility for the area during the Depression. The great emphasis on the human-interest element of construction makes this a good counterpart to the more engineering-oriented exhibit

Charming Boulder City is unusual in that it's the only place in Nevada where you can't gamble.

at the Dam itself. *1305 Arizona St., Boulder City.* **Hotel** 📞 *702/293-3510. www.boulderdamhotel.com.* **Hoover Dam Museum** 📞 *702/294-1988. www.bcmha.org. Admission $2 adults, $1 children & seniors. Open 10am–5pm Mon–Sat, noon–5pm Sun. Closed Jan 1, Easter Sunday, Mother's Day, Thanksgiving & Christmas Day.*

Take U.S. 93 South to the Nevada-Arizona border. Pass the turnoff for Lake Mead, and as you near the dam you'll see the parking structure on your left. Parking fee is $7, cash only. Note that this drive can get very backed up on Sundays and the end of holiday weekends, so if you must visit on those days, go early in the morning or late in the day.

⑤ ★★★ Hoover Dam. The star of the show and a wonder of the modern, engineering world. You may not realize how beautiful a monolithic structure can be until you behold the dam. Note how the design reflects the Art Deco period so influenced by the post–King Tut-tomb-discovery Egyptian revival. Construction on this National Historic Landmark lasted from 1931 to 1936 and, once completed, the face of the Southwest was changed forever. Anytime someone turns on a light switch in California or Nevada, they can thank the Hoover Dam engineers and the workers who gave so much (more than 100 people died during construction) to make it come true. ⏱ *2 hr. Off S. 93 South.* 📞 *866/730-9097 or 702/494-2517. www. usbr.gov/lc/hooverdam. Admission $11 adults; $9 seniors, military & dependents; $6 children 7–16; free for kids under 7. Open 9am–6pm, last admission at 5:15pm.*

⑥ Visitor's Center. All the information you could possibly want about Hoover Dam is contained in this three-level exhibition and information center. Videos, interactive displays, photos, and more help illustrate what a massive feat this was. Because of post-9/11 security issues, there are no longer extensive tours of the interior. Currently (subject to change), admission to the center includes a partly guided, partly self-guided tour of the dam, including a 500-foot (152m) elevator ride down to one of the generators, a journey through a tunnel drilled through rock, and a trip to the observation deck overlooking Lake Mead. *See bullet* ④ *above.*

⑦ ★★ Winged Figures of the Republic. Should you opt to walk the dam on your own, stop on the Nevada side to pay homage to these 30-foot-high (9.1m) winged mythological figures representing the higher nature of all humankind (they were designed by sculptor Oskar J. W. Hansen). The bronze-shelled statues were originally erected, along with an astrological star chart, as a memorial to higher intelligence, but after World War II were rededicated to the men who built the dam, plus their little mascot dog. *Off S. 93 South. Free admission.*

The huge Winged Figures of the Republic *guard the entrance to Hoover Dam on the Nevada side.*

Lake Mead is known both for its scenery and for its outdoor recreational opportunities.

8 ★ **Elevator Towers.** Exhibits on local flora and fauna are found on the dam's elevator towers, thus combining nature and industry. Note how the clock on the tower on the Nevada side gives one time, and the one on the Arizona side another; the latter is on Mountain Standard Time, 1 hour ahead of the former—except during daylight saving time, because Arizona does not observe it. *See bullet* **4** *above; just viewing the exterior is free.*

Get a cup of joe or a burger at the classic greasy spoon **9** **Coffee Cup Diner.** *512 Nevada Hwy., Boulder City.* ☎ *702/294-0517. $.*

Take U.S. 93 North to Lakeshore Dr./NV 166.

10 **Alan Bible Visitors Center.** Staffed by eager, knowledgeable locals, Lake Mead's main visitor center is a great place to pick up information on area recreational activities. Do explore its small but interesting exhibits on local nature and history. It's also here that you pay your fee for the Lake Mead scenic drive (see bullet **11**). ⏱ *20 min. 4 miles northeast of Boulder City, on U.S. 93 at NV 166.* ☎ *702/293-8990. Open 8:30am–4:30pm daily, except Thanksgiving, Christmas & New Year's Day.*

Follow the scenic Lakeshore Dr./NV 166 into Lake Mead National Recreational Area.

11 ★★★ **Lake Mead.** Created in 1935 by the building of Hoover Dam (and named for the commissioner of the Bureau of Reclamation at the time), Lake Mead is the largest man-made lake in the United States. The best way to view the lake (whose beauty isn't lessened by its artificial origins) is to take its 30-mile (48km) scenic drive. Expect colorful desert landscape, panoramic views, and mountain vistas. There are several beaches and campgrounds along the way, with plenty of opportunities for various recreational activities. The water is a bit chilly and the beaches are rocky, so it's used more for fishing and sailing purposes than swimming. ⏱ *1½ hr.; more if you indulge in the recreational facilities.* www.nps.gov/lame. *Entry fee $5 per vehicle, $3 per person walking or biking. Open daily, 24 hr. though some spots in the park have shorter hours (inquire at visitors center, bullet* **10***).*

The scenic route becomes Northshore Rd. and from here you can head to the Valley of Fire or take U.S. 93/95 North back to Las Vegas.

Valley of Fire State Park

1. **Valley of Fire State Park Entrance**
2. **Visitor's Center**
3. **Rainbow Vista**
4. **Mouse's Tank**
5. **Seven Sisters**
6. **Cabins**
7. **Petrified Logs**
8. **Elephant Rock**
9. **Lost City Museum**
10. **Inside Scoop**

Unpaved road
Hiking trail
(approximate route)

0   2 mi
0   2 km

Overton

Duck Rock

White Domes

LAKE MEAD NAT'L RECREATION AREA

VALLEY

OF FIRE

STATE

PARK

Rainbow Vista 3
Silica Dome
Baseline Mesa
To Overton Beach & Lake Mead

Mouse's Tank 4
Petrified Log
Natural Arch

Visitor Center 2
Cabins 6   7

Pinnacles
Petrified Logs
Seven Sisters 5
Elephant Rock 8

Atlatl Rock
Clark Memorial
Charlie's Spring

Beehives

Northshore Dr.

←To 15

For those who think a desert is brown, flat, and featureless, the Valley of Fire comes as a shock. This almost otherworldly tundra of brilliant red sandstone formations was created 150 million years ago as wind twisted and shaped the landscape into what could be called a Jurassic zoo of creaturelike configurations. The man-made structures that make Las Vegas a marvel have nothing on what nature can do, given enough time. **START: From Las Vegas, take I-15 North to exit 75 (Valley of Fire turnoff); trip time is 1 hour. For a more scenic route, take I-15 North, then take Lake Mead Boulevard East to Northshore Road/NV 167 and proceed to the Valley of Fire exit; trip time is 1½ hours. Be sure to bring plenty of water.**

---

1 **Valley of Fire State Park Entrance.** As you enter the 25,000-acre (10,117-hectare) park (Nevada's oldest state park) on a windy little road, the first major sight will be on your left. The Atlatl Rock was a basic training camp for Native American tribes in the area (an *atlatl* was a stick used to throw spears) and is full of old petroglyphs. Men came here for coming-of-age ceremonies and to learn hunting and survival skills. ⏱ *5 min. 60 miles (97km) NE of Las Vegas, Overton, NV. http://parks.nv.gov/vf.htm. Admission $6 per car. Open daily, sunrise to sunset.*

Valley of Fire State Park is filled with beautiful and eerie rock formations, and is home to some of the best scenery in the state.

2 Visitor's Center. Accessed from the Old Arrowhead road (the first car road running from Los Angeles to Salt Lake City), this is where you can purchase various materials concerning information on the park, talk to park rangers, and check out some small displays on the local landscape. Be sure to pick up a map before you head into the park. ⏱ *15 min. NV 169, 6 miles (9.7km) west of Northshore Rd.* ☎ *702/397-2088. Open daily 8:30am–4:30pm, except for Christmas Day.*

3 Rainbow Vista. From the visitor's center, drive through this palette of multicolored sandstone, all the colors of the spectrum splashed down to earth. The drive dead-ends at the pure white silica domes. At this point, you can take a hiking trail to a movie site where they filmed the bawdy western *The Professionals* (1966) with Burt Lancaster and Lee Marvin. A bit of the set is still there. ⏱ *1 hr. round-trip for gardens; 1 hr. for hike.*

4 Mouse's Tank. Take a hike down a deep sandy wash (no sandals, shoes only) with many well-executed petroglyphs lining the way. The glyphs are the most ancient and historic in the Southwest, thousands of years old—even the local Paiute people don't know who did them. The titular Mouse's Tank (named for a fugitive who hid out here in the 1890s) lies at the end of the hike and is a natural sandstone bowl *tanaha*, which is a hole in the desert that fills up when it rains (don't come here after a storm), but it's something of a let-down post-petroglyphs. ⏱ *30 min.*

5 Seven Sisters. Named after an Indian legend describing how the seven stars of the big Dipper were created, these girls are seven huge red rock formations of Mesozoic sandstone. It was originally an ancient sand dune that hardened and cracked over the years, and erosion has separated it into seven distinct shapes with one little brother in the middle. ⏱ *15 min.*

Heat Alert

Daytime temperatures in the Valley of Fire can reach 120°F (49°C) in the height of summer. This tour is best done in late fall, early spring, and winter, when the climate is more tolerable. Even during those times, carry at least a gallon of water per person.

Some of the detailed petroglyphs found on the hiking trail to Mouse's Tank.

An ancient pueblo village is one of the top attractions at the Lost City Museum.

6 Cabins. These native stone structures are now used for picnicking (bring fixings along with you to the park), but were originally constructed in the 1930s by the Civilian Conservation Corps to provide nighttime shelter for weary travelers. It's a good location for taking a breather before hitting the road again. ⏱ *15 min.*

7 Petrified Logs. These prime examples of fossilized wood have been fenced off to prevent treasure hunters from walking off with them. It's believed that the colorful trunks are the remnants of a forest, whose trees were washed into this area about 225 million years ago. ⏱ *10 min.*

8 Elephant Rock. This red stone formation is easily accessed via a short trail from the main park road. And it really does look like the head of a giant pachyderm. Can we say prime photo op? ⏱ *10 min.*

From Valley of Fire, follow NV 169 southeast toward Scenic Loop Rd. Make a left to stay on NV 169 into Overton. NV 169 becomes S. Moapa Valley Blvd. 30 min.

9 Lost City Museum. A charming little museum focusing on an ancient Anasazi village (named Pueblo Grande de Nevada because the Pueblo Indians occupied it after the Anasazi disappeared) discovered in the area in 1924. Along with exhibits whose contents date back

some 12,000 years, there are some displays on the area's 19th-century Mormon settlers. ⏱ *30 min. 721 S. Moapa Valley Blvd./NV 169, Overton, NV. ☎ 702/397-2193. http://dmla. clan.lib.nv.us/docs/museums/lost/ lostcity.htm. Admission $3 adults, $2 seniors 65+, free for kids 18 & under. Open 8:30am–4:30pm daily. Closed Thanksgiving Day, Dec 25 & Jan 1.*

A sweet old-fashioned ice-cream parlor, **10 Inside Scoop** also offers soups, sandwiches, and box lunches for picnics inside the park. *395 S. Moapa Valley Blvd. ☎ 702/ 397-2055. $.*

To get back to Vegas, head northeast on S. Moapa Valley Blvd./NV 169 toward S. Pioneer Rd. Merge onto I-15 South to Las Vegas. ●

One of the immense Seven Sisters, giant rock formations set inside the Valley of Fire; see p 143.

The
Savvy Gambler

Playing the **Games**

As you walk through the labyrinthine twists and turns of a casino floor, your attention will likely be dragged to the various games and, your interest piqued, your fingers may begin to twitch in anticipation of hitting it big. Before you put your money on the line, it's imperative to know the rules of the game you want to play.

Most casinos offer free gambling lessons at scheduled times on weekdays. This provides a risk-free environment for you to learn the games that tickle your fancy. Some casinos follow their lessons with low-stakes game play, enabling you to put your newfound knowledge to the test at small risk. During those instructional sessions, and even when playing on your own, dealers in most casinos will be more than happy to answer any questions you might have. Remember, the casino doesn't need to trick you into losing your money . . . the odds are already in their favor across the board; that's why it's called gambling.

Another rule of thumb: Take a few minutes to watch a game being played in order to familiarize yourself with the motions and lingo. Then go back and reread this section—things will make a lot more sense at that point Good luck!

Players Clubs

If you gamble, it definitely pays to join a players club. These so-called clubs are designed to attract and keep customers in a given casino by providing incentives: meals, shows, discounts on rooms, gifts, tournament invitations, discounts at hotel shops, VIP treatment, and (more and more) cash rebates. Join a players club (it doesn't cost a cent to sign up), and soon you too will be getting those great hotel-rate offers—$20-a-night rooms, affordable rooms at the luxury resorts, even free rooms. (This is one way to beat high hotel rates in Vegas.) Of course, your rewards are often greater if you play in just one casino, but your mobility is limited.

When you join a players club (inquire at the casino desk), you're given something that looks like a credit card, which you must insert into an ATM-like device whenever you play. Yes, many casinos even have them for the tables as well as the machines. (Don't forget to retrieve your card when you leave the machine, as I sometimes do.) The device tracks your play and computes bonus points.

Which players club should you join? Actually, you should join one at any casino where you play because even the act of joining usually entitles you to some benefits. It's convenient to concentrate play where you're staying; if you play a great deal, a casino hotel's players-club benefits may be a factor in your accommodations choice. Consider, though, particularly if you aren't a high roller, the players clubs Downtown. You get more bang for your buck because you don't have to spend as much to start raking in the goodies.

Previous Page: There are a myriad number of card games that you can play in Las Vegas.

Another advantage is to join a players club that covers many hotels under the same corporate umbrella. For example, MGM MIRAGE runs The Mirage, Bellagio, MGM Grand, and more, and their players club offers discounts and point awards at all of their properties.

One way to judge a players club is by the quality of service you receive when you enroll. Personnel should politely answer all your questions (for instance, is nickel play included,

and is there a time limit for earning required points?) and be able to tell you exactly how many points you need for various bonuses.

Maximizing your players club profits and choosing the club that's best for you is a complex business. If you want to get into it in depth, order a copy of Jeffrey Compton's **The Las Vegas Advisor Guide to Slot Clubs** ($9.95 plus shipping), which examines just about every facet of the situation (☎ **800/244-2224**).

Baccarat

The ancient game of baccarat, or chemin de fer, is played with eight decks of cards. Firm rules apply, and there is no skill involved other than deciding whether to bet on the bank or the player. No, really—that's all you have to do. The dealer does all the other work. You can essentially stop reading here. Oh, all right, carry on.

Any beginner can play, but check the betting minimum before you sit down, as this tends to be a high-stakes game. The cards are shuffled by the croupier and then placed in a box called the "shoe." Players may wager on "bank" or "player" at any time. Two cards are dealt from the shoe and given to the player who has the largest wager against the bank, and two cards are dealt to the

croupier, acting as banker. If the rules call for a third card, the player or banker, or both, must take the third card. In the event of a tie, the hand is dealt over. **Note:** The guidelines that determine if a third card must be drawn (by the player or banker) are provided at the baccarat table upon request.

The object of the game is to come as close as possible to the number 9. To score the hands, the cards of each hand are totaled and the *last digit* is used. All cards have face value. For example: 10 plus 5 equals 15 (score is 5); 10 plus 4 plus 9 equals 23 (score is 3); 4 plus 3 plus 3 equals 10 (score is 0); and 4 plus 3 plus 2 equals 9 (score is 9). The closest hand to 9 wins.

Size Counts . . . Sort Of

For those who desire a more informal environment in which to play baccarat, casinos offer minibaccarat, played on a normal-size table no larger than a blackjack table. There is no substantive difference between baccarat and its little brother. It's simply a matter of size and speed—the size of your bankroll and the speed with which you may build it (or lose it). Table stakes in minibaccarat tend to be lower, and the hands proceed at a much faster pace.

Each player has a chance to deal the cards. The shoe passes to the player on the right each time the bank loses. If the player wishes, he or she may pass the shoe at any time.

Note: When you bet on the bank and the bank wins, you are charged a 5% commission. This must be paid at the start of a new game or when you leave the table.

Big Six

Big Six provides pleasant recreation and involves no study or effort. The wheel has 56 positions on it, 54 of them marked by bills from $1 to $20. The other two spots are jokers, and each pays 40 to 1 if the wheel stops in that position. All other stops pay at face value. Those marked with $20 bills pay 20 to 1, the $5 bills pay 5 to 1, and so forth. The idea behind the game is to predict (or just blindly guess) what spot the wheel will stop at and place a bet accordingly.

Blackjack

The dealer starts the game by dealing each player two cards. In some casinos, they're dealt to the player faceup, in others facedown, but the dealer always gets one card up and one card down. Everybody plays against the dealer. The object is to get a total that is higher than that of the dealer without exceeding 21. All face cards count as 10; all other number cards, except aces, are counted at their face value. An ace may be counted as 1 or 11, whichever you choose it to be.

Starting at his or her left, the dealer gives additional cards to the players who wish to draw (be "hit") or none to a player who wishes to "stand" or "hold." If your count is nearer to 21 than the dealer's, you win. If it's under the dealer's, you lose. Ties are a push and nobody wins. After all the players are satisfied with their counts, the dealer exposes his or her facedown card. If his or her two cards total 16 or less, the dealer must "hit" (draw an additional card) until reaching 17 or over. If the dealer's total exceeds 21, he or she must pay all the players whose hands have not gone "bust." It is important to note here that the blackjack dealer has no choice as to whether he or she should stay or draw. A dealer's decisions are predetermined and known to all the players at the table.

If you're a novice or just rusty, do yourself a favor and buy one of the small laminated cards available in shops all over town that illustrate proper play for every possible hand in blackjack. Even longtime players have been known to pull them out every now and then, and they can save you from making costly errors.

How to Play

Here are eight "rules" for blackjack:

1. Place the number of chips that you want to bet on the betting space on your table.

2. Look at the first two cards the dealer starts you with. If you wish to "stand," then wave your hand over your cards, palm down (watch your fellow players), indicating that you don't want any additional cards. If you elect to draw an additional card, you tell the dealer to "hit" you by tapping the table with a finger (watch your fellow players).

3. If your count goes over 21, you are "bust" and lose, even if the dealer also goes "bust" afterward.

4. If you make 21 in your first two cards (any picture card or 10 with an ace), you've got blackjack. You will be paid 1½ times your bet, provided the dealer does not have blackjack too, in which case it's a push and nobody wins.

5. If you find a "pair" in your first two cards (say, two 8s or two aces), you may "split" the pair into two hands and treat each card as the first card dealt in two separate hands. You will need to place an additional bet, equal to your original bet, on the table. The dealer will then deal you a new *second* card to the first split card and play commences as described above. This will be done for the second split card as well. *Note:* When you split aces you will receive only one additional card per ace and must "stand."

6. After seeing your two starting cards, you have the option to "double down." You place an amount equal to your original bet on the table and you receive only one more card. Doubling down is a strategy to capitalize on a potentially strong hand against the dealer's weaker hand. *Tip:* You may double down for less than your original bet, but never for more.

7. Anytime the dealer deals himself or herself an ace for the "up" card, you may insure your hand against the possibility that the hole card is a 10 or face card, which would give him or her an automatic blackjack. To insure, you place an amount up to one-half of your bet on the "insurance" line. If the dealer does have a blackjack, you get paid 2 to 1 on the insurance money while losing your original bet: You break even. If the dealer does not have a blackjack, he or she takes your insurance money and play continues in the normal fashion.

8. *Remember:* The dealer must stand on 17 or more and must hit a hand of 16 or less.

Look, but Don't Touch!

1. **Never touch your cards (or anyone else's),** unless it's specifically stated at the table that you may. While you'll only receive a verbal slap on the wrist if you violate this rule, you *really* don't want to get one.

2. **Players must use hand signals to indicate their wishes to the dealer.** All verbal directions by players will be politely ignored by the dealer, who will remind players to use hand signals. The reason for this is the "Eye in the Sky," the casino's security system, which focuses an "eye" on every table, and must record players' decisions to avoid accusations of misconduct or collusion.

Professional Tips

Advice of the experts in playing blackjack is as follows:

1. *Do not* ask for an extra card if you have a count of 17 or higher, *ever*.

2. *Do not* ask for an extra card when you have a total of 12 or more if the dealer has a 2 through 6 showing in his or her "up" card.

3. *Ask* for an extra card or more when you have a count of 12 through 16 in your hand if the dealer's "up" card is a 7, 8, 9, 10, or ace.

There's a lot more to blackjack strategy than the above, of course. So consider this merely as the bare bones of the game. Blackjack is played with a single deck or with multiple decks; if you're looking for a single-deck game, your best bet is to head to a Downtown casino.

A final tip: Avoid insurance bets; they're sucker bait!

Craps

The most exciting casino action is usually found at the craps tables. Betting is frenetic, play is fast-paced, and groups quickly bond while yelling and screaming in response to the action.

The Possible Bets

The craps table is divided into marked areas (Pass, Come, Field, Big 6, Big 8, and so on), where you place your chips to bet. The following are a few simple directions.

PASS LINE A "Pass Line" bet pays even money. If the first roll of the dice adds up to 7 or 11, you win your bet; if the first roll adds up to 2, 3, or 12, you lose your bet. If any other number comes up, it's your "point." If you roll your point again, you win, but if a 7 comes up again before your point is rolled, you lose.

DON'T PASS LINE Betting on the "Don't Pass" is the opposite of betting on the "Pass Line." This time, you lose if a 7 or an 11 is thrown on the first roll, and you win if a 2 or a 3 is thrown on the first roll.

If the first roll is 12, however, it's a push (standoff), and nobody wins. If none of these numbers is thrown and you have a point instead, in order for you to win, a 7 will have to be thrown before the point comes

up again. A "Don't Pass" bet also pays even money.

COME Betting on "Come" is the same as betting on the Pass Line, but you must bet after the first roll or on any following roll. Again, you'll win on 7 or 11 and lose on 2, 3, or 12. Any other number is your point, and you win if your point comes up again before a 7.

DON'T COME This is the opposite of a "Come" bet. Again, you wait until after the first roll to bet. A 7 or an 11 means you lose; a 2 or a 3 means you win; 12 is a push, and nobody wins. You win if 7 comes up before the point. (The point, you'll recall, was the first number rolled if it was none of the above.)

FIELD This is a bet for one roll only. The "Field" consists of seven numbers: 2, 3, 4, 9, 10, 11, and 12. If any of these numbers is thrown on the next roll, you win even money, except on 2 and 12, which pay 2 to 1 (at some casinos 3 to 1).

BIG 6 AND 8 A "Big 6 and 8" bet pays even money. You win if either a 6 or an 8 is rolled before a 7. Mathematically, this is a sucker's bet.

ANY 7 An "Any 7" bet pays the winner 5 for 1. If a 7 is thrown on the first roll after you bet, you win.

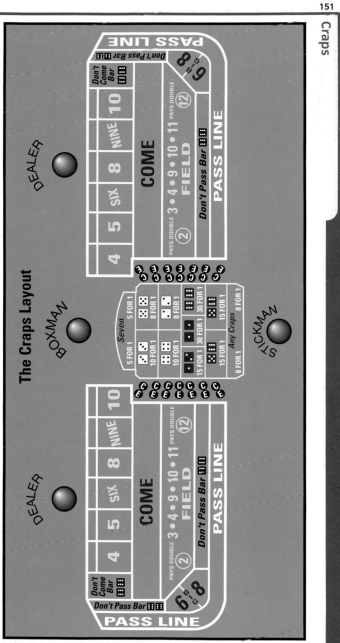

A typical craps table.

DICE PROBABILITIES

NUMBER	POSSIBLE COMBINATIONS	ACTUAL ODDS	PERCENTAGE PROBABILITY
2	1	35:1	2.8%
3	2	17:1	5.6%
4	3	11:1	8.3%
5	4	8:1	11.1%
6	5	6.2:1	13.9%
7	6	5:1	16.7%
8	5	6.2:1	13.9%
9	4	8:1	11.1%
10	3	11:1	8.3%
11	2	17:1	5.6%
12	1	35:1	2.8%

"HARD WAY" BETS In the middle of a craps table are pictures of several possible dice combinations together with the odds the casino will pay you if you bet and win on any of those combinations being thrown. For example, if double 3s or 4s are rolled and you had bet on them, you will be paid 7 to 1. If double 2s or 5s are rolled and you had bet on them, you will be paid 9 to 1. If either a 7 is rolled or the number you bet on was rolled any way other than the "Hard Way," then the bet is lost. In-the-know gamblers tend to avoid "Hard Way" bets as an easy way to lose their money.

ANY CRAPS Here you're lucky if the dice "crap out"—if they show 2, 3, or 12 on the first roll after you bet. If this happens, the bank pays 7 to 1. Any other number is a loser.

PLACE BETS You can make a "Place Bet" on any of the following numbers: 4, 5, 6, 8, 9, and 10. You're betting that the number you choose will be thrown before a 7 is thrown. If you win, the payoff is as follows: 4 or 10 pays at the rate of 9 to 5; 5 or 9 pays at the rate of 7 to 5; 6 or 8 pays at the rate of 7 to 6. "Place Bets" can be removed at any time before a roll.

Some Probabilities

The probability of a certain number being rolled at the craps table is not a mystery. As there are only 36 possible outcomes when the dice are rolled, the probability for each number being rolled is easily ascertained. See the "Dice Probabilities" chart in this section to help you in case you decided it was more fun to pass notes or sleep during your math classes.

So 7 has an advantage over all other combinations, which, over the long run, is in favor of the casino. You can't beat the law of averages, but if you can't beat 'em, join 'em. (Play the "Don't Pass" bet.)

Poker

Poker is the game of the Old West. There's at least one sequence in every Western where the hero faces off against the villain over a poker hand. In Las Vegas, poker is a tradition, although it isn't played at every casino.

There are lots of variations on the basic game, but one of the most popular is **Hold 'Em.** Two cards are dealt facedown to the players. After a betting round, five community cards (everyone can use them) are dealt faceup on the table. The player makes the best five-card hand, using their own cards and the "board" (the community cards), and the best hand wins. The house dealer takes care of the shuffling and the dealing and moves a marker around the table to alternate the start of the deal. The house rakes 1% to 5% (it depends on the casino) from each pot. Most casinos also provide tables for playing Seven-Card Stud,

Omaha High, and Omaha Hi-Lo. A few will even have Seven-Card Stud Hi-Lo split. To learn how these variations are played, either read a book or take lessons.

Warning: If you don't know how to play poker, don't attempt to learn at a table. Card sharks are not a rare species in Vegas; they will gladly feast on fresh meat (you!). Find a casino that provides free gaming lessons and learn, to paraphrase Kenny Rogers, when to hold 'em, and when to fold 'em.

Pai Gow Poker

Pai gow poker (a variation on poker) has become increasingly popular. The game is played with a traditional deck plus one joker. The joker is a wild card that can be used as an ace or to complete a straight, a flush, a straight flush, or a royal flush. Each player is dealt seven cards to arrange into two hands: a two-card hand and a five-card hand. As in standard poker, the highest two-card hand is two aces, and the highest five-card hand is a royal flush. The five-card hand *must* be higher than the two-card hand (if the two-card hand is a pair of sixes, for example, the five-card hand must be a pair of sevens or better).

Any player's hand that is set incorrectly is an automatic loser. The object of the game is for both of the players' hands to rank higher than both of the banker's hands. Should one hand rank exactly the same as the banker's hand, this is a tie (called a "copy"), *and the banker wins all tie hands.* If the player wins one hand but loses the other, this is a "push," and no money changes hands. The house dealer or any player may be the banker. The bank is offered to each player, and each player may accept or pass. Winning hands are paid even money, less a 5% commission.

Caribbean Stud Poker

Caribbean stud poker is yet another variation of poker that is gaining in popularity. Players put in a single ante bet and are dealt five cards facedown from a single deck; they play solely against the dealer, who receives five cards, one of them

faceup. Players are then given the option of folding, or may call by making an additional bet that is double their original ante. After all player bets have been made, the dealer's cards are revealed. If the dealer doesn't qualify with *at least an*

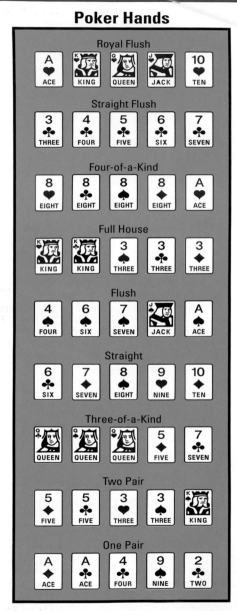

All the major poker hands.

ace/king combination, players are paid even money on their ante and their call bets are returned. If the dealer does qualify, each player's hand is compared to the dealer's. On winning hands, players receive even money on their ante bets, and call bets are paid out on a scale according to the value of their hands. The scale ranges from even money for a pair, to 100 to 1 on a royal flush, although there is usually a cap on the maximum payoff, which varies from casino to casino.

An additional feature of Caribbean stud is the inclusion of a progressive jackpot. For an additional side bet of $1, a player may qualify for a payoff from a progressive jackpot. The jackpot bet pays off only on a flush or better, but you can win on this bet even if the dealer ends up with a better hand than you do. Dream all you want of getting that royal flush and taking home the jackpot, but the odds of it happening are astronomical; so don't be so quick to turn in your resignation letter. Most veteran gamblers will tell you this is a bad bet (from a strictly mathematical standpoint, it is), but considering that Caribbean stud already has a house advantage that is even larger than the one in roulette, if you're going to play, you might as well toss in the buck and pray.

Let It Ride

Let It Ride is another popular game that involves poker hands. You place three bets at the outset and are dealt three cards. The dealer is dealt two cards that act as community cards (you're not playing against the dealer). Once you've seen your cards, you can choose to pull the first of your three bets back, or "Let It Ride." The object of this game is to get a pair of 10s or better by combining your cards with the dealer's. If you're holding a pair of 10s or better in your first three cards, you want to let your bets ride the whole way through. Once you've decided whether to let your first bet ride, the dealer exposes one of his or her two cards. Once again you must make a decision to take back your middle bet or keep on going. Then the dealer exposes the last of his or her cards; your third bet must stay. The dealer then turns over the hands of the players and determines whether you've won. Winning bets are paid on a scale, ranging from even money for a single pair up to 1,000 to 1 for a royal flush. These payouts are for each bet you have in play. Like Caribbean Stud, Let It Ride has a progressive jackpot that you can win for high hands if you cough up an additional dollar per hand, but be advised that the house advantage on that $1 is obscene. But hey, that's why it's called gambling.

3-Card Poker

3-Card Poker is rapidly gaining popularity and now you'll find at least one table in most major Vegas casinos. It's actually more difficult to explain than to play. For this reason, I recommend watching a table for a while. You should grasp it pretty quickly.

Basically, players are dealt three cards with no draw and have to make the best poker hand out of those three cards. Possible combinations include a straight flush (three sequential cards of the same suit), three of a kind (three queens, for example), a straight (three sequential cards of any suit), a flush (three cards of the same suit), and a pair (two queens, for example). Even if you don't have one of the favored combinations, you can still win if you have cards higher than the dealer's.

On the table you'll see three betting areas—the Ante, the Play, and the Pair Plus. There are actually two games in one on a 3-Card Poker table—"Pair Plus" and "Ante and Play." You can play the Pair Plus, the Ante, or both. Place your chips in the areas you want to bet in.

In Pair Plus, you are betting only on your hand, not competing against anyone else at the table or the dealer. If you get a pair or better, depending on your hand, the payoff can be pretty fab—Straight Flush: 40 to 1, Three of a Kind: 30 to 1, Straight: 6 to 1, Flush: 4 to 1, Pair: 1 to 1.

In Ante and Play, you are betting that your hand will be better than the dealer's but are not competing against anyone else at the table. You place an Ante bet, you view your cards, and then, if you decide you like your hand, you place a bet in the Play area equal to your Ante bet. If you get lousy cards and don't want to go forward, you can fold, losing only your Ante bet and your Pair Plus bet, if you made one. Once all bets are made, the dealer's hand is revealed—he or she must have at least a single queen for the bet to count; if not, your Ante and Play bets are returned. If you beat the dealer's hand, you get a 1 to 1 payoff but there is a bonus for a particularly good winning hand: Straight Flush: 5 to 1, Three of a Kind: 4 to 1, Straight: 1 to 1.

Your three cards are dealt. If you played only Pair Plus it doesn't matter what the dealer has—you get paid if you have a pair or better. If you don't, you lose your bet. If you played the Ante bet you must then either fold and lose the Ante bet or match the Ante bet by placing the same amount on the Play area. The dealer's hand is revealed and payouts happen accordingly. Each hand consists of one fresh 52-card deck.

Roulette

Roulette is an extremely easy game to play, and it's really quite colorful and exciting to watch. The wheel spins and the little ball bounces around, finally dropping into one of the slots, numbered 1 to 36, plus 0 and 00. You can place bets "Inside" the table and "Outside" the table. Inside bets are bets placed on a particular number or a set of numbers. Outside bets are those placed in the boxes surrounding the number table (see picture below). If you bet on a

specific number and it comes up, you'll be paid 35 to 1 on your bet. Bear in mind, however, that the odds of a particular number coming up are actually 38 to 1 (don't forget 0 and 00!) so the house has an advantage the moment you place an Inside bet. For payoffs on Outside bets, such as Red/Black, Odd/Even, and so forth, see the drawing below. The methods of placing single-number bets, column bets, and others are fairly obvious. The dealer will be

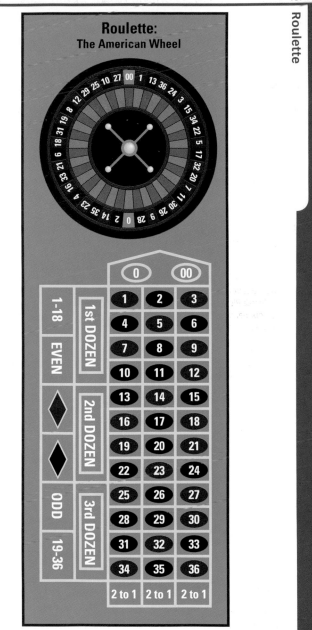

A typical roulette table.

happy to show you how make many interesting betting combinations, such as betting on six numbers at once. Each player is given different-colored chips so that it's easy to follow the numbers you've bet on.

Some typical bets are indicated by means of letters on the roulette layout depicted in the figure. The winning odds for each of these sample bets are listed. These bets can be made on any corresponding combinations of numbers.

Slots

You put the coin in the slot and pull the handle. What, you thought there was a trick to this?

Actually, there is a bit more to it. But first, some background. Old-timers will tell you slots were invented to give wives something to do while their husbands gambled. Slots used to be stuck at the edges of the casino and could be counted on one hand, maybe two. But now they *are* the casino. The casinos make more from slots than from craps, blackjack, and roulette combined. There are some 115,000 slot machines (not including video poker) in the county. Some of these are at the airport, steps from you as you deplane. It's just a matter of time before the planes flying into Vegas feature slots that pop up as soon as you cross the state line.

But in order to keep up with the increasing competition, the plain old machine, where reels just spin, has become nearly obsolete. Now, they are all computerized and have added buttons to push, so you can avoid getting carpal tunnel syndrome from yanking the handle all night. (The handles are still there on many of them.) Many don't even have reels any more, but are entirely video screens, which offer a number of little bonus extras that have nothing to do with actual play. The idea is still simple: Get three (sometimes four) cherries (clowns, sevens, dinosaurs, whatever) in a row and you win

something. Each machine has its own combination. Some will pay you something with just one symbol showing; on most, the more combinations there are, the more opportunities for loot. Some will even pay if you get three blanks. Study each machine to learn what it does. **Note:** The **payback** goes up considerably if you bet the limit (from 2 to as many as 45 coins).

Progressive slots are groups of linked machines (sometimes spread over several casinos) where the jackpot gets bigger every few moments (just as lottery jackpots build up). Bigger and better games keep showing up; for example, there's Anchor Gaming's much-imitated **Wheel of Gold,** wherein if you get the right symbol, you get to spin a roulette wheel, which guarantees you a win of a serious number of coins. **Totem Pole** is the Godzilla of slot machines, a behemoth that allows you to spin up to three reels at once (provided you put in the limit).

Other gimmick machines include the popular **Wheel of Fortune** machines; slots that have a gorilla attempt to climb the Empire State Building, heading up as you win; and machines with themes like Elvis or the Three Stooges. And, of course, there are always those **giant slot machines,** gimmicky devices found in almost every casino. They may not win as often as regular slots (though there is no definite word on it one way or the other), but not only are they just plain fun to spin, they often turn into audience-participation gambling, as watchers gather to cheer you on to victory.

Nickel slots, which for a long time had been overlooked, relegated to a lonely spot somewhere by a back wall because they were not as profitable for the casinos as quarter and dollar slots, are making a comeback. Many machines now offer a 45-nickel maximum (meaning a larger bet on those machines than on the five-quarter-maximum slots), and gamblers have been flocking to them. As a result, more cash is pocketed by the casino (which keeps a higher percentage of cash off of nickel slots than it does off of quarter slots), which is happy to accommodate this trend by offering up more and more nickel slots. (See how this all works? Are you paying attention?)

The biggest trend in Vegas, though, is the use of cashless machines. When gambling with these machines, players insert their money, they play, and when they cash out, they get—instead of the comforting sound of coins cascading out into the tray—a little paper ticket with their total winnings on it. (Those of us who find the sound of the coins pouring out a comfort are only slightly pleased to learn that the noise plays, as a computer-generated audio effect, when the ticket is disgorged.) Hand in your ticket at a cashier's window and you get your winnings. It's not

nearly as viscerally satisfying, but it is the wave of the future; many of the casinos are already entirely cashless, and the rest are on their way. Why take this cheap thrill from us? Because it saves gambling time (instead of waiting for the flow of coins to stop, you can grab your ticket and pop it into another machine), it saves maintenance time (keeping the machines stocked with coins), and the casinos no longer need worry about having enough quarters on hand. I am not pleased about this.

Are there surefire ways to win on a slot machine? No. But you can lose more slowly. The slot machines use minicomputers known as random number generators (RNGs) to determine the winning combinations on a machine; depending on how many numbers have been programmed into the RNG, some machines are going to be "looser" than others. A bank of empty slots probably (but not certainly) means the machines are tight. Go find a line where lots of people are sitting around with trays full of money. (Of course, yours will be the one that doesn't hit.) A good rule of thumb is that if your slot doesn't hit something in four or five pulls, leave it and go find another. It's not as though you won't have some choice in the matter. Also, each casino has a bank of slots that they advertise as more loose or with a bigger payback. Try these. It's what they want you to do, but what the heck.

Sports Books

Most of the larger hotels in Las Vegas have sports-book operations, which look a lot like commodities-futures trading boards. In some, almost as

large as theaters, you can sit comfortably, occasionally in recliners and sometimes with your own video screen, and watch ballgames, fights, and, at some casinos, horse races on huge TV screens. To add to your enjoyment, there's usually a deli/bar nearby that serves sandwiches, hot dogs, soft drinks, and beer. As a matter of fact, some of the best sandwiches in Las Vegas are served next to the sports books.

Sports books take bets on virtually every sport (and not just who'll win, but what the final score will be, who'll be first to hit a home run, who'll be MVP, who'll wear red shoes, you name it). They are best during important playoff games or big horse races, when everyone in the place is watching the same event—shrieking, shouting, and moaning, sometimes in unison. Joining in with a cheap bet (so you feel like you too have a personal stake in the matter) makes for bargain entertainment.

Video Poker

Rapidly gaining on slots in popularity, video poker works the same way as regular poker, except you play against the machine. You are dealt a hand, you pick which cards to keep and which to discard, and then you get your new hand. And, it is hoped, you collect your winnings. This is somewhat more of a challenge and more active than slots because you have some control (or at least the illusion of control) over your fate, and it's easier than playing actual poker with a table full of folks who probably take it very seriously.

There are a number of varieties of this machine, with **Jacks or Better, Deuces Wild,** and so forth. Be sure to study your machine before you sit down. (The best returns are offered on the **Bonus Poker** machines; the payback for a pair of Jacks or better is two times your bet, and three times for three of a kind.) The Holy Grail of video-poker machines is the 9/6 (it pays nine coins for a full house, six coins for a flush), but you'll need to pray a lot before you find one in town. Some machines offer **double down:** After you have won, you get a chance to draw cards against the machine, with the higher card the winner. If you win, your money is doubled and you are offered a chance to go again. Your money can increase nicely during this time, and you can also lose it all very quickly, which is most annoying.

Technology is catching up with video poker, too. Now they even have touch screens, which offer a variety of different poker games, blackjack, and video slots—just touch your screen and choose your poison. ●

The
Savvy Traveler

WELCOME
TO Fabulous
DOWNTOWN
LAS VEGAS
NEVADA

Before You Go

Government Tourist Offices

For advance information, call or write the **Las Vegas Convention and Visitors Authority**, 3150 Paradise Rd., Las Vegas, NV 89109 (☎ **877/ VISIT-LV** or 702/892-0711; www.visit lasvegas.com).

For information on all of Nevada, including Las Vegas, contact the Nevada **Commission on Tourism** (☎ **800/638-2328**; www.travel nevada.com).

The Best Times to Go

Most of a Las Vegas vacation is usually spent indoors, so you can have a good time here year-round. That said, the most pleasant seasons in this area are spring and fall (when crowds are everywhere and prices are high), especially if you want to experience the great outdoors. Summers here mean ultrahigh temps, but also fewer crowds and lower prices. Winters can get downright cold, so you can forget about using the hotel pool (almost all are outdoors and many close from Labor Day to Memorial Day); but prices in early December and mid-January usually descend into good-value territory.

Holidays (especially New Year's) in Vegas are a mob scene—and for Vegas, "holiday" includes Super Bowl Sunday, anytime during the NCAA Basketball Championships (especially the Final Four), boxing matches, and all other important pro and college sporting events. Hotel prices skyrocket not only during the holidays, but also when big conventions and special events take place. If a major convention is to be held during your trip, you might want to change your date. You can check convention dates by contacting the **Las Vegas**

Convention and Visitors Authority (☎ **877/VISIT-LV** or 702/892-7575; www.visitlasvegas.com).

Festivals & Special Events

Before you arrive, contact the **Las Vegas Convention and Visitors Authority** (☎ **877/VISIT-LV** or 702/ 892-7575; www.visitlasvegas.com), or the **Chamber of Commerce** (☎ **702/735-1616**; www.lvchamber. com), to find out what other events are scheduled during your visit. Once you're in town, check *Las Vegas Weekly* (www.lasvegas weekly.com), the free magazines you'll find in your hotel room, or **www.lasvegasevents.com**.

MAR. The start of spring sees the running of two of the most important **NASCAR/Winston Cup** races in the country. Held at the **Las Vegas Motor Speedway**, 7000 Las Vegas Blvd. N. (☎ **800/644-4444**; www. lvms.com), the Sam's Town 300 and the UAW-DaimlerChrysler 400 attract thousands of racing fans each year.

JUNE. The annual **CineVegas Film Festival** (☎ **702/992-7979**; www. cinevegas.com), usually held in early June, is growing in popularity and prestige, with film debuts from both independent and major studios, plus lots of celebrities hanging around for the big parties. The **World Series of Poker,** held at **The Rio All-Suite Hotel & Casino** (3700 W. Flamingo Rd.; ☎ **800/PLAY-RIO**) in June, July, and August, is *the* gambling event in Vegas, featuring high-stakes gamblers and showbiz personalities. There are daily events with entry stakes ranging from $125 to $5,000. For a chance at the main event's $12-million purse, players must ante up

---

Previous Page: The Strip might be more famous today, but Downtown Las Vegas is where it all began.

LAS VEGAS'S AVERAGE TEMPERATURES (°F/°C) & PRECIPITATION

	JAN	FEB	MAR	APR	MAY	JUNE
High °F	57	63	69	78	88	99
High °C	14	17	21	26	31	37
Low °F	37	41	47	54	63	72
Low °C	3	5	8	12	17	22
AVG. PRECIP.						
(in.)	.59	.69	.59	.15	.24	.08
(cm)	1.5	1.8	1.5	.4	.6	.2

	JULY	AUG	SEPT	OCT	NOV	DEC
High °F	104	102	94	81	66	57
High °C	40	39	34	27	19	14
Low °F	78	77	69	57	44	37
Low °C	26	25	21	14	7	3
AVG. PRECIP.						
(in.)	.44	.45	.31	.24	.31	.40
(cm)	1.1	1.1	.8	.6	.8	1.0

$10,000. You can crowd around the tables and watch for free, or if you want to avoid the throngs you can catch a lot of it on TV. For more information visit **www.worldseriesofpoker.com**.

OCT. Pro golf's best players hit the greens at the televised 4-day PGA **Frys.com Open** (☎ **702/242-3000**), which is played at TPC Summerlin and TPC at the Canyons in October.

NOV. Some of the world's top comics and comedy troupes laugh it up at **The Comedy Festival** (☎ **800/634-6661;** www.thecomedyfestival.com). The event also includes workshops, film festivals, and more. Held in mid-November, its primary host casino is Caesars Palace.

DEC. The **National Finals Rodeo** (☎ **866/388-3267** or 702/739-3267; www.nfrexperience.com) is the Super Bowl of rodeos, attended by about 200,000 people each year, suddenly turning Vegas into Cowboy Country. Order tickets as far in advance as possible. In mid-December, the winners of college football's Mid-American Conference and the Big West conference square off

against each other in the **Las Vegas Bowl.** The action takes place at the 32,000-seat Sam Boyd Stadium. Call **702/732-3912** or visit www.lvbowl.com for ticket information. **New Year's Eve** is the biggest day of the year on the Vegas calendar; reserve your hotel room early (and be prepared to pay top dollar). Downtown, at the Fremont Street Experience, there is a big block party with two dramatic countdowns to midnight at 9pm (midnight on the East Coast) and midnight. The Strip is usually closed to street traffic and hundreds of thousands of people pack the area for the festivities.

Weather

Vegas isn't always hot, but when it is hot, it's melting. Still, the humidity averages a low 22% and even on hot days there's apt to be a breeze. Also, except on the hottest of summer days, there is relief at night, when temperatures drop by as much as 20°F. Keep in mind, however, that this is the desert and it's not hot year-round; it can get quite cold, especially in the winter. That summer breeze can become a cold, biting, strong wind of up to 40 mph (64kmph) and more in winter. And there are entire portions of the year when you won't be using your hotel pool at all (even if you want to, because most of the hotels close huge chunks of their fabulous pool areas for "the season," which can be as long as from Labor Day to Memorial Day). If you aren't traveling at the height of summer, bring a jacket. Also remember sunscreen and a hat—even if it's not all that hot, you can burn easily and very quickly.

Useful Websites

- **www.vegas4visitors.com:** A sweeping and comprehensive site on Las Vegas, with lots of practical advice and strong opinions.

- **www.lvchamber.com:** The Chamber of Commerce's official website has a calendar of events, lots of practical tips, info on getting married in Vegas, and more.

- **www.vegas.com:** Using resources from the city's free weeklies, this site features plenty of locally written reviews and opinions.

- **www.lasvegasadvisor.com:** Veteran Vegas bargain hunter Anthony DeCurtis gives out all sorts of valuable tips, plus trivia, and lots of cool info.

- **www.visitlasvegas.com:** The Convention and Visitor Bureau's official site is well organized by subject matter and offers lots of information and practical tips on hotels, dining, entertainment, and more. There's also information on discount vacation packages.

- **www.travelaxe.net:** This site's ultrauseful (and free) program can help you search multiple hotels' sites at once. It has lots of hotel options for Las Vegas.

Cellphones

It's a good bet your phone will work in Las Vegas, but take a look at your wireless company's coverage map on its website before heading out.

Car Rentals

If you stick to one section of the Strip, or concentrate solely on Downtown, then you technically don't need a car. But I strongly suggest getting one, especially if you plan on doing some serious touring or are staying off the Strip. Parking won't cost you anything beyond valet tips on the Strip, and a car will definitely make it easier to get around.

National companies with outlets in Las Vegas include **Alamo** (☎ **877/227-8367;** www.goalamo.com), **Avis** (☎ **800/230-4898;** www.avis.com), **Budget** (☎ **800/527-0700;** www.budget.com), **Dollar** (☎ **800/800-3665;** www.dollar.com), **Enterprise** (☎ **800/736-8227;** www.enterprise.com), **Hertz** (☎ **800/654-3131;** www.hertz.com), **National** (☎ **800/227-7368;** www.nationalcar.com), **Payless** (☎ **800/729-5377;** www.paylesscarrental.com), and **Thrifty** (☎ **800/847-4389;** www.thrifty.com).

If you're visiting from abroad and plan to rent a car in the United States, keep in mind that foreign driver's licenses are usually recognized in the U.S., but you should get an international one if your home license is not in English.

For decent car-rental rates, consult the major travel websites (Travelocity.com, Expedia.com) to comparison shop. You should also check out **Breezenet.com,** which offers domestic car-rental discounts with some of the most competitive rates around.

Getting **There**

By Plane

The following airlines have regularly scheduled flights into Vegas (some of these are regional carriers, so they may not all fly from your point of origin): AeroMexico, Air Canada, Alaska Airlines, Allegiant Air, Aloha Air, American/American Eagle, Ameri-can Trans Air, Continental, Delta/Skywest, Frontier Airlines, Harmony Airways, Hawaiian Airlines, Japan Airlines, JetBlue, Mexicana Airlines, Midwest Airlines, Northwest Airlines, Philippine Airlines, Southwest Airlines, Spirit Airlines, Ted Airlines, United Airlines, U.S. Airways, and Virgin Atlantic Airways.

Las Vegas is served by **McCarran International Airport** (☎ 702/261-5211; www.mccarran.com), just a few minutes' drive from the southern end of the Strip, where the bulk of casinos and hotels are concentrated. This big, modern airport is rather unique in that it includes several casino areas with more than 1,000 slot machines.

Getting to your hotel from the airport is a cinch. **Bell Trans** (☎ 800/274-7433; www.bell-trans.com) runs 20-passenger minibuses daily between the airport (shuttles depart just west of the baggage-claim area) and all major Las Vegas hotels and motels (7:45am–midnight). Several other companies offer similar ventures—just stand outside on the curb, and one will be flagged for you. Cost is determined by distance, but the range is about $5.50 per person each way to the Strip and Convention locations to $7 to Downtown. Other similarly priced shuttles run 24 hours and can be found in the same place.

Even less expensive are **Citizens Area Transit (CAT)** buses (☎ 792/CAT-RIDE; www.rtcsouthernnevada.com/cat). The no. 108 bus departs from the airport and takes you to the Stratosphere, where you can transfer to the no. 301, which stops close to most Strip- and Convention Center–area hotels. The no. 109 goes from the airport to the Downtown Transportation Center (at Casino Center Blvd. and Stewart Ave). Bus fares are $2 for adults, 60¢ for seniors and children 6 to 17, and free for children under 6. It's cheaper than a shuttle, but it might not be enough to put up with the added hassle (buses do not stop in front of hotel main entrances, while shuttles do—you could be in for a long walk if you opt for the bus), especially if you have luggage.

You can also take a taxi from the airport to the Strip (around $13–$14) or Downtown (about $30); the maximum number of passengers allowed in a cab is five (infants and kids included).

By Car

The main highway connecting Las Vegas with the rest of the country is **I-15;** it links Montana, Idaho, and Utah with Southern California. From the east, take **I-70** or **I-80** west to Kingman, Arizona, and then **U.S. 93** north to Downtown Las Vegas (Fremont St.). From the south, take **I-10** west to Phoenix and then U.S. 93 north to Las Vegas. From San Francisco, take **I-80** east to Reno and then **U.S. 95** south to Las Vegas.

Getting **Around**

By Public Transportation

The **no. 301** bus operated by **CAT** (☎ 702/CAT-RIDE; www.rtc southernnevada.com/cat) plies a route between the Downtown Transportation Center (at Casino Center Blvd. and Stewart Ave.) and a few miles beyond the southern end of the Strip. The fare is $2 for adults, 60¢ for seniors and children 6 to 17, and free for children under 6. A low $5 buys an all-day pass. CAT buses run all day and are wheelchair accessible. Exact change is required.

The Deuce (☎ **702/CAT-RIDE;** www.rtcsouthernnevada.com/deuce) is a fleet of 24-hour double-decker buses that run the length of the Strip and operate extended routes to Downtown, the South Strip Transfer Center (near but not at the airport), and the Paradise Road/Convention Center area. A one-way ride is $2 for adults, $1 for seniors 62 and older and children 6 to 17, and free for those under 6. A remarkably cheap $5 buys you an all-day pass that lets you get on and off as many times as you like and also lets you ride other RTC buses all day. Exact change is required.

Also available is a classic street-car replica run by **Las Vegas Strip Trolley** (☎ **702/382-1404;** www.striptrolley.com). Like the buses, it runs northward from Hacienda Avenue, stopping at all major hotels en route to the Sahara, and then loops back from the Las Vegas Hilton. It does not, however, go to the Stratosphere or Downtown. Trolleys run about every 15 minutes daily between 9:30am and 1:30am. The fare is $2.50 for a single one-way ride or $6.50 (free for children under 5) for an all-day pass. Exact change is required.

By Taxi

Cabs line up in front of all major hotels and are an easy way to get around town (if not the cheapest). Cabs charge $3.20 at the meter drop and 25¢ for each additional ⅛ mile, plus an additional $1.20 fee for being picked up at the airport; time-based penalties are assessed when you get stuck in a traffic jam. You can often save money by sharing a cab—up to five people can ride for the same fare. Do not attempt to hail a taxi from anywhere but an approved stand when you're on the Strip; it's illegal for cabs to pick up fares off the street.

Cab companies in the area include **Desert Cab Company** (☎ 702/386-9102), **Whittlesea Blue Cab** (☎ 702/394-6111), and **Yellow/Checker Cab/Star Company** (☎ 702/873-2000).

By Monorail

The Las Vegas Monorail (www.lv monorail.com) is a rider's best shot at getting from one end of the Strip to the other with a minimum of frustration (though the expense can add up). The 4-mile (6.4km) monorail route runs from the MGM Grand at the southern end of the Strip to the Sahara at the northern end, with stops at Paris/Bally's, The Flamingo, Harrah's, the Las Vegas Convention Center, and the Las Vegas Hilton along the way. Keep in mind that some of the physical stops are not as geographically close as their namesakes, so there can be an unexpected additional (*very* long) walk from the monorail stop to wherever you need to go.

Trains can accommodate more than 200 passengers (standing and sitting) and make the end-to-end run in about 15 minutes. Operating hours are Monday through Thursday from 7am to 2am and Friday through Sunday from 7am to 3am. Fares are an expensive $5 for a one-way ride, no matter what distance you travel; discount multiride/multiday passes are sold and can bring the price of a ride down to about $3.50. Kids ages 5 and under ride free.

By Car

If you plan on venturing beyond the immediate area surrounding your hotel, a rental car is your best bet (if not a must). The Strip is too spread out for walking (and often Las Vegas is too hot or too cold to make those strolls pleasant), Downtown is too far away for a cheap cab ride, and public transportation is often ineffective in getting you where you want to go. You should note that places with addresses some 60 blocks east or west of the Strip are actually less than a 10-minute drive—provided there is no traffic.

Having advocated renting a car, I should warn you that traffic is getting worse, and it's harder and harder to get around town with any certain swiftness. A general rule of thumb is to avoid driving on the Strip whenever you can, and avoid driving at all during peak rush hours (8–9:30am and 4:30–6pm). Notable back roads that can help you access the major hotels while avoiding the Strip include Harmon Avenue, Koval Lane, and Frank Sinatra Drive. Get yourself a good map (most Vegas car-rental agencies hand out excellent ones) and familiarize yourself with chosen routes before you set out.

Parking in Vegas is usually a pleasure because all the casino hotels offer free valet service. That means for a mere $1 to $2 tip you can park right at the door, though valet parking usually fills up on busy nights (or is offered to guests only on busy evenings). In those cases, you can use the gigantic self parking lots that all hotels have.

On Foot

The best way to navigate Downtown is on your own two feet, especially in the Glitter Gulch area on Fremont Street, which is now pedestrian-only. Walking also makes sense on the Strip, if you're going short distances and want to avoid traffic tie-ups. I know people who walk up and down the Strip as a matter of course, but despite the flat terrain, it can get very tiring (especially when it might very well be a mile from your room to a hotel's entrance). Keep in mind the following:

1. **Distances in Las Vegas can be very deceiving.** That hotel that looks really close to where you're standing may be more than a mile away. And if it's broiling hot outside or freezing cold (and it can get very chilly in winter), that may be the longest mile you've ever walked.

2. **Don't even think of jaywalking.** Pushing your luck in this area will likely result in you getting hurt. Badly. Use the provided escalators and pedestrian walkways to cross the Strip and its major side streets.

3. **Make use of indoor walkways and free shuttles.** A free monorail connects Mandalay Bay with Luxor and Excalibur (and indoor walkways connect all three hotels as well), and a free tram shuttles between The Mirage and TI Las Vegas. And you can walk from Paris Las Vegas to Bally's without ever stepping outside.

Fast **Facts**

APARTMENT RENTALS Note that most home and apartment rentals in Las Vegas are located off the Strip and that a car becomes a necessity if you go this route. **Las Vegas Home Solutions** (☎ 800/856-2426 or 702/361-7474; www.lasvegashome solutions.com) is a service-oriented company that manages 50 or so homes in the Vegas area. Another reputable option, **Las Vegas Retreats** (☎ 888/887-0951 or 702/966-2761; www.lasvegasretreats. com), offers slightly more upscale accommodations.

AREA CODES The area code for Las Vegas is **702.**

ATMS/CASHPOINTS An ATM (automated teller machine) is pretty much right at your elbow no matter where you are in Vegas, particularly in casinos.

The **Cirrus** (☎ 800/424-7787; www.mastercard.com) and **PLUS** (☎ 800/843-7587; www.visa.com) networks span the globe; look at the back of your bank card to see which network you're on, then call or check online for ATM locations in Vegas.

Be sure you know your personal identification number (PIN) and daily withdrawal limit before you depart. *Note:* Remember that many banks impose a fee every time you use a card at another bank's ATM, and that fee can be higher for international transactions (up to $5 or more) than for domestic ones (which typically run $2–$3 in Las Vegas).

BABYSITTERS Contact **Around the Clock Child Care** (☎ 800/798-6768 or 702/365-1040). In business since 1987, this reputable company clears its sitters with the health department, the sheriff, and the FBI and carefully screens references. Rates are $70 for 4 hours for one or two children, $15 for each additional children,

hour, with surcharges for additional children and on holidays. Call at least 3 hours in advance.

BANKS Banks are generally open from 9 or 10am to 5 and sometimes 6pm, and most have Saturday hours.

BUSINESS HOURS Casinos and most bars are open 24 hours a day. Stores generally open between 9 and 10am and close between 7 and 8pm Monday through Saturday; on Sunday they usually open around 11am and close by 6pm. Stores in the casino hotels sometimes keep longer hours.

CONSULATES & EMBASSIES All embassies are located in the nation's capitol, Washington, D.C. Some consulates are located in major U.S. cities and most nations have missions to the United Nations in New York City. For addresses and phone numbers of embassies in Washington, D.C., call (☎ 202/555-1212), or log on to www.embassy. org/embassies.

CUSTOMS U.S. airports have considerably beefed up security clearances in the years since the terrorist attacks of 9/11, and clearing Customs and Immigration can take as long as 2 hours, especially on summer weekends.

DENTISTS Hotels usually keep lists of dentists, should you need one. For dental referrals, you can also call the **Southern Nevada Dental Society** (☎ 702/733-8700; www. sndsonline.org) weekdays from 9am to noon and 1 to 5pm; when the office is closed, a recording will tell you who to call for emergency service.

DINING Vegas is used to all kinds, so unless a restaurant specifies a dress code (and if you're headed to a "name" restaurant, be sure to check in advance), business-casual attire should get you in anywhere. Always make reservations way in advance for higher-end locations (a month early isn't unheard of).

In the budget department, you'll almost always save money by splurging at lunch instead of dinner; prices can be 20% to 50% less at lunchtime in some fancy restaurants. Most restaurants start serving lunch between 11:30am and noon; dinner usually starts at around 5:30pm.

DOCTORS Hotels usually keep lists of doctors, should you need one. For physician referrals, call the **Desert Springs Hospital** (☎ **702/ 388-4888;** www.desertsprings hospital.net). Hours are Monday to Friday from 8am to 8pm and Saturday from 9am to 3pm.

DRUGSTORES There's a 24-hour **Walgreen's** (which also has a 1-hr. photo) at 3763 Las Vegas Blvd. S. (☎ **702/739-9638**), almost directly across from the Monte Carlo. **CVS** is a large 24-hour drugstore and pharmacy close to the Strip at 1360 E. Flamingo Rd , at Maryland Parkway (☎ **702/731-5373** for the pharmacy, 702/737-0595 for general merchandise). **White Cross Drugs,** 1700 Las Vegas Blvd. S. (☎ **702/382-1733**), will make pharmacy deliveries to your hotel during the day.

ELECTRICITY Like Canada, the United States uses 110–120 volts AC (60 cycles), compared to 220–240 volts AC (50 cycles) in most of Europe, Australia, and New Zealand. If your small appliances use 220–240 volts, you'll need a 110-volt transformer and a plug adapter with two flat parallel pins to operate them here. Downward converters that change 220–240 volts to 110 -120 volts are difficult to find in the United States, so bring one with you.

EMERGENCIES Dial ☎ **911** to contact the police or fire department or to call an ambulance.

EVENT LISTINGS In order to make sure the show you want isn't dark during your visit, or to see what headliner has hit town, you can check events through the following: The *Las Vegas Review Journal* (www. lvrj.com) is the city's daily paper, and its Friday edition carries a special "Weekend" section with a guide to shows and other entertainment options. *City Life* (www.lasvegascity life.com) and *Las Vegas Weekly* (www.lasvegasweekly.com) are free weekly alternative papers with plenty of club and bar listings. *Show Biz Weekly* (www.showbizweekly.com) and *What's On* (www.whats-on.com) are the free magazines you usually find in your hotel room. They are mostly rehashes of press releases, but often have discount coupons for some shows, buffets, and more.

FAMILY TRAVEL Think twice (and then again) before you bring kids to Vegas these days. The "Vegas is for families" concept died years ago, so not only is there considerably less to do with children, but you have to do it while constantly distracting them from casinos, four-story-tall billboards featuring nearly bare bottoms, and other adult material. On top of that, some casino hotels ban children if they aren't guests of that property—and they will check your room keys for proof. If you must bring your children to town, I suggest you look at our special Vegas with Kids tour on p 31. Another good source of information is *Frommer's Las Vegas with Kids.*

GAMBLING LAWS You must be 21 years of age to enter, much less gamble in, any casino. If you look young, carry your identification with you as you may be asked to prove your age. Most casinos are open 24 hours a day.

HOLIDAYS Banks, government offices, post offices, and many stores, restaurants, and museums are closed (but not the casinos!) on the following legal national holidays: January 1 (New Year's Day), the third Monday in January (Martin Luther King Day), the third Monday in February (Presidents' Day), the last Monday in May (Memorial Day), July 4 (Independence Day), the first Monday in September (Labor Day), the second Monday in October (Columbus Day), November 11 (Veterans' Day/Armistice Day), the fourth Thursday in November (Thanksgiving Day), and December 25 (Christmas). The Tuesday after the first Monday in November is Election Day, a federal government holiday in presidential-election years (held every 4 years, and next in 2008).

For more information on holidays see "Festivals & Special Events," earlier in this chapter.

HOSPITALS   Emergency services are available 24 hours a day at **University Medical Center,** 1800 W. Charleston Blvd., at Shadow Lane (☎ **702/383-2000;** www.umc-cares. org); the emergency-room entrance is on the corner of Hastings and Rose streets. **Sunrise Hospital and Medical Center,** 3186 Maryland Pkwy., between Desert Inn Road and Sahara Avenue (☎ **702/731-8080;** www. sunrisehospital.com), also has a 24-hour emergency room.

For more minor problems, try the **Harmon Medical Urgent Care Center**—the closest to the Strip—at 105 E. Harmon at Koval Lane, near the MGM Grand (☎ **702/796-1116;** www.harmonmedicalcenter.com). It's open 24 hours, it has X-ray machines, and there is a pharmacy on-site.

INSURANCE   For Domestic Visitors: Trip-cancellation insurance will help retrieve your money if you have to back out of a trip or depart early, or if your travel supplier goes bankrupt. Trip cancellation traditionally covers such events as sickness, natural disasters, and State Department

advisories. The latest news in trip-cancellation insurance is the availability of **"any-reason"** cancellation coverage—which costs more but covers cancellations made for any reason. You won't get back 100% of your prepaid trip cost, but you'll be refunded a substantial portion. **TravelSafe** (☎ **888/885-7233;** www.travelsafe.com) offers this coverage, and Expedia offers any-reason cancellation coverage for its air-hotel packages.

For details, contact one of the following recommended insurers: **Access America** (☎ 866/807-3982; www.accessamerica.com); **Travel Guard International** (☎ 800/826-4919; www.travelguard.com); **Travel Insured International** (☎ 800/243-3174; www.travelinsured.com); and **Travelex Insurance Services** (☎ 888/457-4602; www.travelex-insurance.com).

Medical Insurance: Although it's not required of travelers, health insurance is highly recommended. Most health-insurance policies cover you if you get sick away from home—but check your coverage before you leave.

International visitors should note that unlike many European countries, the United States does not usually offer free or low-cost medical care to its citizens or visitors. Doctors and hospitals are expensive, and in most cases will require advance payment or proof of coverage before they render their services. Packages such as **Europ Assistance's "Worldwide Healthcare Plan"** are sold by European automobile clubs and travel agencies at attractive rates. **Worldwide Assistance Services, Inc.** (☎ **800/777-8710;** www.worldwide assistance.com), is the agent for Europ Assistance in the United States. Though lack of health insurance may prevent you from being admitted to a hospital in nonemergencies, don't worry about being left on a street corner to die: The American way is to fix you now and bill the living daylights out of you later.

Insurance for British Travelers: Most big travel agents offer their own insurance and will probably try to sell you their package when you book a holiday. Think before you sign. **Britain's Consumers' Association** recommends that you insist on seeing the policy and reading the fine print before buying travel insurance. **The Association of British Insurers** (☎ 020/7600-3333; www. abi.org.uk) gives advice by phone and publishes *Holiday Insurance,* a free guide to policy provisions and prices. You might also shop around for better deals: Try **Columbus Direct** (☎ 020/7375-0011; www. columbusdirect.net).

Insurance for Canadian Travelers: Canadians should check with their provincial health-plan offices or call **Health Canada** (☎ 866/225-0709; www.hc-sc.gc.ca) to find out the extent of their coverage and what documentation and receipts they must take home in case they are treated in the United States.

Lost-Luggage Insurance: On flights within the U.S., checked baggage is covered up to $2,500 per ticketed passenger. On flights outside the U.S. (and on U.S. portions of international trips), baggage coverage is limited to approximately $9.07 per pound, up to approximately $635 per checked bag. If you plan to check items more valuable than what's covered by the standard liability, see if your homeowner's policy covers your valuables, get baggage insurance as part of your comprehensive travel-insurance package, or buy Travel Guard's "BagTrak" product.

If your luggage is lost, immediately file a lost-luggage claim at the airport, detailing the luggage

contents. Most airlines require that you report delayed, damaged, or lost baggage within 4 hours of arrival. The airlines are required to deliver luggage, once found, directly to your house or destination free of charge.

INTERNET ACCESS Many Las Vegas hotels offer Internet service through their room TVs with a wireless keyboard (provided) or through Wi-Fi (wireless fidelity). Figure, on average, that you'll pay about $13 a day for the privilege.

To find cybercafes in your destination, check **www.cybercaptive.com** and **www.cybercafe.com**.

More and more hotels, cafes, and retailers are signing on as Wi-Fi "hot spots." Mac owners have their own networking technology, Apple Air-Port. To find public Wi-Fi hot spots at your destination, go to **www.jiwire. com**; its Hotspot Finder holds the world's largest directory of public wireless hot spots.

LIMOUSINES Hotels will often provide airport limos for high rollers or VIP guests—in the latter case, that often means someone merely staying in a higher-level room. Ask and see. Otherwise, try **Las Vegas Limo** (☎ 888/696-4400 or 702/736-1419) or **Bell Trans** (☎ 888/274-7433 or 702/384-2283).

LIQUOR LAWS The legal age for purchase and consumption of alcoholic beverages is 21; proof of age is required and often requested at bars, nightclubs, and restaurants, so it's always a good idea to carry ID when you go out.

Beer, wine, and liquor are all sold in all kinds of stores pretty much around the clock, plus cocktail waitresses are ready to ply you moments after you sit down at a slot machine or gaming table. You won't have a hard time finding a drink in this town.

Do not carry open containers of alcohol in a car or any public area at isn't zoned for alcohol consumption. Note that it is also forbidden to have an open container of alcohol in a vehicle, even if you're the passenger. The Strip and Fremont Street in Downtown Las Vegas are the only areas in town where you can have open containers on public sidewalks; otherwise, the police can fine you on the spot. And nothing will ruin your trip faster than getting a citation for DUI ("driving under the influence"), so don't even think about driving while intoxicated.

LOST PROPERTY   Be sure to tell all of your credit card companies the minute you discover your wallet has been lost or stolen, and file a report at the nearest police precinct. Your credit card company or insurer may require a police report number or record of the loss. Most credit card companies have an emergency toll-free number to call if your card is lost or stolen; they may be able to wire you a cash advance immediately or deliver an emergency credit card in a day or two. Visa's U.S. emergency number is ☎ **800/847-2911** or 410/581-9994. American Express cardholders and traveler's check holders should call ☎ **800/221-7282.** MasterCard holders should call ☎ **800/307-7309** or 636/722-7111. For other credit cards, call the toll-free number directory at ☎ **800/555-1212.**

MAIL & POSTAGE   At press time, domestic postage rates were 26¢ for a postcard and 41¢ for a letter. For international mail, a first-class letter of up to 1 ounce costs 90¢ (69¢ to Canada and Mexico); a first-class postcard costs the same as a letter. For more information go to **www.usps.com** and click on "Calculate Postage."

MONEY   Vegas runs on money, in all its forms. Most places, except the smallest stores and restaurants, take credit cards. The gaming tables and slot machines run on cold hard cash. If you prefer using traveler's checks, they are accepted in many places in Las Vegas.

American Express (☎ **800/807-6233;** ☎ **800/221-7282** for card holders); **Visa** (☎ **800/732-1322**); and **MasterCard** (☎ **800/223-9920**) all issue traveler's checks.

Be sure to keep a copy of the traveler's checks serial numbers separate from your checks in the event that they are stolen or lost. You'll get a refund faster if you know the numbers.

PARKING   Free valet parking is one of the great pleasures of Las Vegas and well worth the $1 or $2 tip (given when the car is returned) to save walking a city block from the far reaches of a hotel parking lot. Valet service can fill up late on weekend nights, but the self-parking lots are vast.

PASSPORTS   International visitors should always keep a photocopy of their passport with them when traveling. If your passport is lost or stolen, having a copy significantly facilitates the reissuing process at a local consulate or embassy. Keep your passport and other valuables in your room's safe or in the hotel safe. See "Consulates & Embassies," earlier in this chapter, for more information.

POLICE   For nonemergencies call ☎ **702/795-3111.** For emergencies, call **911.**

SAFETY   While otherwise quite safe for a big city, in Las Vegas vast amounts of money are always on display, and criminals find many easy marks. At gaming tables and slot machines, men should keep wallets well concealed and out of reach of pickpockets, and women should keep handbags in plain sight (on laps). If you win a big jackpot, ask the pit boss or slot attendant to cut you a check rather than give you cash; it's also perfectly reasonable to ask security to escort you to your car. Outside casinos, popular spots for pickpockets and thieves are restaurants and outdoor shows. Stay alert. Unless your hotel room has an in-room safe, check your valuables in a safe-deposit box at the front desk.

SMOKING Smoking has been banned in Vegas restaurants, and in any bar that serves food. And most poker rooms in Las Vegas do not permit smoking. Otherwise, Las Vegas remains quite smoker-friendly.

SPECTATOR SPORTS Las Vegas isn't known for its sports teams. Except for minor-league baseball and hockey, the only consistent spectator sports are those at UNLV. For the pros, if watching Triple A ball (in this case, a Los Angeles Dodgers farm team) in potentially triple-degree heat sounds like fun, the charmingly named and even-better merchandized **Las Vegas 51s** (as in Area 51, as in alien-themed gear!) are a great bet. This ball team's schedule and ticket info are available by calling ☎ **702/386-7200** or online at **www.lv51.com**. Ice hockey might be a better climate choice; get info for the **Las Vegas Wranglers** at **www.lasvegaswranglers.com** or by calling ☎ **702/471-7825.**

The **Las Vegas Motor Speedway** (p 35) is a major venue for car racing that draws major NASCAR events to Las Vegas.

Because the city has several top-notch sporting arenas, important annual events take place in Las Vegas. The PGA Tour's **Frys.com Open** takes place in Las Vegas each October. The **National Finals Rodeo** is held in UNLV's Thomas and Mack Center each December. From time to time, you'll also find NBA exhibition games, professional ice-skating competitions, or gymnastics exhibitions.

Finally, Las Vegas is well-known as a major location for boxing matches. These are held in several Strip hotels, most often at Caesars or the MGM Grand, but sometimes at The Mirage. Tickets are hard to come by and quite expensive.

Tickets to sporting events at hotels are available either through **Ticketmaster** (☎ 702/893-3000; www.ticketmaster.com) or through the hotels themselves.

TAXES Sales tax is 7%. The Clark County hotel room tax is 9%, and in Henderson it's 10%. The United States has no value-added tax (VAT) or other indirect tax at the national level. Every state, county, and city may levy its own local tax on all purchases, including hotel and restaurant checks and airline tickets. These taxes will not appear on price tags.

TAXIS See "By Taxi" in "Getting Around," earlier in this chapter.

TELEPHONES For **directory assistance** ("information"), dial 411; for long-distance information, dial **1,** then the appropriate area code and **555-1212.** Hotel surcharges on long-distance and local calls are astronomical, so you're usually better off using a **cellphone** or **public pay telephone**, which you'll find clearly marked in most public buildings and private establishments as well as on the street. Pay phones do not accept pennies, and few will take anything larger than a quarter.

Most long-distance and international calls can be dialed directly from any phone. **For calls within the United States and to Canada,** dial 1 followed by the area code and the seven-digit number. **For other international calls,** dial 011 followed by the country code, the city code, and the number you are calling.

CKETS To avoid surcharges and obtain better seating options, it's best to go through the box office for the show in question (some box offices can be accessed online). Top-draw shows can sell out months in advance, so try to order tickets as early as possible. Ticket agencies generally charge obscene markups and should be consulted only if you're desperate. For more information on buying discount tickets, check out p 119.

TIPPING You can get tip fatigue in Vegas, but try to remember that this city runs on the service sector and tipping is often an important part of certain workers' income. In hotels, tip bellhops at least $1 per bag ($2–$3 if you have a lot of luggage) and tip the chamber staff $1 to $2 per day (more if you've left a disaster area). Tip the doorman or concierge only if he or she has provided you with some specific service (for example, calling a cab for you or obtaining difficult-to-get theater tickets). Tip the valet-parking attendant $1 to $2 every time you get your car.

In restaurants, bars, and nightclubs, tip service staff 15% to 20% of the check, tip bartenders 10% to 15%, tip checkroom attendants $1 per garment, and tip valet-parking attendants $1 per vehicle.

As for other service personnel, tip cab drivers 15% of the fare; tip skycaps at airports at least $1 per bag ($2–$3 if you have a lot of luggage); and tip hairdressers and barbers 15% to 20%.

TOILETS There are large, clean, and often rather glamorous toilets scattered throughout every hotel casino. Just look for the signs. Some city restaurants and bars may reserve their restrooms for patrons. You can avoid arguments by paying for a cup of coffee or a soft drink, which will qualify you as a patron.

TOURIST OFFICES The main tourist office is the **Las Vegas Convention and Visitors Authority,** 3150 Paradise Rd., Las Vegas, NV 89109 (☎ **877/VISIT-LV** or 702/892-0711; www.visitlasvegas.com). They're open daily from 9am to 5pm.

Another excellent source of information is the **Las Vegas Chamber of Commerce,** 3720 Howard Hughes Pkwy., #100, Las Vegas, NV 89109 (☎ **702/735-1616;** www.lvchamber.com). Ask them to send you their *Visitor Guide,* which contains extensive information about accommodations, attractions, and more. They can answer all your Vegas questions. They are open Monday to Friday from 8am to 5pm.

TOURS Just about every hotel in town has a tour desk offering a seemingly infinite number of sightseeing opportunities in and around Las Vegas.

Gray Line (☎ **800/634-6579;** www.grayline.com) is a reputable company with a rather comprehensive roster, including 5- to 6-hour city tours (both day and evening), half-day excursions to Hoover Dam and Red Rock Canyon, and full-day trips to the Grand Canyon in Arizona. Call for details or inquire at your hotel's tour desk, where you'll also find free magazines with coupons for discounts on select tours.

For unique, personalized tours of the city and of the surrounding desert countryside, check out Char Cruze and her highly recommended **Creative Adventures** (☎ **702/893-2051**; www.creativeadventuresltd.net). A fourth-generation local, Char is a seemingly endless source of history and legend. Part raconteur, part lecturer, she's thorough, interesting, and reliable.

TRAVELERS WITH DISABILITIES On the one hand, Las Vegas is fairly well equipped for travelers with disabilities, with virtually every hotel having accessible rooms, ramps, and other requirements. On the other hand, the distance between hotels (particularly on the Strip) makes a vehicle of some sort virtually mandatory for most people with disabilities, and it may be extremely strenuous and time-consuming to get from place to place (even within a single hotel, because of the crowds).

Even if you don't intend to gamble, you still may have to go through the casino, and casinos can be quite difficult to maneuver in, particularly for a guest in a wheelchair. Casinos are usually crowded, and the machines and tables are often laid out close together, with chairs, people, and other items blocking easy access. You should also consider that it is often a long trek through larger hotels between the entrance and the room elevators (or, for that matter, anywhere in the hotel), and then add a crowded casino to the equation.

Organizations that offer a vast range of resources and assistance to travelers with disabilities include **MossRehab** (☎ 800/CALL-MOSS; www.mossresourcenet.org); the **American Foundation for the Blind (AFB)** (☎ 800/232-5463; www.afb.org); and **SATH (Society for Accessible Travel & Hospitality)** (☎ 212/447-7284; www.sath. org). **AirAmbulanceCard.com** is now partnered with SATH and allows you to preselect top-notch hospitals in case of an emergency.

Access-Able Travel Source (☎ 303/232-2979; www.access-able.com) offers a comprehensive database on travel agents from around the world with experience in accessible travel; destination-specific access information; and links to such resources as service animals, equipment rentals, and access guides.

Many travel agencies offer customized tours and itineraries for travelers with disabilities. Among them are **Flying Wheels Travel** (☎ 507/451-5005; www.flyingwheelstravel. com) and **Accessible Journeys** (☎ 800/846-4537 or 610/521-0339; www.disabilitytravel.com).

Flying with Disability (www.flying-with-disability.org) is a comprehensive information source on airplane travel. **Avis Rent a Car** (☎ 888/879-4273) has an "Avis Access" program that offers services for customers with special travel needs. These include specially outfitted vehicles with swivel seats, spinner knobs, and hand controls; mobility scooter rentals; and accessible bus service. Be sure to reserve well in advance.

British travelers should contact **Holiday Care** (☎ 0845-124-9971 in UK only; www.holidaycare.org.uk) to access a wide range of travel information and resources for seniors and travelers with disabilities.

WEATHER For current weather conditions, the radio station 970 FM does regular weather reports. You can also consult **www.weather.com**.

A Brief **History**

1831–48 Artesian spring waters of Las Vegas serve as a watering place on the Old Spanish Trail.

1855 Mormon colony of 30 missionaries establishes settlement just north of today's Downtown. Unsuccessful in its aims, the colony disbands in 1858.

1864 President Lincoln proclaims Nevada the 36th state of the Union. Las Vegas, however, is still part of the Territory of Arizona.

1865 Gold prospector Octavius D. Gass builds Las Vegas Ranch, the first permanent settlement in Las Vegas, on the site of the old Mormon colony.

1880s Due to the past 2 decades' mining fever and the fervor for westward migration, the population of Nevada soars to more than 60,000 in 1880. The Paiutes are forced onto reservations.

1895 San Francisco inventor Charles Fey creates a three-reel gambling device—the first slot machine.

1907 Fremont Street, the future "Glitter Gulch," gets electric lights.

1909 Gambling is made illegal in Nevada, but Las Vegas pays little heed.

1928 Congress authorizes construction of Boulder Dam 30 miles from Vegas, bringing thousands of workers to the area. Later, Las Vegas will capitalize on the hundreds of thousands who come to see the engineering marvel.

1931 Gambling is legalized once again.

1932 The 100-room Apache Hotel opens in Downtown.

1933 Prohibition is repealed. Las Vegas's numerous speakeasies become legit.

1934 The city's first neon sign lights up the Boulder Club Downtown.

1941 The luxurious El Rancho Vegas becomes the first hotel on the Strip. Downtown, the El Cortez opens.

1942 The Last Frontier opens 2 miles south of El Rancho Vegas.

1946 Benjamin "Bugsy" Siegel's Flamingo extends the boundaries of the Strip. Sammy Davis, Jr., debuts at the El Rancho Vegas. Downtown (now dubbed "Glitter Gulch") gets two new hotels: the Golden Nugget and the Eldorado.

1947 United Airlines inaugurates service to Las Vegas.

1948 The Thunderbird becomes the fourth hotel on the Strip.

1950 The Desert Inn adds country club panache to the Strip.

1951 The first of many atom bombs is tested in the desert just 65 miles from Las Vegas. Frank Sinatra debuts at the Desert Inn.

1952 The Club Bingo (opened in 1947) becomes the desert-themed Sahara. The Sands' Copa Room enhances the city's image as an entertainment center.

1954 The Showboat pioneers buffet meals and bowling alleys in a new area of Downtown.

1955 The Strip gets its first high-rise hotel, the nine-story Riviera, which pays Liberace the unprecedented sum of $50,000 to open its showroom.

1957 The Dunes introduces bare-breasted showgirls in its *Minsky Goes to Paris* revue. The most luxurious hotel to date, the Tropicana, opens on the Strip.

1958 The 1,065-room Stardust opens as the world's largest resort complex with a spectacular show from France, the *Lido de Paris*.

1959 The Las Vegas Convention Center goes up, presaging the city's future as a major convention city.

1960 A championship boxing match, the first of many, takes place at the Convention Center. El Rancho Vegas, the Strip's first property, burns to the ground.

1963 McCarran International Airport opens.

1966 The Aladdin, the first new hotel on the Strip in 9 years, is soon eclipsed by the unparalleled grandeur of Caesars Palace. The Four Queens opens in Downtown. Howard Hughes takes up residence at the Desert Inn; he buys up big chunks of Las Vegas and helps erase the city's gangland stigma.

1967 Elvis Presley marries Priscilla Beaulieu at the Aladdin.

1968 Circus Circus gives kids a reason to come to Las Vegas.

1973 The ultraglamorous 2,100-room MGM Grand assumes the mantle of "world's largest resort." Siegfried & Roy debut at the Tropicana.

1976 Pioneer aviator Howard Hughes dies aboard a plane en route to a Houston hospital. Dean Martin and Jerry Lewis make up after a 20-year feud.

1979 A new international arrivals building opens at McCarran International Airport.

1980 McCarran International Airport embarks on a 20-year, $785-million expansion program. A devastating fire destroys the MGM Grand, leaving 84 dead and 700 injured.

1981 Siegfried & Roy begin a record breaking run in their own show, *Beyond Belief*, at the Frontier.

1982 A Las Vegas street is named Wayne Newton Boulevard.

1989 Steve Wynn makes headlines with his spectacular Mirage, fronted by an erupting volcano.

1990s The family-friendly medieval Arthurian realm of Excalibur opens as the new "world's largest resort" titleholder with 4,032 rooms, a claim it relinquishes when the MGM Grand's new 5,005-room mega resort/theme park opens in 1993, with a *Wizard of Oz* theme. Other properties geared toward families open in the 1990s, most notably Luxor, with its pyramid and Egyptian motifs, and the pirate-themed Treasure Island. The rock-'n'-roll Hard Rock, Mandalay Bay, Bellagio, New York–New York, The Venetian, and Paris Las Vegas carry concept gaming resorts to new heights. Celebrity chefs come to town.

2004 The Strip Monorail debuts.

2005 Wynn Las Vegas, the first major new casino resort to open in 5 years, debuts on the Strip.

2006 The Red Rock Resort opens off the Strip.

2007 The Stardust is demolished to make way for the new Echelon Place. The Aladdin is renamed Planet Hollywood.

Toll-Free Numbers **& Websites**

Airlines
AIR CANADA
☎ *888/247-2262*
www.aircanada.ca
AIRTRAN AIRLINES
☎ *800/247-8726*
www.airtran.com

ALASKA AIRLINES/HORIZON AIR
☎ *800/252-7522*
www.alaskaair.com
AMERICAN AIRLINES
☎ *800/433-7300*
www.aa.com

...AIRLINES
☎ 800/1-FLY-ATA
vw.ata.com

...ONTINENTAL AIRLINES
☎ 800/525-0280
www.continental.com

DELTA AIR LINES
☎ 800/221-1212
www.delta.com

FRONTIER AIRLINES
☎ 800-432-1359
www.frontierairlines.com

HAWAIIAN AIRLINES
☎ 800/367-5320
www.hawaiianair.com

NORTHWEST AIRLINES
☎ 800/225-2525
www.nwa.com

SOUTHWEST AIRLINES
☎ 800/435-9792
www.southwest.com

UNITED AIRLINES
☎ 800/241-6522
www.united.com

US AIRWAYS
☎ 800/428-4322
www.usairways.com

VIRGIN ATLANTIC AIRWAYS
☎ 800/862-8621 in the continental U.S.
☎ 0870/380-2007 in Britain
www.virgin-atlantic.com

Major Hotel & Motel Chains

BEST WESTERN INTERNATIONAL
☎ 800/528-1234
www.bestwestern.com

COMFORT INNS
☎ 800/228-5150
www.hotelchoice.com

COURTYARD BY MARRIOTT
☎ 800/321-2211
www.marriott.com/courtyard

CROWNE PLAZA HOTELS
☎ 888/303-1746
www.crowneplaza.com

DAYS INN
☎ 800/325-2525
www.daysinn.com

EMBASSY SUITES
☎ 800/EMBASSY
www.embassysuites.com

FOUR SEASONS
☎ 800/819-5053
www.fourseasons.com

HILTON HOTELS
☎ 800/HILTONS
www.hilton.com

HOLIDAY INN
☎ 800/HOLIDAY
www.ichotelsgroup.com

HOWARD JOHNSON
☎ 800/654-2000
www.hojo.com

HYATT HOTELS & RESORTS
☎ 800/228-9000
www.hyatt.com

INTERCONTINENTAL HOTELS & RESORTS
☎ 888/567-8725
www.ichotelsgroup.com

LA QUINTA INNS & SUITES
☎ 800/531-5900 or 1/866-725-1661
www.lq.com

MARRIOTT HOTELS
☎ 800/228-9290
www.marriott.com

MOTEL 6
☎ 800/4-MOTEL6 (800/466-8356)
www.motel6.com

OMNI
☎ 800/THEOMNI
www.omnihotels.com

RADISSON HOTELS INTERNATIONAL
☎ 800/333-3333
www.radisson.com

RITZ-CARLTON
☎ 800/241-3333
www.ritzcarlton.com

SHERATON HOTELS & RESORTS
☎ 800/325-3535
www.sheraton.com

SUPER 8 MOTELS
☎ 800/800-8000
www.super8.com

TRAVELODGE
☎ 800/255-3050 or 800/578-7878
www.travelodge.com

WESTIN HOTELS & RESORTS
☎ 800-937-8461
www.westin.com

WYNDHAM HOTELS & RESORTS
☎ 800/822-4200 in continental U.S.
and Canada
www.wyndham.com

Index

Photo **Credits**